# The CRY *and the* DEDICATION

In the series

ASIAN AMERICAN HISTORY AND CULTURE,

*edited by Sucheng Chan and David Palumbo-Liu*

A list of books in the series appears at the

back of this volume

· · · · · · · · · · · · · · · · · · · · · · · · · · · · · · · · · · · · · ·

# The **CRY**

# *and the* **DEDICATION**

## CARLOS BULOSAN

*Edited and with an introduction by* **E. SAN JUAN, JR.**

TEMPLE UNIVERSITY PRESS *Philadelphia*

Temple University Press, Philadelphia 19122

Published 1995

Printed in the United States of America

∞ The paper used in this book meets the requirements
of the American National Standard for Information Sciences –
Permanence of Paper for Printed Library Materials,
ANSI Z39.48-1984

Text design by Richard Hendel

Library of Congress Cataloging-in-Publication Data

Bulosan, Carlos.
    The cry and the dedication / Carlos Bulosan: edited and with
an introduction by E. San Juan, Jr.
        p.   cm. – (Asian American history and culture series)
    Includes bibliographical references.
    ISBN 1–56639–295–0. – ISBN 1–56639–296–9 (pbk.)
    1. Philippines – History – 1946–1986 – Fiction.
    2. Guerrillas – Philippines – Fiction.   I. San Juan, E.
(Epifanio), 1938–   .  II. Title.   III. Series.
PR9550.9.B8C79   1995
813'.52 – dc20                                          94-29767

The original typescript for Carlos Bulosan's *The Cry and the
Dedication* is deposited at the University of Washington
Libraries archives.

# CONTENTS

## ACKNOWLEDGMENTS

· · · · · · · · · · · · · · · · · · · · · · · · · · · · · · · · · · · · ·

I want to thank the University of Washington Libraries, Seattle, Washington, for permission to use the original typescript of Bulosan's novel found in the Bulosan collection in their Manuscripts and University Archives section; and in particular, Ms. Karyl Winn, curator of manuscripts, who has supported scholarly endeavors like this to promote the study of the writings of Bulosan.

I am also grateful to the following persons, who supported and facilitated the realization of this project: Professors David Palumbo-Liu and Sucheng Chan, the series editors; Janet Francendese, executive editor of Temple University Press; and Professors Alan Wald, James Bennett, and Tim Libretti. I am most indebted to Delia Aguilar for her encouragement and comradeship in the "long march" to the final rendezvous.

E. San Juan, Jr.

> *Everywhere I roam I listen for my native language with a crying heart because it means my roots in this faraway soil; it means my only communication with the living and those who died without a gift of expression. My dear brother, I remember the song of the birds in the morning, the boundless hills of home, the sound of the language.*
> *— Carlos Bulosan, in a letter of 2 June 1953*

**W**hen I visited the University of Washington archives in the early seventies to examine the papers left by Carlos Bulosan, I came upon a typescript of a novel entitled *The Cry and the Dedication*. As far as I can gather, there is only a passing allusion to this novel, referred to in his letters as *The Hounds of Darkness* (Bulosan 1960:274). He alluded to two other novels he was completing, but this is the only one available in the archives and is the only novel of Bulosan's to be published.

In a letter dated 2 November 1949, Bulosan confessed his "secret dream of writing here a 1,500-page novel covering thirty-five years of Philippine history" (Bulosan 1960:258). This work, intended as part of a series of four novels encompassing a hundred years of Philippine history, was the one he was working on at the time and spanned the years from 1915 to 1950. Another novel was to cover the period from the birth and death of Rizal, and a third novel would run from Rizal's death to the outbreak of World War I. A fourth novel (partly fulfilled in *The Cry and the Dedication*) would cover the 1951–61 period, whose events, the pressure of "historical currents and cross-currents," Bulosan estimated as constituting "a great crisis in Philippine history." Although what really preoccupied him was "a novel covering the ideal friendship, courtship and marriage of a Pinoy and an American white woman," a riposte to the antimiscegenation law that crystallized U.S. racism against Filipinos in the first half of this century, his energies were rechaneled to elucidate a much more profound obsession: the "great crisis" not only in Philippine history but also in his own life and the Filipino diaspora.

What was the nature of this crisis? A brief résumé of Bulosan's life might help contextualize this novel in the light of lived experience and social circumstance.

Born to a poor peasant family in the Philippines in 1911, when the country was ruled as a classic colony of the United States, Bulosan learned the survival craft of workers and peasants resisting the tyranny of landlords, merchant usurers, petty bureaucrats, and comprador agents of the U.S. government. As he recounts in *America Is in the Heart*, the struggle of his family to overcome poverty in his homeland proved futile: Bulosan followed his two brothers, who had fled to the United States in search of a better life. When he landed in Seattle, Washington, in 1931, the community of more than 125,000 Filipino workers in Hawaii and on the West Coast was suffering from the worst crisis of the capitalist world system, the Great Depression of the early thirties. Aside from enduring severe unemployment, intense labor exploitation, and numerous legal prohibitions and exclusions, Filipinos were victims of racist vigilante violence that began in Yakima Valley, Washington, in 1928 and continued through the pogrom of Watsonville, California, in 1930, and onward (Takaki 1989). Since the violent suppression of the revolutionary Philippine Republic in the Filipino-American War 1898–1903), Filipinos in the United States had inhabited a limbo: neither citizens, refugees, nor wards, they were considered "nationals" without a sovereign country – a deracinated, subaltern species. In 1935 Filipinos were threatened with deportation to a neocolony called the Philippine Commonwealth. Bulosan's analysis of his experience in the United States, from his arrival to the beginning of World War II, can be condensed in passages from his letters (circa 1937–38):

> I was completely disillusioned when I came to know this American attitude [of race hatred]. If I had not been born in a lyrical world, grown up with honest people and studied about American institutions and racial equality in the Philippines, I should never have minded so much the horrible impact of white chauvinism. I

shall never forget what I have suffered in this country because of racial prejudice. . . . And we were all thousands of miles from our islands, alone (without even our women) in a strange, and often hostile, country. . . . Most of us will die here because we can work here, and when we can work we will make a life for ourselves. Man always makes a life for himself from whatever he has. . . . Do you know what a Filipino feels in America? He is the loneliest thing on earth [surrounded by] beauty, wealth, power, grandeur. But is he a part of these luxuries? . . . He is enchained damnably to his race, his heritage. He is betrayed, my friend. (Bulosan 1960:191–93)

On the eve of Pearl Harbor, Bulosan summed up his years as a labor organizer, journalist, and exile: "Yes, I feel like a criminal running away from a crime I did not commit. And the crime is that I am a Filipino in America" (Bulosan 1960:199).

Parallel to the peasant insurgency in the Philippines in the first three decades of U.S. colonial rule, the resistance of Filipino workers to capital may offer the subtext of the "crime" Bulosan was fleeing from, the latent inverted content to the manifest dream of success. This began with the organization of one of the first unions in Hawaii in 1919, the Filipino Federation of Labor, which spearheaded industrywide multiracial strikes in 1920, 1924, and later (Chan 1991). In 1934, to cite one other milestone, the Filipino Workers Association organized the militant strikes of 1934 in Salinas, El Centro, Vacaville, and the cotton fields of San Joaquin Valley, California. Drawing from this reservoir of experience, the Filipino Agricultural Workers Organizing Committee (led by Bulosan's contemporaries Larry Itliong and Philip Vera Cruz) conducted the path-breaking grape strike of 1965, the matrix of what became the United Farm Workers of America (Scharlin and Villanueva 1992). Bulosan became involved in this historic trend when he befriended activists in the Congress of Industrial Organizations (CIO) and the United Cannery, Agricultural, Packing and Allied Workers of America (UCAPAWA). In 1934 he helped edit *The New Tide*, a bi-monthly workers' magazine, and other newspapers, which brought him in contact with progressive writers and radical intellectuals.

After years of extreme privation and persecution, Bulosan was confined at the Los Angeles General Hospital (1935–38) for tuberculosis and kidney problems. The comradeship of intelligent American women friends and the self-education he acquired by a guided reading of books from the public library, Bulosan confessed, "opened all my world of intellectual possibilities – and a grand dream of bettering society for the working man." While in the hospital, Bulosan began writing poems (accepted by Harriet Monroe for *Poetry* magazine) and stories satirizing feudal despotism and patriarchal authority that would constitute the best-selling *The Laughter of My Father*, published in 1944 and reprinted in several languages. Bulosan depicted the resistance culture of the peasantry and plebeians of his childhood years. In response to the philistine dismissal of these folkloric vignettes as commercialized exotic humor, Bulosan stressed the allegorical/didactic cast of his imagination: "My politico-economic ideas are embodied in all my writings. *Laughter* is *not* humor; it is satire; it is indictment against an economic system that stifled the growth of the primitive, making him decadent overnight without passing through the various stages of growth and decay" (Bulosan 1960:273). In this terrain of a subjugated milieu where commodification eroded all pieties, Bulosan celebrated the carnivalesque wit of his father and the quiet resourcefulness of his mother, that "dynamic little peasant woman" who sold salted fish in the public market of Binalonan and nurtured her son's adventurous and daring spirit.

With *Laughter*, Bulosan enjoyed a measure of worldwide fame. Three previous books of poetry, *Chorus for America* (1942a), *Letter from America* 1942b), and *The Voice of Bataan* (1943c) went unnoticed. Earlier, his piece on "Freedom from Want" made him a celebrity when it was published in the *Saturday Evening Post* (1943a) and displayed in the Federal Building in San Francisco; its most memorable sentence proclaimed: "But we are not really free unless we use what we produce." The publication of *America* in 1946 climaxed this itinerary of the artist's apprenticeship. At the outset of the Cold War, Bulosan unwittingly became the hero of a stereotyped immigrant success story, one that his failed, homeless, lost protagonists had tried to imagine but could not duplicate in life.

While *America* gestures toward a Popular Front politics against global fascism, this quasi-autobiographical montage of Filipino lives is essentially an exercise in nationalitarian self-inscription. Bulosan was trying to remap his journey and waystations across an uneven, disintegrated landscape: "I want to interpret the soul of the Filipinos in this country. What really compelled me to write was to try to understand this country, to find a place in it not only for myself but my people" (San Juan 1991:172). *America*, then, is more properly conceived as a testimony to those years of struggle against denigration of one's nationality, class exploitation, and racist violence – in effect, it functions as a critique of the paradigm of ethnic assimilation. The narrative returns to what Amilcar Cabral calls "the source" to recover a submerged tradition of indigenous revolutionary culture rooted in more than three hundred years of anticolonial insurgency. The key to *America's* nonorganic artistic form is the often ignored first part, in which the narrator describes the effects of semifeudal, iniquitous property relations maintained by the U.S. colonial state. Of crucial importance is the 1927 Colorum uprising (Chapter 8) in his province, the site of conscientization and source of Bulosan's solidarity with anarchists and communists during the Spanish Civil War. Given the groundwork of Part One, the narrator can easily make the connection between Franco's fascism supported by Filipino landlords and compradors and the violence of U.S. agribusiness and the state's coercive agencies (Allen 1993). His simplistic version of the United Front strategy against world fascism explains the melodramatic, sentimental praise of Whitmanian democracy and the deployment of the utopian metaphor of "America" as a classless, nonracist society, motifs that pervade the texts of this period.

The terror of the Cold War quickly vaporized this utopian "America." Amid McCarthy-era witchhunts and FBI surveillance in the fifties, Bulosan was a blacklisted writer in danger of being deported with Chris Mensalvas and Ernesto Mangaoang, veteran leaders of the International Longshoreman's and Warehouseman's Union (ILWU), Local 37, whom Bulosan knew during the days of the UCAPAWA. The union had asked him to edit their 1952 *Yearbook*, a task that consolidated the socialist politics he expressed in "My Education": "Writing was not sufficient. . . . I drew inspiration from my active participation in the worker's movement. The most decisive move that the writer could make was to take his stand with the workers" (Bulosan 1982:35). Bulosan's role as union journalist and defender of the democratic rights of the Filipino community demonstrated that, contrary to allegations of self-induced ruin and obscurity, he was as fertile and combative as ever; he confessed how "writing is a pleasure and a passion to me – what drives me is the force of the idea, the historical fact" (Bulosan 1960:260). Bulosan renewed his radical commitment in his editorial for the 1952 *Yearbook*: "I believe that the unconditional unity of all workers is our only weapon against the evil designs of imperialist butchers and other profiteers of death and suffering to plunge humanity into a new world war." The U.S. armed aggression against the Korean people under the banner of the United Nations (shades of the recent Gulf War), and by proxy against Filipino workers and peasants, was then in full blast.

Aware of the configuration of heterogeneous forces, Bulosan affirmed once more the ethics of solidarity with all the oppressed, not just the proletariat, in his poem "If You Want to Know What We Are." At this juncture, his predicament acquired a new urgency: he was no longer confronting Japanese fascism, which had brutalized his brothers and sisters a decade ago. He was now confronting the power of U.S. finance capital assaulting the freedom and dignity of Filipino peasants and workers, ruthlessly destroying their homes, bodies, and spirits under the aegis of a CIA-sponsored populist hero, Ramon Magsaysay (Constantino and Constantino 1978). In the same yearbook, Bulosan rallied to the cause of the Huks (acronym for "People's Liberation Army") who were fighting not only feudal landlords and compradors but also the returned invader, U.S. military forces. This repetition of 1898 provided the leitmotif of *rendez-vous* – literally, "present yourself" – subtending the theme of "national liberation" of this novel. He also sympathized with Amado Hernandez, the great insurrectionary poet and union leader, who was imprisoned in 1950 for such alleged subversive activities as an unwavering advocacy of social justice, popular democracy, and genuine national independence.

In the midst of the depression, Bulosan speculated that "the greatest art will appear in a happy world of free men, but this new world will not come without pain and struggle." Although he hoped that "a common vision of a peaceful, creative future" could be realized by all humanity, he was not naive. In 1943 he was learning dialectics: "The old world is dying, but a new world is being born . . . from the chaos that beats upon us all" (Bulosan 1943b:646). At the juncture of world-transforming upheavals in the fifties as *pax Americana* entered its epoch of decline, Bulosan summed up his passage through the ordeal of living in the United States as one that bridged the Filipino war of resistance against U.S. Manifest Destiny at the turn of the century, the struggle of people of color in the thirties, and the communist-led Huk rebellion in the late forties and fifties. His project of critique and social transformation was inscribed in a suppressed tradition of dissidence, which is only now being resuscitated (San Juan 1991). In a provocative idiom that emulated the polemic verve of the 1896 *ilustrado* propagandists (e.g., Jose Rizal, Marcelo del Pilar), Bulosan denounced "the vicious lies of the capitalist press and yellow journalism, the warmongering of big business, the race-hating hysteria of reactionary organizations" at the height of the unconscionable McCarthy period. Such fiery words were penned by Bulosan when he was the beleaguered editor of the *1952 Yearbook*, a position that in retrospect one can regard as emblematic of his achievement in making the praxis of writing consonant with the labor of migrant workers in North America and with the history of the resistance of people of color everywhere.

In a 1947 letter, Bulosan reflected on the responsibility of the Filipino writer to intervene in the crisis of the *ancien regime* sweeping the country: "We should work like common people, absorbing, learning, remembering. It is only when we know the depth of the human soul, its tranquillity and violence, its magnificence and fragility, that we are really capable of writing something of significance and importance. . . . The Philippines is undergoing a great tragedy: why are the writers not challenged by it?" (Bulosan 1960:234). In *Laughter*, in numerous essays and letters, and in *America*, Bulosan bewailed the evils of "absentee landlordism" patronized by the U.S. government – when the United States conquered the islands in the first decades, they coopted the landed elite in administering minor local affairs – that plagued his family and millions of disenfranchised peasants in the Philippines, evils against which the Huks were fighting.

Around the time he was completing this narrative of guerrillas representing a coalition of sectors and classes with determinate peculiarities (1954–55) he expressed the fundamental principle of his vocation and the driving force behind this text:[1]

> What impelled me to write? The answer is – my grand dream of equality among men and freedom for all. To give literate voice to the voiceless one hundred thousand Filipinos in the United States, Hawaii, and Alaska. Above all and ultimately, to translate the desires and aspirations of the whole Filipino people in the Philippines and abroad in terms relevant to contemporary history.
>
> Yes, I have taken unto myself this sole responsibility. (Kunitz 1955:145)

What is striking in this credo is the urge to conceive of the Filipino diaspora (now affecting 65 million Filipinos) as a central phenomenon that defines the singular historical specificity of the Philippines in the wake of three hundred years of Spanish mercantile colonialism and almost a century of U.S. domination. Bulosan's project of articulating heterogenous voices, desires, and interests in order to synthesize them coincides with the central motivation informing his previous works, like *Laughter* and *America:* "to utilize our common folklore, tradition and history in line with my socialist thinking" (Bulosan 1960:261). This goal of coordinating aesthetic and political agendas is further elaborated in another letter: "[Filipino writers] should rewrite everything written about the Philippines and the Filipino people from the materialist, dialectical point of view – this being the only [way] to understand and interpret everything Philippines. . . . The material is inexhaustible. But always they should be written for the people, because the people are the creators and appreciators of culture" (Bulosan 1960:268). In a letter written a year before he died, Bulosan encapsulated his historical-materialist orientation in these words:

Life is a collective work and also a social reality. Therefore the writer must participate with his fellow men in the struggle to protect, to brighten, to fulfill life. Otherwise he has no meaning – a nothing. . . . If the writer has any significance, he should write about the world in which he lives: interpret his time and envision the future through his knowledge of historical reality. (Bulosan 1960:271).

I

In the spirit of Bulosan's counsel, I outline here only a few suggestions for interpreting key themes and episodes in *The Cry and the Dedication*. It is perhaps advisable to read the novel first before proceeding so as not to circumscribe one's horizon of expectations.

The historical parameter of the *fabula* embraces the political upheavals of the forties and fifties, when the Philippines, despite nominal independence, still functioned as the only Asian neocolony of the United States that supplied cheap raw materials and labor power and served as a market for expensive industrial goods. From 1898 to 1946, through "free trade" and other neocolonizing legislation, the United States perpetuated a semifeudal economy in which a landed oligarchy, in return for its assistance in pacifying the "natives," was allowed to take over as long as U.S. interests (economic and military) were safeguarded. In 1903, 29 percent of farmers were landless tenants; by 1946, the figure had soared to 40 percent, with tenants paying 50 to 75 percent of their crops as rent to landlords (Bayani 1976). Rural poverty and *cacique* abuses had intensified since Bulosan left his hometown in the twenties. In addition, the enormous destruction of World War II had left the country impoverished and heavily dependent on U.S. largesse, which was given in exchange for military control and economic-political ascendancy (Labor Research Association 1958). The passage of the infamous Bell Act of 1946 (which allowed U.S. business to exploit fully the national patrimony) and other treaties required the forcible silencing of nationalist voices and the maintenance of an unjust status quo; this soon precipitated civil war as outraged workers and peasants took up arms against the client government seeking to preserve the old inequalities – the point of *in medias res* when Bulosan's novel begins.

During and after the war, resistance against the Japanese occupation had rekindled the indigenous revolutionary spirit of the Indonesians, Vietnamese, Chinese, and Filipinos, among others. But while the Chinese and Indonesians succeeded in winning autonomy, the Filipino masses organized by the Huks lost whatever freedom they had won – to the old occupier. They never arrived at the site that the prophetic singer of the native's return, Aimé Césaire, once called the "rendezvous of victory." Those who fought against the Japanese encountered only treachery and betrayal at the hands of their American "liberators" and their lackeys. The onset of the Cold War, however, brought forth not only a reactionary tide of repression but also the decline of *pax Americana* signaled by the triumph of the People's Liberation Army in China in 1949 and the U.S. debacle in Korea at about the time the CIA was transplanting to Vietnam its newly tested counterinsurgency schemes in the Philippines. The postwar popularity of the Huks and the phenomenal growth of the Communist Party of the Philippines (founded in 1930 as a worker-peasant alliance) may be attributed to their resolute leadership in fighting the brutal Japanese occupation assisted by puppet collaborators (landlords, compradors, bureaucrats) – the very same politicians in the colonial regime whom General Douglas MacArthur would reward with economic and political privileges (Chapman 1987).

Such reversals and denouements were not strange to Bulosan. In *America* he displaced the predicament of exile in a way that would engage the paradoxes and ironies at the heart of this novel. If his composite memoir wrestled with the disjunction of past and present, the antinomies of dream and reality, and then conclude with a homily that all victims are united in the crusade for freedom, justice, and equality, such a textual strategy was no longer viable. The problem for the artist now became how to translate this ecumenical unity of antifascist forces into dramatic terms, into cogent symbolic action. For the first time, the convergence of the Cold War and U.S. counterinsurgency in the Philippines afforded

Bulosan an extraordinary shock of recognition in which he grasped the linkage between the national democratic agenda of the Huks and the agitation of multiracial workers in the United States, a moment of vindication in which he seized the present as history – analogous to the messianic "Now-Time" of Walter Benjamin (1969) and as the fulfillment of the promises given to now muted, vanquished, but still unpacified martyrs of the revolution.

In structuring his novel, Bulosan was also exploring the predicament of exile and confronting the task of calculating one's bearings in the postwar era. We have here a field of political-ethical forces representing the uneven and unsynchronized maldevelopment of the country. In this arena, the chief concern of the actors is how to establish linkages and channels of communication to bring people, races, classes, and genders into contact. In designing this project, the contingencies of space and time are textualized in the mutations of ideas, passions, impulses of memory and hope that fragment and at the same time reconstitute individuals. In registering these changes, the archive of Marxist critique lends Bulosan a precision instrument for mapping the conflict of wills, interests, and desires. Since the proletariat as a universal class – defined as the main producer of social wealth and the only agency that can liberate humanity from class bondage and reification – has no country in the ultimate reckoning, Bulosan's account of peasant/worker revolts in the neo-colony transcends its geographical provenance. By suturing revolts occurring thousands of miles away from the U.S. mainland with the resistance of class-conscious organized workers on the West Coast exploited by monopoly capital, Bulosan's writing practice is able to capture the emergent totality of the struggle of all dominated people. In particular, this multiracial spearhead of the struggle in the United States during the forties derives from the antifascist Popular Front around the world that climaxed the narrator's search, in *America*, for a coherent pattern or overarching purpose that would give meaning to his nomadic, deracinated existence.

We have here the advent of a new genre: the transnational allegory of a Third World imagination. In the interaction of overlapping generations and incommensurable lifeworlds, Bulosan delineates the evolution of the popular democratic movement against colonial barbarism into an anti-imperialist united front. When he portrays guerrillas seeking to free the masses from semifeudal bondage and neocolonial subalternity, he is also confronting the main source of violence against his race and nation: the rule of U.S. finance capital. And so it turns out that the Huk insurgency is a pretext or figure that transcodes in the local context the struggle of oppressed people of color in "the belly of the beast" and the formidable task of purging the beast from the colonized "native" psyche. In the last analysis, one cannot divorce the autochtonous struggle of the Filipino masses for justice and independence from the fight of Third World nationalities ("internal colonies," in one formulation) in the United States for the exercise of the right to self-determination, including the right of secession.

Although living thousands of miles away from the islands, Bulosan never left the Philippines in mind and heart – he never became a U.S. citizen. Vicariously he joined the peasant revolt against despotic landlords, avaricious compradors, and corrupt bureaucrat-capitalists – the local clients/agents of the U.S. elite. One might say that he was engaged in the same struggle on two fronts. It was in this dialectic between the concrete practice of Bulosan the artist and the historical pressures of his identity-on-trial as a Filipino migrant (unable to return home, choosing a permanent state of transition) that this novel germinated. Because Bulosan consciously integrated the Filipino struggle for complete and true independence with the migrants' efforts to oppose racist violence, he discovered in the process the resources of a critical and transformative imagination. Such a discovery is essentially the governing principle, the controlling vision, of this narrative – so far the first and only sophisticated rendering of that epoch in Philippine history whose repression up to now only begets its relentless repetition.

The schema of this novel has a daunting simplicity. It can be conceived as a mimesis, an inventory if you like, of a constellation of attempts and failures – a continuum of desire with its flux of traumas and sublimations. The history of the struggles of the Filipino people for genuine independence displays such a trajectory, a series of truncated flights toward a series of rendezvous: first, with the 1896 anti-Spanish revolution and the subsequent war against

U.S. aggression (1898–1902), then with the insurrections of the twenties and thirties (such as the Tayug revolt described in Chapter 8 of *America*), and finally, with the Huk-led resistance against the Japanese and their Filipino collaborators, which was suppressed after the war by U.S.-supported "puppet" regimes. Each journey yields lessons of fidelity often betrayed, alliances tested, and trust sometimes regained. While the final meeting with destiny (the attainment of the objectives of the struggle) is deferred or postponed, the process of moving toward it – with its accumulation of nuanced experiences, its actualization of human potential – eventually comes to define the substance of national liberation. As Salud Algabre, leader of the 1935 Sakdal rebellion, once said, "No uprising fails. Each one is a step in the right direction" (Sturtevant 1976:296). In effect, the ordeal of the quest, the encounter with one's self (the collective agent) mediated through alterity, becomes the constitutive element in the project of achieving true autonomy or self-determination.

The plot also exhibits a geometric simplicity.[2] It is structured around the journey of seven guerrilla partisans who are attempting a rendezvous in the capital city of Manila with an expatriate from the United States bearing help, or more precisely, "instructions" on how to secure funds from friends overseas. The protagonists are thus assigned a mission to establish contact with the world outside, traversing villages and towns, crossing boundaries of every kind. Linkages, empathies, and affinities are consequently drawn across ruptures, divides, suspicions. The journey of the seven guerrillas involves a reconaissance of contested terrain, a wager of loyalties in a time of betrayals and broken promises. Before they enter the inhospitable terrain of the city, the guerrillas are required – there seems to be no plausible reason, a lack whose supplement may elicit the key to deciphering the novel's rationale – to return to their home villages to reunite with their families or to "settle accounts" with them. At those sites, we find their individual life histories unfold their antinomies and contradictions, a drama over which the "spirit of place" presides, the matrix of an emergent symbolic order. In the process, the guerrillas discover who their friends and enemies are. "Reunion" thus engenders schisms and demarcations. Less horizontal than vertical, this movement is both advent and departure, strategically offensive and defensive at the same time. This is in turn overshadowed by an enigmatic figure at the end who, as a messenger of solidarity and succor, also bears the stigmata of violation ("vital disfigurement") and anonymity. Dante, the only person who can recognize the expatriate, returns to his hometown only to meet his death, thus aborting the original script.

While this overview indicates the chronotope of homecoming as the model of the final rendezvous (thus its impossibility) and the organizing principle of the incidents, we are not sure what generic expectations to have until the characters are more concretely fleshed out. As though anticipating this, the author himself has obliged and provided (in a handwritten sheet in the archives) a table of correspondences anatomizing his characters and their "humours," here reproduced verbatim:

Hassim – brooding
(city [Manila] proletarian self-taught) (factory worker)
Dante – detached
(seen other lands, other peoples) (educated proletarian)
Old Bio – compassionate
(unlettered peasant of the old generation)
Dabu – laughing (peasant of young generation:
went 3rd grade; then cane plantation worker)
Legaspi – slow but decisive when he acts
(unlettered peasant of young generation)
(rice field worker) (village)
Mameng – silent
(once a grade school teacher)
(finished high school) (town woman)
Linda Bie – philosophical
(college graduate: middle family: provincial capital)

One may remark in passing how this carefully outlined character system with its implied scenarios attests to Bulosan's divergence from the paradigm of the "typical" in conventional realism. The counterpointing of subjective (agency) and objective (institution) elements and the articulation of dynamic social tendencies and their dialectical resolution are regulated by the geometric schema, which reinforce the allegorical cast of the novel's structure. This manifests both antipicaresque and counterpastoral tendencies. One perceives the antipicaresque impulse in its conversion of the traditional rogue into a partisan band of "outlaws," a move that undermines hierarchy and questions the legitimacy of the social order. Meanwhile, the counterpastoral thrust resonates in passages that subvert the still seductive myth of the harmonious and innocent countryside. Both aspects are meant to defamiliarize the techniques usually associated with the adventure/war novel – most by American veterans of World War II – set in the tropic isles.

Deploying the chronotope of a pilgrimage to the city where each station becomes a pretext for testing/interpellating each character, the narrative links rural and urban, center and margin, past and present, the morality of the village and the demystifying telos of the socialist project. Everything becomes problematized: each character discovers a shifting void in the psyche – the death of loved ones, changes in the physical environment, a lingering *ressentiment,* and so on. What the text unfolds in antithesis is the quest for a resolution in the solidarity of the underground movement (vis-à-vis the individualism of the market), a quest repeatedly blocked by the inertia of tributary customs and bourgeois property relations.

One rendering of the "crisis" Bulosan had in mind (noted in my opening) can be illustrated by Chapters Ten to Thirteen, the second rendezvous. Legaspi returns to his hometown after five years of absence. Instead of reuniting, this visit dis-members. Legaspi's brother, a traitor-agent of the class enemy, is killed by the insurgent chief Hassim in a violent scuffle witnessed by the whole family. With a theatrical gesture, Hassim tries to console the aggrieved father, delivering a speech on proletarian humanism. He invokes the "only one true flag . . . the flag of the working class everywhere in the world. . . . There is no bowing to the flag of the working class we represent, because it is a symbol of liberation from exploitation and the achievement of human dignity. . . . We are not slaves. We are free men. . . . " This poignant episode ends with the father's recognizing Hassim as one of his sons, more exactly a substitute, a symbolic affiliation based on adherence to a political ideal that transcends bloodties, filial piety, the Oedipal law. This transcendence of proletarian allegiance over familial bond is meant to resolve Legaspi's predicament. It also functions as a sign foreshadowing Dante's fatal wounding by his brother – their estrangement is a symptom of the weakening of the conservative disciplinary regimes of patriarchal family and church – and the subsequent renewal of guerrilla comradeship in the wake of their withdrawal from enemy terrain. It allegorizes a transition in which social contact supersedes kinship; the clan dies only to be reborn from group sacrifice as a community of equals, the nation conceived as an artifact.

Before focusing on the thematic logic of Dante's homecoming and the compensatory efficacy of the ending, I want to pose certain questions for readers to puzzle out: Is the first rendezvous in Old Bio's town a reaffirmation of tradition, organic folk togetherness, and patriarchal supremacy, all of which are designed to guarantee village self-sufficiency? Is the second rendezvous an instance of "revolutionary" justice superseding primordial ties, as well as a repudiation of the mystique of aristocratic honor? Is the third rendezvous – the spectacle of horror and the indiscriminate carnage that follows – testimony to the power of the spirit of revenge and a displacement of patriarchal wrath in the son's obedience to filial duty? Coming quickly after their disruption of the wedding festival (Chapter Fifteen), Dabu's wild vengeance implies a breakdown of discipline and the return of *lex talionis*, of archaic residues. Much more problematic is the fact that each site of the rendezvous, each occasion for restaging the presentness of the past, proves to be precarious if not hostile ground; the enemy lurks everywhere, the town hall serving as its bastion and the police its private army. There is as yet no mass base or zone of freedom for the revolution, despite Dimasalang's dictum that "where there is oppression, we have friends everywhere." Indeed the struggle may be "one and indivisible all over the planet"; lacking hegemony, however, this remains a sectarian view. A foretaste of the revolutionary will evolving toward its self-defined rendezvous is shown in the fraternal exchange with the group's double (another guerrilla formation) in the last chapter, already prefigured in the recruitment of father and son earlier, and in the potential of erotic transcendence in those rare scenes invested with the charisma of Mameng/Alicia.

After the emotional reunion of Mameng with her mother and sister, the only encounter with the past where blood is not spilled, we witness in the next rendezvous Dante's outburst of anger at his brother-priest for failure to recognize a personal debt, thus provoking his death. With the past mediated by verses from alien/European culture heroes, San Juan de la Cruz and Francis Thompson – uncanny symptoms of pre-Oedipal longing or sacramentalizing death drive? – we observe Dante's last act of ordering Dr. O'Brian to heed Old Bio, "an act that took him thirty-five years to arrive at and execute, which was the ultimate fusion of his two selves; he, Dante, who was an American one moment and a Filipino the next, complete now at the very door of death." In what sense does this scene reconcile Dante's past (revived in the fratricide) with his present? Is this rendezvous with his local past (his presentation of self to his blood brother) a means of rescuing his "American" double? Or is it a punishment inflicted on his guilty self for leaving home? Is Dante trying to exorcise the hatred of the white world (evoked by the memory of the howling mob in San Diego) that once overwhelmed him before he lost consciousness?[3]

Before Dante dies, however, he settles accounts with the past in the person of Dr. Jack O'Brian, a self-confessed hater of Filipinos, who fails to save his life. It seems to me that Bulosan here contrives a somewhat forced catharsis when he peremptorily declares that Dante, no longer remembering but apprehending danger, achieves the "ultimate fusion of his two selves," the American and the Filipino. Despite this implausible if utopian gesture, this scene nonetheless illuminates part of Bulosan's motivation on which I have commented earlier: re-membering as a gathering together of fragments to reconstitute the whole; anamnesis as exchange of gifts (memories), with the novel serving as amanuensis and compensating for the imbalance in the psychic economy of the colonized. What the journey then enacts is the crossing of boundaries (physical and spiritual) to establish the possibilities of communicative action, a strategy of exchanging space for time – the classic guerrilla maneuver. Recall that in the first chapter Hassim, in a dialogue with Old Bio, talks about Dante's book, in which the old revolutionary

figures prominently; a text tracing Philippine history "from the revolutionary viewpoint, from Chief Lapu-Lapu and his pagan men who killed Magellan and most of his mercenary soldiers and drove the others to their boats and thence to Spain, to the formation of the underground in Mt. Arayat, where Alipato took the military leadership in this our latest struggle against tyranny." In this sense the narrative form replicates what it is trying to convey, evincing in the process the locutionary difficulties accompanying the performance.

Both the personal and historical crises which I pointed out earlier can be resolved, it seems, only by Dante's sacrifice, inasmuch as this immediately leads to the dismantling of the original plan and the recognition of the collective double. In retrospect, the libidinally charged rendezvous with Felix Rivas (the author's quasi double; a reincarnation of Felix Razon in *America*) turns out to be a symptom of a collective predicament. In effect, Rivas functions as the empty space and the signifier of the negative; further, he serves as a metaphoric vehicle for the illusion of dependency, the colonial *habitus* of demanding recognition/acknowledgment from the master's gaze. Disfigured or virtually castrated, Rivas thus becomes the telltale icon of a disappeared hope, a trust sold out; of a scandalous betrayal that may be said to configure the underlying structure of a long-repressed contradiction between the United States and the Philippines of which Filipinos abroad (for whom Bulosan acted as spokesman) were the living embodiment.

So then the participants in this allegorical pilgrimage are cut off from their destination in the city, with two more rendezvous involving Linda Bie and Hassim postponed and the whole mission aborted. Their fortuitous rescue by another group of armed peasants intimates the discovery of the real objective or meaning of their final rendezvous, which I would like to underscore: the encounter with others whose sharing of a common purpose yields the gift of mutual recognition. Doubting this proposition, one can inquire further: Is this denouement Bulosan's emblematic figure of self-reliance or even autarky? Does it express a covert insistence on privileging the supremacy of the mass line?[4] All these questions find their answers in the repetitions of the narrative scheme, a pattern that focuses less on punctual chronology than on salvaging relics of messianic time from mutilated life histories, a re-member-ing via going back, with each homecoming or rendezvous conceived both as self-discovery and a presenting of self, or its "rendering back," for the Other.

We can finally venture the hypothesis that Dante's plight epito-mizes the contradictions of individualist, "free enterprise" ideology ripened in a Third World neocolony undergoing mutations and distortions, a crisis whose long-range implications cannot yet be fully spelled out except as a negation of the moribund status quo. Dante's death would then signify the historical obsolescence of the petit bourgeoisie, more exactly bourgeois liberal ideology, and in particular the neocolonized intelligentsia caught between its obses-sion with Western lifestyles and the reality of class antagonisms. We sympathize with Dante's situation as he tries to bury the nightmare of the past, incapable of exorcising its specters until he himself assumes the role of victimizer; and in this self-estranged position, he is delivered from suffering by the violence of his brother-priest. We can now conceive of Dante as a figure for the fragmented body of the nation, a body cut up and its members dispersed around the world today as in the past as "warm body export," their labor power treated as bargain commodities for sale. Dante the "unprodigal" son whose body now blends with one inalienable earth (localized in Philippine soil) remains an enigmatic personification of the Filipino exile torn from his still occupied homeland. His experiences can then be read as the allegory of Bulosan as dismembered culture hero, of the worker robbed of the fruits of his alienated labor and therefore of his life, of the peasant dispossessed of the land he had made fruitful, and of the millions of women (mothers, sisters, wives) who in the march of imperial progress were forced to make the absolute sacrifice.[5]

At this point, the novel's closure inserts a caesura in our medita-tion and provokes the following speculation. The ending might be understood as a parable in miniature: the incidence of Dante's sacrifice leads to his group's rescue by a counterpart band of antilandlord partisans who have already demarcated a territory for themselves, perhaps a token of decentralized grassroots politics in gestation. A politics of hope is also insinuated here with a detour in nostalgia for the organic community, leading finally to a redemptive rescue. The novel's closure then compensates for the sentimental and melodramatic excess the earlier incidents might have produced, for the insensitivity to the "woman question," and other improbabilities. It neutralizes somewhat the essentializing tendency of liberal humanism immanent in the self-deceptive misrecognition of Dante's bifurcated self, the duplicities in each of the protagonists, and all other contradictions that are exposed but are deliberately left unresolved.

In the end, Hassim displaces Dante as the undisputed central intelligence of the narrative, distancing Bulosan from his own predicament. In response to the American doctor's racist harangue, Hassim "knew that he had to say something to this proud man [Dante] to remember him by. He had to grapple with space and time, wrest away from the silence of the years a land called America and fling it upon this room, beside this proud man, and point to towns and cities where fragments of Dante's life had been lost and where drops of his blood had been spilled to make the soil of that land rich for vegetation." Connotations revolving around the Orphic and Osiris myth charge this passage with a prophetic force oriented to a future redemption. In Chapter One, Hassim's character operates as a totalizing consciousness bridging past and present, opening the space for the intervention of a utopian Now-Time: Old Bio was confused by "what Hassim had said about their revolutionary tradition, then what they were fighting for in the underground, and now about himself and the revolution against Spain. Time and space seemed to converge in Hassim's mind freely" and this "resilient thinking" is what enables Old Bio to be transported in time. Of crucial significance is this passage in Chapter Fourteen, the middle of the book, where Hassim distinguishes the peace of childhood and the peace of commitment:

Was there no other meaning of life? Hassim could look back to the beginning, almost at the end of time, and seek out among the wreckage of other lives, all that he had known, if there was another, more tangible than what he had found among his companions in these last few hectic years. But he could not find any: for there at the beginning was a false peace, the peace of childhood that took nourishment from the unfailing roots of parenthood; not the peace of awareness, of knowing the world and the people in it, and their relations to each other as they were striving to weave a motif as a setup of their pattern of living. It was the false peace of childhood, deeply embedded in his memory and everybody's memory; yet he knew that from it started the yearning for real peace, the peace that came with maturity and awareness; and in it were first revealed the magic casements that revealed the dawn and murmur of real peace, becoming more murmurous and brighter as awareness grew, as it grew steadily until it became an imperishable reality. So that was the beginning of real peace after all, he thought.

A dialectic of past and future is being negotiated in Hassim's mind, culminating in a "peace of awareness" (lived by Hassim and his comrades in the guerrilla struggle), the genesis of "an imperishable reality." But it is ultimately Hassim's invocation of Dante's fertilizing blood that allows this text to function as the conscience of all oppressed nationalities, people of color whose labor and its fruits have been expropriated by capital and whose spirit is now being stirred up to reclaim what has been alienated from it. Bulosan's novel thus critiques the utopian humanism of *America* and rewrites it in the allegory of revolutionary praxis.

II

Given the ambitious scope of the themes woven in the novel, one can claim that *The Cry* is a magnificent achievement by a Filipino artist of world stature, a counterhegemonic text rendering in allegorical terms the tragic *agon* of a neocolonial formation such as the Philippines, a cultural performance equaled only by Jose Rizal's novels, the poetry of Amado Hernandez, and the films of Lino Brocka.[6]

This novel is the only narrative of this magnitude by a self-taught writer born of the peasantry that successfully integrates (albeit in a problematic form) the anti-imperialist people's war in the Philippines with the self-transmuting experience of Filipino migrants, wandering vendors of cheap labor in the United States, in the first half of this century. It develops with compelling intensity the theme of combined class, national, and racial struggles traversing the unsynchronized time-space of *America*, as well as the theme of collective renewal by satiric demystification elaborated in *Laughter*. Those themes are then rearticulated and syncopated in this novel through the lives of typical but fully concretized characters whose internal complexities surface in the feud between blood relations, in recurrent antagonisms that explode phallocentric authority, feudal patronage, and the ideological apparatuses of neocolonial subordination. In effect, one is tempted to read these internal splits as symptoms of the underlying structural mutations suffered by the body politic. Plot and characters can then be properly glossed as allegorizing tropes for the conflicts that fragment the populace along class, gender, and racial lines, suspending the claims of kinship and other organic ties for the sake of a larger ethicopolitical affiliation such as "the Filipino people" or "the national-popular forces" – rubrics of a symbolic identity-in-process – without which all resistance against the consolidated power of capital remains dispersed and futile.

From the perspective of the nineties, Dolores Feria, Bulosan's trusted literary confidante, speculates on Bulosan's prescience: "The novel, as it would have to be, is largely an ideological construct with only an allegorical resemblance to the factual nitty-gritty of day-to-day revolutionary tactics. What is most impressive is the power that the book succeeds in generating in spite of its obvious factual lapses. For the fictional journey of Hassim (was he a stand-in for the Persian poet whom Bulosan said had influenced his poetry?) and his six companions on their way to Rendezvous 7 is merely a journey in the time continuum from the Hukbalahap bases of the late 1940s to the New People's Army of 1969 and subsequent years. It was Bulosan's only way of coming to terms with a historic phase from which circumstances had totally excluded him and yet for which he had waited for 25 years."[7]

In that framework, I suggest that the narrative be interpreted as a transnational allegory of a new kind, to modify Fredric Jameson's heuristic category. It performs a mapping of the complex, ever- shifting constellation of social/psychic forces underlying that con- juncture when the hegemonic "language" of U.S. liberalism disin- tegrates on collision with the heteroglossia (to use Bakhtin's term) of its victims. It is in this light that Bulosan may be said to decenter the monologic discourse of U.S. supremacy by deploying the oppositional voices of his underground agents, catching off balance the phalanx of ideological mechanisms used to reproduce subalterns and sustain the parasitic regime of capital. The novel aims to dramatize the crisis of this system, of U.S. hegemony, as it is being challenged by the organized force of peasants, workers, and intellectuals – the first serious challenge since the Filipino-American War of 1898–1902.

Because of his incisive critique of U.S. imperialist domination and its racist violence coexisting with tributes to the idea of "America" as a creation of mass democracy, Bulosan has become a battlefield of political contestation. Were he alive today, he would most likely relish this position of being the medium through which life-and-death questions, formerly muted or sidetracked, are released into a phantom "public sphere" for debate. In a dependent formation such as the Philippines, however, what preponderates in intellectual circles is not so much reason as hope and fear, the twin passions of the modality of finite existence, which Spinoza considered barriers for enjoying freedom. One can argue that *The Cry* challenges the omnipotence of these barriers, even if indirectly, in the fixations and defense mechanisms of his protagonists. Not that Bulosan was trying to fabricate an ingenious Aesopian discourse to outwit the police; his effort to craft a transnational allegory had no traditional precedents, hence its novelty may annoy conformist taste. The conventional mode of reception is certainly blind to the way Bulosan transforms the motif of the journey (as elaborated, for instance, in Goethe's *Wilhelm Meister*) into a cognitive-aesthetic cartography of the vicissitudes of U.S.-Philippine relations. Nor is it sensitive to the way Bulosan's discursive method interweaves the more subtle ideological "war of position" with the largely economistic conception of the "war of maneuver" rendered by doctrinaire realism (Libretti 1994). This is understandable because the problem of hegemony (the mix of force and consent enabling social reproduction) that preoccupies this novel and his other writings has not really been addressed by critics with a historical materialist rigor. What we need is a politically transformative approach to cultural texts like Bulosan's that would be cognizant of the specific audiences for whom he was writing, the circulation and reception of his texts in changing environments, the dialectical play of forces overdetermining his writing practice, and the limits and possibilities of the semiotic codes and genres within which he was operating. The present essay is only a preliminary contribution toward inventing such a materialist approach.

At the peak of the Cold War, Bulosan expressed (in a testament cited earlier) the synthesizing vision of his art, his project of striving to concretize the "grand dream of equality among men and freedom for all," a dream immanent in "the desires and aspirations of the whole Filipino people," which he vowed to actualize as his "sole responsibility." This task of interpellating a Filipino subjectivity-in-process coeval with the emergence of a truly sovereign Filipino nation is one that Bulosan accepted as he straddled the boundaries between two worlds, the Southeast Asian colony and the Western metropolis, collapsing the distinction between center and margin in the process of dramatizing the psychological and ethical dilemmas of the characters in this novel. One can propose that in general Bulosan's writings assumed the responsibility of unleashing the transgressive impulses locked in folklore, indigenous tales and songs, newspaper accounts, oral and graphic testimonies, journals, propaganda, and other intractable practices of quotidian life – forces and energies that can be harnessed for popular democratic emancipation.

In trying to fulfill the mandate of his responsibility, Bulosan envisioned a just, egalitarian, convivial world – a socialist society that would emerge from the cultural awakening and political mobilization of the multiracial working class in the United States. He prophesied such an event being catalyzed by the defeat of imperialism at the hands of the armed organized masses in the Third World.

Bulosan died before his insight could be partly confirmed by the popular democratic victories in Cuba, Vietnam, Nicaragua, and several countries in Africa. The struggle for "national liberation" is still raging in the country of his birth. In Bulosan's description of how Filipino workers in his lifetime united with progressive sections of U.S. society in their fight against predatory capital, in his affirmation that workers and oppressed nationalities in metropolis and periphery constitute the principal motive force in the making of world history, Bulosan composed a powerful testimony to the immense potential of "the wretched of the earth" to transform exploitative structures and uncover the wellspring of beauty and freedom in the self-renewing creativity of cooperative labor. Celebrating the sanctity of life and solidarity of the "common" people, Bulosan hoped in his works not merely to give pleasure and knowledge but also and above all to disturb the peace of tyrants and empower the masses with the spirit of revolt. Given this achievement, Bulosan's name today has come to symbolize the implacable revolutionary will of people of color everywhere combating racist oppression and exploitation by transnational capital, fighting for the right of self-determination, for justice and human dignity.

## NOTES

1. In 1991, Dolores Feria proposed a correction to the editor's hypothetical dating of the novel (San Juan 1986) by adducing certain biographical circumstances surrounding its composition. She calculated the time of writing as between 1949 and 1952, a period when Bulosan drifted between Los Angeles and Stockton, associating with people who were then distributing Taruc's autobiography, *Born of the People*, published in 1953. Bulosan's article on the capture of the Huk Politburo, "Terrorism Rides the Philippines," appeared in August 1952 in the *Yearbook* he edited. The idea of a guerrilla march and rendezvous could have been inspired only by the strategic marches vividly recounted in Taruc's memoir. The age of Dante, Bulosan's fictional surrogate, coincides with Bulosan's age in 1953. I would strongly suggest that the book was begun sometime in 1952 or 1953 and was completed in 1955 when, in a letter to Florentino Valeros, Bulosan first mentioned the early title of this novel, *The Hounds of Darkness* (Bulosan 1960:274).

2. Obvious similarities exist between the characters of Old Bio and Hassim with the old man and the hero of Ernest Hemingway's *For Whom the Bell Tolls:* parallels involving characterization, setting, arrangement of incidents, and so on can also be found. But I have not found any reference to Hemingway's novel in Bulosan's letters. In my opinion, the actual model for this novel is Luis Taruc's *Born of the People*, published in 1953 by International Publishers.

3. In contrast to Dante's dichotomized self, Bulosan experienced his own spiritual reconstitution/rebirth, as captured by this confession in a letter to Dorothy Babb (2 July 1942):

> In spite of everything that has happened to me in America I am not sorry that I was born a Filipino. When I say "Filipino" the sound cuts deep into my being – it hurts. . . .
>
> I will never forget you: never. I will never forget what you have given me. I hope you are happy. As for myself, I don't care if I am happy or not.
>
> I am proud that I am a Filipino. I used to be angry, to question myself. But now I am proud. (Bulosan 1982:81)

4. One of the problems the text seeks to articulate and resolve (see especially Chapters Six to Ten) is the tension between centralized vanguard leadership and the democratic participation of all citizens in a "people's war."

5. Dante's authorship of *Tales of My Own People*, a book that Mrs. O'Brian places inside his shirt on his death, clearly identifies him with the author, who alludes to a manuscript collection of his stories with the same title (Bulosan 1960:253).

6. First published in a modified version by Tabloid Books (Guelph, Canada) in 1977 with the title *The Power of the People*, the typescript of the novel was shunned by frightened profit-seeking publishers in the Philippines because of the censorship laws of the Marcos dictatorship and because of the danger associated with a blacklisted person like its editor and introducer. Even after the novel finally appeared in Manila in 1986, after the EDSA "People Power" uprising, it was periodically denounced for various reasons. One is Bulosan's alleged "chauvinist" rendition of its woman protagonist, another is the motif of dependency of the guerrillas on external assistance. Both responses refuse to see the centrality of race and nationality, as well as the seemingly incommensurable themes of tutelage, exile, and the problematic of permanent revolution with its anticolonial and anticapitalist phases (Libretti 1994), so that one is inclined to diagnose them as reaction formations, which are more symptomatic

of the malaise of the critics themselves than accurate formulations of what the text is driving at.

7. If I may add a superfluous note: The novel does not claim to be a documentary transcript of the actual Hukbalahap rebellion nor a veridical copy of any empirical happening. While Bulosan uses the names of such Hukbalahap commanders as Linda Bie, Dabu, Dimasalang, his concern is to use the historical frame of the Huk insurrection (1949–52) in order to explore and probe the depth of the political, ideological, and moral changes necessary to transform a whole society whose fate is intertwined with stranded Filipinos in the United States.

## WORKS CITED

Allen, James S. 1993. *The Philippine Left on the Eve of World War II.* Minneapolis: MEP Publications.

Bayani, Samuel P. 1976. *What's Happening in the Philippines.* New York: Far East Reporter.

Benjamin, Walter. 1969. *Illuminations.* New York: Schocken Books.

Bulosan, Carlos. 1942a. *Chorus for America: Six Filipino Poets.* Los Angeles: Wagon and Star.

———. 1942b. *Letter from America.* Prairie City, Illinois: J. A. Decker.

———. 1943a. "Freedom from Want." *Saturday Evening Post* (6 March).

———. 1943b. "Letter to a Filipino Woman." *New Republic* (8 November):645–46.

———. 1943c. *The Voice of Bataan.* New York: Coward McCann.

———. 1944. *The Laughter of My Father.* New York: Harcourt, Brace and Co.

———. [1946.] 1973. *America Is in the Heart.* Seattle: University of Washington Press.

———. 1952. *1952 Yearbook.* Seattle: ILWU, Local 37.

———. 1960. "Sound of Falling Light." Ed. Dolores Feria. *Diliman Review* 8 Nos. 1–3 (January–September):185–278.

———. 1982. *Selected Works and Letters.* Ed. E. San Juan, Jr., and Ninotchka Rosca. Honolulu: Friends of the Filipino People.

Cabral, Amilcar. 1973. *Return to the Source: Selected Speeches.* New York: Monthly Review Press.

Cesaire, Aime. 1969. *Return to My Native Land.* New York: Penguin Books.

Chan, Sucheng. 1991. *Asian Americans.* Boston: Twayne.

Chapman, William. 1987. *Inside the Philippine Revolution.* Quezon City: Ken Inc.

Constantino, Renato, and Letizia Constantino. 1978. *The Philippines: The Continuing Past.* Quezon City: Foundation for Nationalist Studies.

Feria, Dolores. 1991. "Bulosan's Power, Bulosan's People." *Manila Times* (28 April):4.

Jameson, Fredric. 1986. "Third World Literature in the Era of Multinational Capitalism." *Social Text* 15:65–88.

Kunitz, Stanley, ed. 1955. *Twentieth Century Authors.* New York: H. W. Wilson.

Labor Research Association. 1958. *U.S. and the Philippines.* New York: International Publishers.

Libretti, Tim. 1994. "U.S. Literary History and Class Consciousness: Towards a Theory of Proletarian Literature." Ph.D. dissertation. University of Michigan.

San Juan, E. 1986. "Introduction." In Carlos Bulosan, *The Power of the People.* Manila: National Book Store.

———. 1991. *Writing and National Liberation.* Quezon City: University of the Philippines Press.

———. 1993. *Reading the West/Writing the East.* New York: Peter Lang.

Scharlin, Craig, and Lilia Villanueva. 1992. *Philip Vera Cruz.* Los Angeles: UCLA Labor Center.

Sturtevant, David. 1976. *Popular Uprisings in the Philippines 1840–1940.* Ithaca: Cornell University Press.

Takaki, Ronald. 1989. *Strangers from a Different Shore.* Boston: Little, Brown and Co.

Taruc, Luis. 1953. *Born of the People.* New York: International Publishers.

# The CRY *and the* DEDICATION

**N**ow long shadows were falling upon the hushed silence of the great forest. Dancing violet streaks of the dying sun penetrated the trees, revealing flitting butterflies and crawling insects. Fireflies were flashing their scintillating tiny lamps in the underbrush and there was a slight flutter of frightened wings nearby. Suddenly there was a violent crushing of dry leaves and dead twigs in the wake of a fleeing wild animal. Then cicadas burst into glorious song in a voice so multitudinous the whole forest seemed to float away with its thrilling beauty

Hassim crept quietly on the soft carpet of the pine needles to the edge of the forest. His guide, who was called Old Bio, followed close behind him. They stood side by side near a fallen tree and looked eagerly toward the dark hills beyond the silent valley below them. They scanned the foothills and hillsides to the treetops and back to the foothills, but saw no sign that the other party had arrived from its long trek across the wide plains on the other side of the mountains.

"Are we in the right rendezvous?" Hassim asked.

"Yes."

Hassim's face showed concern. He took a map from his shirt pocket and unfolded it.

"There is no need for that," Old Bio told him. "I am sure we are in the right place."

Hassim knew the old man was right. He said as an apology, "I look at maps because I can't rely on my memory anymore. I have seen so many places, but they all look alike to me. I know you are right about this spot, old man."

Old Bio nodded his head. "I was born in this part of the country," he said. "I know the whole region by heart."

Hassim knew that was true; to hear it from the old man made a definite confirmation of his knowledge.

"They must have been delayed," Hassim said.

"I have great confidence in their guide."

"Do you know him?"

"I know him well. He is a boy who had lived in a village not far from where I was born, and like a grandson to me, considering the fact that I am the oldest living person in this part of the country. I saw every child come into the world in this territory. Look," Old Bio said, pointing to the far end of the valley, "that is his village. On the other side, running westward, is the river where the villagers used to wash their clothes and clean their animals. The farmers dug a canal there years ago so the rice fields will always have an abundant supply of water. There was fighting at the beginning of the war, so I doubt very much if it is still working. You should have seen the grain they produced in those fields."

Hassim noted a wistful reminiscence in Old Bio's voice. Looking in the direction of the old man's pointing finger, he took the field glasses from the pocket of his sweat-soaked khaki shirt, wiped the lenses with his sleeve, and adjusted the eyepieces until the river showed like a taut blue ribbon stretching westward across a wide plain and disappearing in the darkening horizon into a tall black mountain that stood guard against heavy storms and the yearly encroachments of the angry sea; and as he screwed down the lenses to the village, he saw the coconut trees clearly and the remains of burned houses and the mass of rubble that was once the town hall; and he saw that the village was deserted because there was neither man nor beast within the periscope of his vision. He saw the awful emptiness of the place and the river stretching westward into the coming night.

"It looks deserted," he said.

"Yes. The people left after the last raid of the enemy," Old Bio explained. "Those who had survived the terror. But they were very few."

"I commanded a squadron of the underground against that raid," Hassim told him. "But we arrived too late. Our courier met difficulties in penetrating enemy lines and reaching our bivouacs."

Old Bio turned to his companion, and his whole being suddenly surged with conflicting emotions; an inner voice told him to study Hassim's face and remember it as long as he lived. But in the gathering darkness, he saw only the sharp profile of an intelligent peasant face, unsmiling and brooding to the point of agony.

"They killed one of our best men," Hassim said as if in after-thought. "Lising is the name. The younger brother."

"I remember him," Old Bio said, turning his face away from Hassim. He looked down the darkening valley. Then back to Hassim's face, he saw again the impeccably dressed young Lising in his glittering black eyes, incredibly alive and piercing now that the sun was gone.

Hassim's eyes were used to the darkness of night and the dead silences of the forest. His were eyes that lived vividly in the night and the silences. His were eyes that revealed their agonizing visual memory when remembering unforgettable events of the past, re-flecting them in lucid images and deflecting them sharply upon your conscience, so that they seared your mind until your face became contorted with pain, because of that horrible remem-brance.

It was this momentary revelation of Hassim's fierceness that disturbed the old man, even more so now, for it seemed unbelieva-ble to him that this young man of twenty-one could strike fear of tremendous proportions in the heart of the enemy. So he repeated to confirm what he already knew, "I remember him."

"Do you remember how they tried to make Cy a traitor?" Hassim asked.

"The first director of the Political Committee?" Old Bio an-swered, turning his face away again. There was a rising note of respect in his voice, even though he tried to suppress it. "How can I forget him when it was you, alone, who rescued him? How can I forget when a whole division of the enemy pursued you to the jungle where you had hidden Cy so that our people could nurse him back to life? Everybody in the plains was talking about you then, Hassim. You were the bright evening star that shown gloriously in the dark sky of our peasant life."

"I am glad you have not forgotten him," Hassim said almost inaudibly. He put the field glasses back in his pocket. The night had come now. He saw the old man's long white hair shining in the darkness and his gray stubble beard whose fringes reminded him of the tangled roots of a dead banana tree. But he had long ago cast flattery aside, knowing it would lead him to self-immolation and softness if he accepted it foolishly. It was one of the cardinal rules of the underground, that a leader should not think of himself as a separate entity from the group or consider his achievements as his personal glory. He said, to depersonalize the incomparable achievement of that rescue, "I will never forget Cy. He opened my eyes to the world."

"Many of us will not forget him."

Hassim turned to the dark hills. It was still quiet. The valley below them was now strangely ominous in the darkness. He felt a little disquieted. He knew the other party had to cross unfriendly territories to make time. He had long ago known the hazards of secret missions such as this one tonight, and in that knowledge he hoped they had all come through successfully. He could not even offer a prayer; that was taken away from him.

The old man spoke again. "Tell me, Hassim," he said, "is it true that you joined the underground when you were only sixteen?"

"Seventeen," Hassim corrected him.

"Are you from this part of the country?"

"No, Old Bio. I was born in Bicol, but I grew up in Manila."

"You speak our local dialect fairly well."

"I have worked and fought with your people since the beginning of the war, as you already know. I have just organized a mass base up north, where you located me for the present mission. I speak a little now of the mountain people's dialect."

"Ay." Old Bio sighed. "I wish I were young again so I could work with you to the very end."

"You will see the end."

"I will see the end?" There was hope mingled with regret in the old man's voice. "The enemy will be destroyed? I would like to see that day."

"You will live to see it, and beyond that day, when we establish a system of government emanating from the needs and desires of our people." Hassim was not brooding now. He felt, from the old man's tone of voice, a sincerity that thawed down his consecrated distance, which was often his shield and weapon when he was sent on secret missions, and seized him completely defenseless. Now he felt light and self-effacing. "You are still a strong man, making me run like a schoolboy across the plains this afternoon," he complimented Old Bio.

"Did I do that to you, Hassim?" Old Bio said, bewilderment enriching his voice.

"You sure did," Hassim answered, smiling a little. And he added, "Tell me, is it true that you defied two hundred soldiers with twelve men for ten months in one of these mountains during the revolution against Spain?"

"Where did you hear that?" Old Bio asked, his feeling of importance growing.

"I read it in one of our history books."

"An educated man wrote about me?"

"It is a newly written book," Hassim explained. "It is done by one of our men called Dante, tracing our history from the revolutionary viewpoint, from Chief Lapu-Lapu and his pagan men who killed Magellan and most of his mercenary soldiers and drove the others to their boats and thence to Spain, to the formation of the underground in Mt. Arayat, where Alipato took the military leadership in this our latest struggle against tyranny."

"Ay," Old Bio cried with delight. "I have heard of Dante but never saw him."

"He is too well known to the intelligence corps of the enemy. Of course, Dante is not his real name."

"What is his real name?"

"You will soon know."

"What part of the country did he come from?"

"That nobody knows. He speaks most of our dialects fluently."

"Ay," Old Bio said again, thinking of the book where his name was written. It was not vanity but a feeling of victory. All that fighting in the past had not been in vain. Then he frowned, knowing that even if he saw the book he would not be able to read it. Suddenly he asked Hassim, "Are you an educated man?"

"Not in the formal sense. As I told you a moment ago, Cy opened my eyes to the world. I am what professors call a self-educated man."

"Times have changed," Old Bio murmured. "I could not have done that under the Spanish regime. You could be garroted for possessing the most elementary books, even the Bible."

"That is why their government was overthrown by the revolutionary Katipunan organization. You can't hide knowledge; it belongs to the world. Education belongs to the people. Education is the prerogative of a system, if it wants to survive chaos. A system that tries to perpetuate itself on ignorance and slavery does not last. You see," Hassim touched the old man to emphasize his point, "mass education is one of the things we are fighting for. Our first objective is to destroy the enemy in such a way that he won't be able to reorganize himself, completely vanished from our midst and his poison purged to the last sediment of thought from the minds of those who believe him. Another thing is the exploitation of all our natural resources for all to share and use, each according to his needs and capabilities to produce."

"Is that possible?"

"Theoretically, yes. But we will have to give up many precious personal luxuries and enterprises to make it practically possible."

"We are used to living on almost nothing," Old Bio said. "And, besides, greed seems to be the common commodity nowadays."

"That, too, shall be done away with," Hassim said, his voice beginning to vibrate with excitement. But he suddenly remembered that he was talking about the old man's youth, during the revolution against Spain, so he said in a low voice, "Tell me about your war against two hundred soldiers, Old Bio."

For a moment, Old Bio was confused by the sudden change of subjects in their discussion. He was trying to assimilate what Hassim had said about their revolutionary tradition, then what they were fighting for in the underground, and now about himself and the revolution against Spain. Time and space seemed to converge in Hassim's mind freely, brilliantly, and compellingly, so that the old man was at a loss. And when he was able, at last, to keep track of Hassim's resilient thinking, he was suddenly transported to another time. He saw again the young man that he had been at eighteen, barefoot, hiding behind a big rock with a *campilan** in one hand and

*A cutlass.

a homemade gun in the other, shouting orders to twelve determined men and defiance to two hundred well-armed soldiers crouching on the mountainside.

"Ay, that is what I call fighting," Old Bio said, remembering. And peering in the darkness to the left of them, he pointed to the rocky peak of a mountain standing tall and inscrutable above the plains. "That is it, Hassim. That was my fortress and castle for ten long months of retreat and advance. When the canailles finally sent three emissaries under a flag of truce and told me to surrender, I said to them, 'We will die first in this mountain before we surrender to you Spanish dogs!' And that was that: they never saw their camps again." He laughed, remembering long-forgotten men under his command. Then he shouted into the night, his voice suddenly fierce and magnificent, "We will die first in this mountain before we surrender to you Spanish dogs!"

Hassim felt the sudden magnificence of the old man's voice. He, too, saw Old Bio as a young man, bold and defiant, shouting orders of no surrender to his twelve bedraggled men. And he thought, he must have been truly great. Now he is an old man, but he must have been a leader of men. You have to give it to him, for even though he is seventy now, he is still a brave man. The young and the old, joining at last the two ends of a protracted great tradition, that is something I will never forget until the day I die. . . .

"How did you live?" Hassim asked. "How did you get your provisions?"

"At night I used to send down two of my men to the villages at the base of the mountain," Old Bio said. "But when it became impossible we ate grass and the leaves of trees, and finally, we ate the bark and roots of every living thing on the mountaintop. Even those did not last long, so we started boiling stones in plain water. Luckily there was a stream on the other side of the mountain, away from the bivouacs of the enemy and unapproachable from the plain because it was walled up by a rough scaffolding of huge rocks and boulders. That was some dish. Then we ate most of our garments. One of my men who had a pair of shoes wept like a child when we cut the leather into shreds and cooked it. Ay, those were great days. Only Old Bio is left now to fight the new dogs in our country!"

"You are still a fighting man," Hassim said with sincerity.

"Yes, we are the same now," Old Bio said sadly. "We have no more family to go back to when it is all over."

Hassim reached for the old man's shoulder and pressed it ever so gently, to let him know that he understood his loss; and in that light pressure the old man realized there was no need for tears, so he shook away the gathering mist in his eyes and returned the pressure. They were standing in the darkness with their private thoughts, looking toward the dark hills beyond the silent valley below them and down, down, down to the plains where they had worked and laughed with their families and neighbors and friends, and it seemed so long ago now that they were living in the jungle and waiting in the night for the other party with the message that would fling them into far and unknown battlements of freedom.

Hassim did not know the exact details of his new assignment. He only knew that he was going to the city with six men who had been picked out from the underground to accompany him. He was lucky to have the old man for a guide because he knew the mountains and the plains. He did not give any importance to what happened to himself when infiltrating enemy lines and entering unfriendly towns; so he was glad indeed to have the old man, but would definitely refuse to accept his judgments. He knew the peasants of the plains. They were stubborn when resisting ideas foreign to their tradition, but were sentimental and oftentimes their emotions dictated their judgments. And they were superstitious to the point of idiocy. Still, their belief in the innate humanity of man was utterly dedicated and deathless. Surely Hassim, who himself had come from the peasants of the south, could rely on no other in his many secret missions but the peasants everywhere, from this day and forever. The valorous deeds of the peasants were magnificent, as he himself knew. So from the very beginning of the underground his fate was inextricably intertwined with theirs. Now beyond this palpable and trembling fate, beyond that hour when they reached their destination, their collective fate would be crystallized beyond doubt, beyond all reasoning and reckoning, and the destiny of the whole peasantry would be shaped irrevocably, unalterably, in success or in defeat, as he himself knew.

Old Bio shifted his weight from one foot to the other. He saw the flowing skyline where it crescented the quivering rim of the tree-tops on the dark hills beyond the valley below them. The automatic rifle was slung on his back and the filtering gray light from the sky glinted sharply on the cold metal of its deadliness. He sighed. He was hungry. He had climbed mountains and waded across rivers and marched through parched lands to guide Hassim to this designated hill, where they were waiting now for the other party to arrive. But he knew he had accomplished a task that a man of his age could not have survived bodily if he did not believe in the righteousness of what he was doing. He shifted his weight again.

"Is Alipato with them?" he asked Hassim.

"No," Hassim said. "Dimasalang is with them. He brings the message from Alipato, but he is going back to the camp."

Fear crossed the old man's mind. No, it was not fear after all. It was a counteracting feeling of fear and courage. Swept over completely by this feeling, he became hungrier. He brushed a rough palm across his face.

"Are you hungry?" he asked.

"A little," Hassim said.

"I will go down to the valley and pick up something."

"Don't bring a carabao."

"If I find one," he said, laughing, "I will carry it up the hill. And I will eat it raw, hide and all."

Hassim laughed, too. He took a bottle of wine from his knapsack and unscrewed the cap with one twist of the wrist, put it between his lips, and swallowed three mouthfuls; wiping the top with his sleeve, he gave it to the old man. Old Bio put the bottle in his mouth and took a long drink, almost without swallowing, so that the red fluid went down his throat like a streamlet falling between two rocks into a cavernous pool, rumbling and regurgitating as it reached his stomach. Then he handed it back to Hassim.

"I will go now," he said.

"I will wait for you here," Hassim told him. "In case they arrive before you come back, I will give you the signal. Wait for me below."

"Do you think they will arrive tonight?"

"I hope so."

"I will watch for your signal."

"Be careful."

But there was no need to advise the old man. He easily scrambled down the steep embankment. When he reached the first ledge that led to a series of ledges, he jumped like a young goat; then he was jumping from ledge to ledge until he disappeared in the tall grass of the dark valley.

Hassim watched the shadow disappear in the darkness. Again he put the bottle in his mouth, and the sudden warmth that the wine spread throughout his body wrapped him with a melancholy feeling and made him think affectionately of the old man. He knew the old man's two sons had been thrown over a high cliff at the mouth of the river in his village by the special police of the town *hacendero**\* and that one of his granddaughters hanged herself after she had been repeatedly raped by fifteen constabulary men. The old man wanted to die then, fighting the enemy with a bolo. But one of Hassim's men dragged him away, and the two of them escaped to the mountains. That was how he joined the underground at the beginning of the war. His services were indeed valuable because he knew the land and the people. And that was why he was sent by his division commander to contact Hassim, who was organizing a mass base for the underground among the friendly peasants in the north. Old Bio had performed his task admirably, for on their way to the rendezvous they had succeeded in evading the enemy. Hassim knew many details concerning the operations of the enemy, being the chief of the underground's counterintelligence unit whose sole responsibility was the gathering of information relating to the atrocities and brutalities committed upon the people by the enemy and the mercenary police of the landlords, and the *tulisanes*, who were outlaw bands of discontented elements operating in the plains and claiming partisan status, but who were actually demanding contributions from the landlords and looting the livestock and produce of belligerent peasants.

Hassim cursed bitterly because of the old man's loss, although he

\*A landlord.

himself lost his father during the long retreat to the mountains, when the commanding general of the enemy personally supervised a three-pronged punitive expedition against the underground that swept across the plains, burning towns and villages as they passed, rolling up the scarred hills that slackened their movement because of their heavy equipment. Then he lost a brother in the mountaintop where they had found refuge all night, when daylight came and planes came also, dropping bombs that shook the mountainside and pulverized the trees. He thought he would never see another day again, but he lived through the terrible bombing and bombardment by heavy artillery. Three of his men who covered the retreat at the base of the mountain were beheaded. But the rest of his division escaped in small groups on the third night and regrouped in a friendly village. And when the enemy's military intelligence discovered they had been there, in that friendly village, it was burned to ashes. Many of the peasants were hanged and beheaded and thrown over the cliff at the mouth of the river. That was the old man's village, and it happened at the beginning of the war and now it was four years later and the old man had not gone back because there was nothing left for him to see. There was only the land now growing tall with lush weeds and grass because there were no trained and loving hands to make it green and beautiful with vegetation again. There were only fond memories now to go back to, but these you could take with you wherever you went hiding and fighting in the jungles and hills and mountains that you knew so well, believing more than ever in the work of the underground and that it alone could bring back what you cherished fondly since birth, and that was your right to have a home and family and a piece of land and some animals to work it with, that was all you wanted, and to make friends with your neighbors, although now, if you ever went back, you went alone and no one was left to receive you because they were all dead, so you would not go back anymore, but would keep on fighting in these jungles and hills and mountains that you knew so well until the whole island was free from the terror.

The terror, Hassim murmured to himself and looked toward the dark hills. The wine was in his head now, and it confused him a little. How long ago was it that he had slept without fear? He could not remember, after all the years of living in the jungle with a loaded gun always in his hand and always fully dressed when sleeping or resting under trees, ready at any moment to strike out into the night with the gun blazing in his hand, alert like a wild animal to sound and smell, because he had to protect the only life he had for the underground. The underground was his life now. He had never known any other life because he was too young when he joined the underground. That was almost at the beginning of time, when he was sixteen going on seventeen, although now he was only twenty-one. His only contact with the past was a bright rainbow of memory flung scimitar-like across the troubled sky of all his world, plunging him enchanted into more and more dangerous missions when that vision shone bright and pointed in his mind. That was his old world, hugged deep in the luminous conduits of his memory, and this new one, the underground, bridging a life of youth and innocence and a life of quick action and harsh decisions, and leading him now into the broad world of acute tenderness and pitiless death.

Pitiless death, Hassim murmured again, still looking toward the dark hills. Then he saw the signal coming through the trees: two short flashes of light, darkness, then a long light. He was suddenly relieved. He took the flashlight from his knapsack and answered it; then, looking down the valley below him, he flashed the light again for the old man. He put back the flashlight in the knapsack and took out the automatic pistol and started climbing down the steep embankment.

There were a few stars in the sky. He could feel the comforting cool light floating like silk in the grass and on the stones. When he came to the edge of the meadow, he felt at once the deadly silence of the place. He thought for a brief moment that he was in the bottom of an abandoned deep dark well. But a slight wind was rising from the other side of the valley toward the hills, and he wanted to believe that it was a wind before rain. He felt relieved because it was safer to travel in the open country when the enemy was sleeping or hiding from the rain. Rain was a smokescreen for the underground. It was good for the land they were fighting for, binding the two, the land and the underground, with its tenuous fecundity. And night was good for the underground, bad for the enemy, separating the two, the enemy and the underground; for darkness was a deadly weapon to one, sudden death to the other. Rain and night, both eternal elements, eternally bound with the eternal struggle of man to be free. Rain and night, born of the elements of the earth where man kneels on his bruised knees to scratch a living, crying to all the world that he should be free.

Hassim looked up at the sky instinctively and knew at once the feasibility of his belief that the first rain of summer was on its way to the plains.

Then he saw the old man coming toward him. Old Bio was carrying something big under his arm.

"They have come?" Old Bio asked."

"Yes."

"Then they are safe."

"They are safe," Hassim repeated.

"I found a melon patch," said Old Bio, patting his burden.

"Anything is good for us."

Old Bio knelt on the grass and cut the melon lengthwise with a spring knife. He could feel the cool juice dripping between his fingers. He got up and gave half of the melon to Hassim. Then they started walking to the dark hills, eating silently. When they crossed the valley the wind became stronger, singing in the tall grass. They came to a deserted farmhouse. They stood at the gate wondering if the people who owned it had been killed or had escaped to the hills like so many others in this part of the country. Then they walked on, scattering the melon seeds in the singing grass.

When they reached the base of the dark hills, Old Bio motioned to Hassim to follow him. There was a narrow trail at the edge of a ravine. The old man seemed to know it well enough because even in the darkness his feet were sure and steady. Hassim followed the old man. And now he could hear the wind whispering softly in the trees. And the trees were thick and tall now because they were in another part of the great forest. Then they saw the other party waiting for them in a clearing surrounded by tall pine trees.

**H**assim knew at once that the man who was standing and silhouetted sharply against the dark trees was Dabu. The unmistakable shock of long black hair on a large head set too close to the broad shoulders was moving in the wind. He was smoking a cigarette carefully cupped in the palm of his hand; the flickering small red glow showed only faintly a few yards away, like a glowworm intrepidly climbing up and down a long blade of grass. There were two others sitting on their hams beside him, but Hassim could not readily identify them. He caught a quick glimpse of the cold gleam of the metal of their guns in the wavering starlight.

When Dabu recognized Hassim, he bent down quickly, shoved the unfinished cigarette under a shoe and crushed it. Then he reached for Hassim's approaching hand. The two men got up, and Hassim knew that they were Legaspi and Dante; and in that knowledge there stalked a frightening realization in his mind, though vaguely understood at the moment, that his mission this time was dangerous indeed. Dabu the merciless, Hassim was thinking when he shook their hands, and now these two, Dante the bitter and Legaspi the fool. . . .

They shook the old man's hand and patted him affectionately on the back.

"Are they all here?" Hassim asked.

"All present and in good health," Dabu said, using the password of the underground.

"I am glad."

"There was a little trouble on the way, but Dimasalang brought fifty of his men and helped us in our passage south."

Hassim looked toward the darkness of the forest and knew surely that Dimasalang's men were hiding there to cover their secret conference.

"How goes it with you?" Dabu broke the temporary silence.

"A little tired," Hassim said.

"Your mission to the north accomplished to the satisfaction of the Political Committee?"

"Accomplished even to my own satisfaction," Hassim said, meaning it because he was a perfectionist. "And it is in good hands now. We will have a good organization there real soon."

"I would like to take over there after this mission," Legaspi said seriously. "It is a new territory and needs competent leadership."

Dabu chuckled. Legaspi dismissed him with the wave of a hand.

"I will recommend you to the Political Committee," Hassim said. Then remembering the old man, who was unable to participate in the conversation because he was still puffing heavily, he said, "I think Old Bio is hungry. We ate a melon a while ago, crossing the valley on our way here."

Dabu patted the old man's back playfully and said, "You will have a whole roast chicken, old one."

"Show me the chicken, son," Old Bio answered. "I will swallow it without chewing. Listen," he said, putting both hands on his stomach. "Do you hear it rumbling?"

They all laughed.

"And if you like goat meat, young and tender," Legaspi titillated the old man's appetite, "There is – "

"Now, now, Legaspi," Dante admonished him.

"What is wrong with goat meat?" Old Bio asked, baffled, not knowing that these three men were always on the verge of laughing when they were thinking of something mischievous that they had done. "I like goat meat. I like it sizzling hot over burning pine cones."

"Well, you know," Legaspi said laconically, winking at the old man.

Old Bio understood Legaspi's implication. He thought, These young rascals are trying to put something over on me. But he said aloud, "Ay, it is not my first time to eat a stolen animal."

"Good Old Bio," Dabu said.

The old man clicked his tongue. He turned to Dante and said, "I have not seen you before."

"This is Dante," Hassim said.

"So you are Dante?" Old Bio leaned over Dante, who was barely five feet tall. "So you are the one who wrote about me in a book?"

"You are a great man," Dante complimented him.

"Ay," Old Bio murmured, pulling his beard.

"Dante takes care of the propaganda department of our organization," Hassim explained. "His job is mostly inside the camp. This is his first time to come out."

"This is Dante's field, old one," Dabu said, tapping his forehead lightly with a finger. "Too much here, but very sour."

"Sour to the enemy, eh?"

"And too bitter."

"Is the enemy so low and foul that he can stomach all that?"

"You said it."

Old Bio peered at Dante's face. Dante was a small man, but he had a way of standing straight on his toes. At first glance you would think that he was six inches taller than his actual height. Now he was standing on his toes, challenging the old man's curious stare. The old man was nearly six feet tall, almost as tall as Hassim , who was the tallest of them all.

Legaspi was fascinated by the old man's curiosity. He said, to intensify his curiosity, "Dante has lived in America, old one."

"You have lived in America?" Old Bio leaned over Dante again, peering at Dante's face.

"Fifteen years," Dante said guardedly.

"Is it true that everybody has an automobile in America?"

"Almost everybody," Dante said. But suddenly remembering that he never had one, he added sarcastically, "Didn't you know, old one? Everybody is rich in that land of the free."

"Ay," Old Bio said, not understanding Dante's sarcasm. He straightened his tall frame and pulled at his beard again. He said, "What a country!"

"Tell the old man about the American women that you have known," Legaspi urged Dante.

"Eh," Old Bio exclaimed with surprise. "You have known some American women?"

Dante nodded his head slightly.

"Tell me about them."

Dabu laughed. Legaspi, who had started the gay mood, pulled at his lower lip, smiling.

Hassim interrupted them. "We should be going," he said.

Old Bio was disappointed. He was expecting an exciting story from Dante, but this Hassim was always on the go. He was always in a great hurry, even when there was no need for it. He sighed deeply.

"Dante will tell you about the American women some other time, Old Bio," Dabu consoled him. Then he said, "Follow me."

They walked single file. Dabu was ahead. Hassim was at the end. The grass was tall in this part of the hill. Dabu made a path with a sapling that he had snatched off a tree. They walked stealthily. Only a man used to forest life could have detected that five men were walking in the darkness, and only he could have understood their presence.

The stars were bright and pointed now. Somewhere in the western horizon, where the angry sea met the gray land, was a quick flash of lightning, bursting with its full glory across the heart of the night and receding farther away west, dying there in the farthest west, where the outer sea spread out to the outside world.

Dabu cocked his head left and right. He knew his ability in a sudden attack, he knew what to do in an emergency. But what of the others? he thought. Surely Hassim can take care of himself, and Dante also. But what of the foolish one, this laughing Legaspi who is always overconfident, and the old man whose eyes are probably bad in the dark? Well, I will take care of them. He chuckled. Then it suddenly came to him that Legaspi could take care of himself and that the old man could take care of himself also. Had not Legaspi fought with him in many battles against the enemy? And had not Old Bio once defied two hundred well-armed soldiers with twelve men for ten months somewhere in these mountains? He frowned with shame.

They entered the forest. The pine needles felt soft and feathery under their shoes. The trees were tall and ancient, rising up to fifty feet or more. Furry ferns were growing in the underbrush and thickets; as Legaspi walked through them, he snatched a handful of the curled tender ends and started eating the slimy plant, although at this very moment he was thinking feverishly of a hilarious joke that he had heard once in a village so he could spring it on the old man when the opportunity came, to see if he could take it. But his mind was not retentive enough; it was even dull at times. He lived from day to day, as though the time of his life were segments of acutely experienced moments to be threaded by a deeply felt common experience somewhere in the future, if he lived long enough to do it himself. Because he could not remember the joke, although it was crawling insinuatingly at the tip of his tongue, he began chewing the tender ferns rapidly and in great amounts, almost choking himself when he swallowed the half-masticated slimy plant. Then he gave up trying to remember the joke, gathered an armful of the ferns, and walked on in silence.

Dante was ahead of Legaspi. He was next to Dabu. He was not thinking of anything in particular. He refused to think at certain moments, and this was one of those moments. When he remembered things that happened to him in the land called America, he was unpredictable, and his serpentlike tongue would lash out words of bitterness one moment and words of great beauty the next. He sometimes perturbed his companions. He was thirty-five years old, older than his companions by almost ten years, except the old man of course, who was walking behind Legaspi. And his hair was completely gray.

Old Bio was thinking of food and the wine in Hassim's knapsack.

Only Hassim was thinking of the magnitude of their mission. Beyond their mission was a diaphanous wall of nonessentials, the unnecessary but natural impediments of a heroic deed. And as they approached the hideout, Hassim felt an electriclike tightening of his body and a heavy weariness began to settle on his mind. He walked automatically, almost like a mesmerized person. He always felt this way before leaping into action, but once it was overcome, for it happened only a minute, his movements were decisive and furiously coordinated with his thoughts. He always came out victorious though afraid, measuring the nearness of death. Would he always be lucky? He would not think of that fatal moment.

They rounded the sharp brow of the hill. Two guards leaped out of the darkness and guided them to the hideout. It was a huge cave, sandy and carpeted with prickly weeds. It smelled of wild animals' dung and the decay of age.

Hassim entered the cave mouth. He saw a flickering candle stuck on a big stone. He saw the shadows of men gathered around the periphery of light. In the four corners, indistinguishable because they were in the darkness, were more men, silent and waiting. Then he saw Dimasalang sitting on the cave floor, in the candlelight; and beside him was Linda Bie, who was blowing noiselessly at a reed flute.

Dimasalang leaped to his feet. He was of average height, tanned by the sun, large-eared and big-throated. His khaki shirt was open at the neck, exposing throbbing large veins. The sleeves were rolled up to the elbows, revealing crisscrossing knotted muscles. There was a swiftness about him that told you in one sweeping glance that he was a man of great ability. And he was. And the underground was proud of him: with two hundred men of the underground he had killed eight hundred of the enemy soldiers in one skirmish, losing only one of his men.

Linda Bie rose slowly when he saw Hassim. He smiled when he recognized the old man. Linda Bie was twenty-two, delicate and almost fragile. He was unlike Dimasalang in many respects: he was not a peasant and he had a good formal education. His father was an influential corporate lawyer in his province who had amassed a sizable fortune that he had divided proportionately among his three sons when he retired. But Linda Bie, drawn to the cause of the revolting peasants by a peasant schoolmate who was working his way through college, flatly refused his inheritance. That was the beginning of his severance with his father and his complete estrangement with the rest of his family, for immediately afterward, his father having stopped his allowance, he joined the peasant union in his province and was later made district organizer. He went into the underground at the beginning of the war, and six months later he was given a division to command. But even now, after four terrible years in the underground, he still had the marked distinctions of the middle class.

Dimasalang grabbed Hassim's hand and embraced the old man. Dabu and Legaspi stood by. Dante disappeared in a corner. Linda Bie saluted Old Bio, who was glad to see the young man again.

"Welcome," Dimasalang greeted them.

"I am glad you came through," Hassim said.

"We had a little trouble. How about you?"

"Luck was at my side, and the old man."

Dimasalang smiled at the old man. "How are you, Old Bio?" he asked.

"I am hungry," he answered.

"I forgot," Hassim said. "The old one wants some goat meat."

Dabu laughed heartily.

"Show him the pot," Dimasalang told Legaspi.

Legaspi motioned to the old man to follow him. They walked to a corner of the cave. And it was then that Hassim saw, when Legaspi lifted the black canvas that separated the main floor of the cave and the interior, a smaller cave, where a pot was boiling on three elongated stones set upright in the form of a triangle. It was then that he saw the back of a woman there, bending over the fire and stirring the pot with a wooden ladle.

Dimasalang noticed his curiosity. But he asked, "Are you hungry?"

"I am, but I can't eat," Hassim said. "Let us discuss the business first."

"It can wait. We will not leave until midnight."

"Did my report from the north come through?"

"It came before we left. Everything was arranged according to your instructions."

"That is good."

"You did a good job."

Hassim nodded his head in silence. He was tired and sleepy. He waved a weak hand toward the darkness of the cave.

"You should rest," Dimasalang said.

"Yes." He turned to Dabu and said, "Will you wake me up in two hours?"

"I will, Hassim."

"Why not have a little whiskey?" Dimasalang suggested. "It will help you to sleep."

"Do you have some around?"

Dimasalang winked at Linda Bie, who disappeared in the darkness and returned with a bottle.

"American," Hassim commented. "How did you get it?"

"We got it on the way here," Dimasalang said.

Dabu smiled mysteriously. Linda Bie fumbled with his flute.

"We have three cases," Dimasalang informed Hassim. "You and your companions will have six bottles, one for each person. We will take the rest to the camp."

Hassim uncorked the bottle and lifted it to his mouth. He closed his eyes and swallowed the stinging fluid. He felt someone tugging at his elbow. He looked aside and saw that it was Old Bio. The old man's Adam's apple was racing up and down; his eyes were critically measuring the whiskey. Hassim gave him the bottle and wiped his mouth with the back of his hand.

Old Bio tore at the leg of a roasted goat and drank three large mouthfuls. He did not know what to do with the bottle, but finally decided to give it to Dimasalang. Then he retreated to the inner cave, belching and breaking wind as he disappeared behind the black canvas.

Dabu wanted to howl but could not. Linda Bie pounded him on the back with a tight fist. Hassim was not interested in their byplay.

"I will sleep now," he said to Dimasalang. "But I would like to know who are coming with me."

"Dabu, Legaspi, Dante, Linda Bie, Old Bio, and Mameng," Dimasalang said .

"Mameng? But why Mameng?"

"You will need her."

"Is that Mameng?" Hassim looked in the direction of the inner cave.

"Yes."

Hassim's throat suddenly went dry. He resented the idea of bringing a woman with him, but there was nothing he could do. It was the decision of the Central Committee, and it was final, so final that even he, Hassim, could not do anything about it. And there was also this Linda Bie, brave but immature politically, and darling of the underground. Why didn't they send somebody else? Why didn't they send Reg, Alipato's brother, for instance? Or Sol, the commander of the Central Division? And Mameng? Why? He was getting sleepy.

Dimasalang was watching Hassim closely. He wondered if Hassim had not been overworked. He had hardly finished his task up north when the new assignment came from the Central Committee. He felt compassion for Hassim. He wished he could contravene the decision, but knew he could not. He remained silent.

Linda Bie noticed Hassim's weariness. Softly, delicately he started playing his flute.

Hassim made a comical gesture with his hand. "I will sleep now," he said.

"Go ahead," Dimasalang told him. "We will discuss the matter when you wake up."

"I will wake you up," Dabu assured him.

Hassim stumbled to a corner of the cave, sat on the ground, leaned against the wall without unstrapping his knapsack, and closed his tired eyes. Linda Bie's music came to him like a faraway whisper, soothing him to sleep. Now his head was like a Ferris wheel; somewhere in his semiconsciousness was the faint tingling of a merry-go-round, and behind it, when it stopped, was calliope music. Where had he heard that? Was it when he was seven years old? Was that the time when his father took him to the provincial carnival and he ate ice cream for the first time? Or was it when he took Consuelo for a long walk around the cigar factory where he had worked for fifty centavos a day? And where was Consuelo now? Consuelo . . .

Hassim shook his tightening head, trying to remember. But the merry-go-round came again, then the Ferris wheel; and he felt the world moving under him, sinking under him. Then the noise in his head stopped, leaving a spreading pain. Then there was Linda Bie's fading flute music again, and sleep came to him like the touch of a sparrow's wings.

Outside the rain began falling, bringing with it the pleasant smell of the meadows and the piney fragrance of the great forest.

## CHAPTER THREE

. . . . . . . . . . . . . . . . . . . . . . . . . . . . . . . . . . . . . .

**H**assim was awakened at midnight in the middle of a dream. When he opened his eyes the cave seemed a momentary illusion, withdrawing slowly away like a faraway nightfall. The darkness around him was still a floating vessel of sleep, overflowing with the bright fragments of his dream. When the old man touched him again, he realized his awkward position. He almost laughed to hide it. But the tenacity of the moment came to him suddenly, violently. In the semidarkness he saw the old man, grave, fully packed, the automatic rifle slung on his back. Jumping to his feet, he saw the flickering candlelight on the other side of the cave and the men sitting around it in silence. The incisive poignancy of the moment struck him full in the face, and immediately he lost all the bright fragments of his dream. And nothing was left but the aching poignancy of the moment.

"Are you ready?" Old Bio asked.

"Yes."

"They are waiting."

"I must have overslept."

"You needed some rest."

"Did you sleep?"

"An hour."

"It is better than nothing."

"That is correct."

"Let us go."

Hassim swung his arms and legs vigorously to hasten the circulation of the blood. Then he walked out of the darkness, following the old man.

They looked at him when he approached the candlelight. He stood for a moment scrutinizing their faces, his shadow flung weirdly across the cave wall. He almost screamed when he saw in their faces the piercing light of their desire to move on in the night. He saw Mameng's unlovely mouth and broken nose. And he suddenly knew, looking at her plain face, that the ugliness of death could not contend with all the beauty in the broad and alien world.

"Are you ill?" Dimasalang asked him.

"I am all right."

"We will discuss the business."

Hassim looked around and noticed that most of the men had left the cave. The black canvas was gone. The pot and the improvised stove were gone. The ashes were covered with sand.

"Where are the others?" Hassim asked.

"They are outside." Dimasalang said.

"Do you expect anything?"

"Precaution and expediency."

Hassim cast a glance at the cave mouth and saw the shadows of two guards and the dark tree trunks beyond them. He saw the leaves of a sapling moving in the wind. How tenderly the wind caresses the leaves, he thought, sitting down among them, between Dimasalang and Dabu.

Legaspi offered him a cigarette, and Linda Bie, who had a flint in his hand, moved to light it. But Hassim had already leaned toward the candle. Mameng noticed his shaking hand. Dante, sitting directly in front of him, was suddenly swept over by a terrible premonition, seeing Hassim's eyes in the soft candlelight. Old Bio steadied his hand. Hassim lit the cigarette and inhaled hard, then exhaled lingeringly, the smoke trailing out of his nostrils magnificently and unfolding above them like a sunflower in full bloom. He felt better. He licked his lips.

"Proceed." he said to Dimasalang.

Now six pairs of eager eyes shifted from Hassim to Dimasalang. Hassim was looking at the glowing tip of his cigarette. Beyond the tiny glow he saw Dimasalang's pistol stuck inside his belt and the pouch of cartridges hanging near it. And he remembered with sadness that there were always guns in the meetings he had attended. And he wondered, waiting for Dimasalang to speak, if there would ever be a meeting without guns, if there would ever be any need for them in the world.

"This mission is of great importance to us," Dimasalang began, looking at their faces. "That is why Hassim has been selected by the Central Committee to take charge of it."

All eyes were shifted back to Hassim, then again to Dimasalang.

"That is why all of you have been selected to accompany Hassim," Dimasalang continued. "Each and every one of you has a specific task to perform. You will discuss the details among yourselves."

"Well?" Hassim said.

Dimasalang cast a sweeping glance at their faces. "It is this, comrades," he said, leaning closer to them, the muscles in his face tightening, his small black eyes glittering darkly. "A man from the United States is waiting in the city with money for our cause."

"How much?" Hassim asked.

"One million pesos. Maybe a little more."

Old Bio whistled softly. Dabu's hand leaped to his thick mop of hair. Legaspi's mouth hung wide open, so great was his astonishment. Dante's curiosity was aroused beyond quelling: the man they were going to meet came from America, the land he could not forget. Even Mameng's broken nose twitched.

Only Linda Bie took the announcement nonchalantly. Money was of no importance to him personally, but he knew that one million pesos could buy many things for them. Ammunition and medicines, for instance. It was something that his successful father had taught him: the value of money. He picked at his teeth, contemplating the tremendous amount.

When Dimasalang knew that his announcement had been carefully digested in their minds, he looked deliberately in the direction of Dante.

"Dante knows the man," he said.

"Yes?" Dante said

"His name is Felix Rivas."

"What?" Dante exclaimed, rising from his crouching position. "Felix Rivas? I thought he was dead!"

"He is very much alive."

They looked at Dante. Disbelief was written all over his face.

"How did you find out I knew him?" he asked.

"We have friends in the United States. That we found out is enough for our present purposes. The important thing is to bring Felix alive to the camp."

"I can't believe that he is still alive. He was dying when I left the United States."

"He is alive, Dante," Dimasalang told him with finality. "And he is one of us."

"You mean he is – ?" Dabu interrupted.

Dimasalang nodded his head vigorously. "That is why Dante is going with you," he explained. "He is the only one who can identify Felix."

"Is there any possibility that the enemy has heard of his presence?" Hassim asked.

"There is. And of course you know the consequences if his presence is discovered."

"The enemy will put a man in his place."

"Naturally. A man exactly like Felix, complete with his disfigurements." Dimasalang looked at Mameng with expressionless eyes. "And I mean vital disfigurements."

"I know Felix a kilometer away," Dante said. "He has a stiff left leg. I was with him when he was operated on. Besides, I have lived with him for years."

"That is so," Dimasalang said.

"Do you have any picture of him?" Hassim asked.

Dimasalang shook his head. Hassim rubbed his eyes, thinking.

"One other thing," Dimasalang said and stopped, hearing footsteps approaching them from outside the cave.

They turned to the cave mouth. Two men entered with their hands up, followed by three guards with carbines. Dabu leaped to his feet and snatched the gun in his knapsack. Dimasalang restrained him with a hand without looking at him. He knew that Dabu was always quick of action.

The two men entered the cave. One of the guards stepped forward, moving sideways, his carbine pointed at the men.

"What is the meaning of this?" Dimasalang asked.

"We found them climbing up the hill," the guard said.

Dimasalang sucked his lips. "What were you doing on this hill?" he demanded.

Silence. Linda Bie lit his flint and went to the men. He lifted it to their faces long enough for the others to see them. They looked alike.

"Well, what were you doing on the hill?" Dimasalang demanded again.

"We heard you were here," the older man said.

"Where did you hear that?"

"In our village."

"Where is your village?"

"About sixty kilometers from here."

"You heard in your village that we were here tonight?"

"Yes."

Dimasalang looked at Hassim, then back to the men. "Why did you come here?" he asked.

Silence. Dimasalang walked toward them, the gun in his hand. He stood before them, his eyes glittering.

"We want to join you," the younger man said.

"Why?"

"They killed our father."

So they are brothers, Linda Bie thought. How tragic that they always come too late.

"Who killed your father?" Dimasalang asked.

"The constabulary men."

"Put your hands down."

They obeyed. The older brother looked at Dimasalang, then at the others, pausing at Hassim's face, and back to Dimasalang.

"Are you Dimasalang?" he asked.

Dimasalang stiffened.

"I recognize Hassim," the younger brother said.

"Which one?" his brother asked.

He pointed to Hassim. "The one beside him is Dabu."

Dabu rocked on his heels.

"Take them outside," Dimasalang told the guards.

"Wait a minute," Hassim said. "Bring them to the light."

The guards shoved them to the candlelight with their guns. The older man glanced at his brother with reproach.

Hassim approached the older man. "Show me your hands," he said.

The older man looked at his brother.

"Show me your hands," Hassim repeated.

Slowly he raised his hands, palms up. Hassim ran his fingers across the man's soft palms, lingering at the fingertips where the skin was as soft as silk. All the black dirt and jungle vine juices could not conceal the damning fact that they were not peasant hands. Hassim looked at the man's eyes: it was a death sentence.

"You," he said to the younger brother. "Show me your hands."

He did not hesitate like his brother. Hassim made the same investigation. He turned to Dimasalang.

"That is what I thought," he said. "Where do these dogs get their information?"

"What?" Dabu exclaimed.

"See for yourself."

Dabu leaped over the stone where the candle was burning and grabbed the two men's hands, examining the palms the way Hassim did it.

"You dogs!" Dabu snarled, slapping their faces. "Where did you get your information?"

"Enough of that," Dimasalang said calmly. "I will find out. Take them away."

They watched them walk silently out of the cave.

"We don't have much time," Dimasalang said, thinking of the two men. "As I was saying, Felix Rivas has instructions from the United States explaining how we could get more money from our friends over there. And there is a possibility that we could get a shipload of arms and medicine."

Old Bio said, "We are not alone?"

"We are not alone, old one," Dimasalang told him. "Where there is oppression, we have friends. When we fight for freedom, we have friends everywhere. Our fight is one and indivisible. So we are not alone, old one."

"Ay."

"Mameng will contact Felix Rivas," Dimasalang continued. "His name now is Mabini."

"How would I approach him?"

"Use a password, Mameng."

"Well?"

"*How is Julie?*" Dimasalang said. "That is the password. You will have to make up the rest."

They murmured the password.

"But it is a woman's name?" Legaspi suddenly exclaimed.

"It is so," Dimasalang said. "And it is better so. Now, is everything clear?"

"Suppose he does not speak our dialect?" Mameng asked.

"He speaks all our dialects and five other languages including English," Dante explained.

"You don't have to worry about that, Mameng," Dimasalang said. "Hassim will tell you your specific job later."

Hassim nodded his head. Dimasalang took a map from his shirt pocket and unfolded it. He spread the map on the stone beside the candle and studied it. The route was marked from numbers one to seven, beginning from the cave where they were hiding to the city. Dimasalang's finger stopped at the spot marked "7", in the city.

"This is the spot," he said, pointing to a street corner. "This is where you will contact Mabini."

Mameng studied the spot and the surrounding area. Dante studied the rendezvous over Mameng's shoulder.

"Can you remember it?" Dimasalang asked.

"Yes."

"You, Dante?"

"I know the place."

"Hassim will take you there."

"Rendezvous Seven," Hassim said.

They nodded their heads in agreement.

"Remember, Hassim," Dimasalang said. "It is imperative that you take him alive. The instructions from the United States are in his head."

Dimasalang saw the surprise in Hassim's face. He said, "That is why you have to take him alive. And of course there are enough of you to carry the money."

"Of course," Old Bio said, trying to imagine the size of the sack containing one million pesos. "I will carry it myself."

"Good Old Bio," Dimasalang said, smiling approvingly at the old man. "But you will not be able to walk a yard. It takes five big sacks to hold that much money."

"That many?"

"Maybe more," Linda Bie said.

Incredulity crossed the old man's face. Then he said, "I had fifty pesos once. I had it in my pocket for over a year."

"What happened to it?" Legaspi asked jokingly.

"The priest took it away when my firstborn son died," he said. They laughed.

"What are you laughing about?" Old Bio asked.

"You will see, old one," Linda Bie said.

"Ah, well." Old Bio sighed.

Dimasalang gave the map to Hassim; then, taking a piece of paper from his pocket, he said, "Your instructions are in here, Hassim."

Hassim took the map and the piece of paper and put them in his pocket. Dimasalang looked at his watch.

"It is one o'clock," he said. "Let us get going."

Dabu went outside and returned with two pistols. "Well, old one," he said to Old Bio, "you will have to give up your rifle."

"Give up my rifle?"

"We will carry pistols."

"But I have never parted with it?"

"You don't want to walk in the streets of the city with that big gun of yours slung on your back, do you?"

Understanding came to the old man. Unwillingly he unslung his rifle and said, "I have been with it for years. Why, it is my right arm."

Dimasalang smiled at him. "I will give you my gun, Old Bio," he said. "Give me your rifle. I will take good care of it."

Old Bio took Dimasalang's gun and caressed it. "You are really giving it to me?"

"For the duration of the trip. And if you make good use of it, you may have it for always."

"Ay."

"Are you ready?" Hassim asked his companions.

They nodded their heads. Dimasalang walked out of the cave, followed by Hassim. Old Bio pinched the candle flame off with his fingers and put the candle in his pocket. Then he followed the others in the darkness. At the back of his mind were similar nights of long ago. His whole body tingled with the memory. He tightened the straps of his knapsack and walked out of the cave.

The rain had stopped. The fragrance of the night met them. They stood under the open sky sniffing the delicious air. Hassim was standing beside the old man, looking skyward. He saw a few stars wetly shedding their pointed lights between the tall columns of trees.

"Are you ready?" Dimasalang asked Hassim.

"Yes."

"Go ahead. We will leave as soon as you are down the first hill."

Hassim was surrounded by his companions now. He looked at their faces and knew that they were ready. He motioned to them to follow him. As he walked downhill, his companions following him, he saw Dimasalang and his men standing darkly under the trees. They stopped at the brow of the hill, before the final descent. Then they walked on in silence.

They stopped again and looked down the silent valley below them. They were standing side by side now, profiled against the dark hill. Then they heard two shots from the direction of the cave.

"That is it," Hassim said.

"Yes," Dabu said.

"What is?" Old Bio asked.

They looked at him. But nobody said anything.

# CHAPTER FOUR

. . . . . . . . . . . . . . . . . . . . . . . . . . . . . . . . . . . . . . .

**T**hey walked all night. When only the Morning Star was left in the sky, Hassim told his companions to rest awhile. They were still in the protective seclusion of the great forest, but the break of day would expose them in the plain, if they chose to continue their trip in broad daylight.

Hassim knew from experience that it was safer to travel at night, although sometimes, when he was passing through friendly towns and villages, he dared daylight to make up for lost time. Those were rare occasions, when he endangered his life. But tonight his mission was the most dangerous in his daring career, perhaps the apogee of all that he had done for the underground. So now he told his companions to rest, under cover of the trees, before the break of day. The pause would give him some time to plan his strategy before they descended to the plain.

They sat under the trees in a circle, smoking cigarettes carefully cupped in the palms of their hands. It was a common practice among them to smoke furtively, for they traveled mostly at night, hiding in the darkness like wild animals when they smelled death stalking nearby.

Only Hassim was not smoking. He was standing outside the circle, looking skyward through the towering treetops. He was watching the vanishing Morning Star and contemplating the brightening horizon. And he was hoping the rain would come again so they would not lose time. The Morning Star vanished, displaced by the spearlike rays of the new sun.

Old Bio exclaimed, looking around the hill with surprise, "Why, it is my own country!"

"It is?" Dabu asked.

"I used to hunt in this forest. Below it is my village."

They looked at Hassim.

"Old Bio is right," he said, smiling.

The old man boasted, "I should know my own country!"

Hassim took the map and the piece of paper where his instructions were written from his pocket. He unfolded them side by side. He studied the code on the piece of paper:

OR: P

R1, OB
R2, Li
R3, D
R4, M
R5, De
R6, La
R7, H

He frowned and looked at the map. So it is a double job, he thought, mentally decoding the code:

OPERATIONAL RENDEZVOUS: POLITICAL

Rendezvous 1, Old Bio
Rendezvous 2, Legaspi
Rendezvous 3, Dabu
Rendezvous 4, Mameng

..........

Chapter
Four

Yes, he thought, it is also a political job. How clever of them to send a person back to his native place and ask the people about local conditions. We are now in Rendezvous 1. I wonder what the old man will feel when I tell him that we are going down the valley together? And it is his own valley.

Hassim scratched a match on a tree trunk. He burned the map and the piece of paper. He watched the fire creeping and when nothing remained but ashes, he crushed the black remnants with the heel of a shoe. Then he turned around to his companions.

It was Dabu who attracted him first. He had not noticed it in the cave, but now he saw the ugly scar on Dabu's neck. The enemy must have tried to hang him when he was gone, he thought. But how did he escape? I will ask him when I have the time. Then, his eyes slowly moving upward, he saw Dabu's masklike face. And for some mysterious reason he turned his face away. He could not stand the challenge in Dabu's staring cold eyes, small and dark and glistening like a snake's before striking. He trembled, realizing at once that those eyes had seen death many times, had taken their terrible shine from the nearness of death, had sucked the horrible image of death, warm death, cold death, decomposing death, death with a mask and without it, death of truth and death of lies, but still death, death, death. He closed his eyes and shook his head violently to dismember in his mind's eye that monstrous image.

When Hassim opened his eyes it was Dante's face that met his scrutiny. And in his face he saw the calm wisdom of age. He saw the roselike mouth, red as though it were a piece of fresh meat, the arrow-shaped nose, the prematurely gray hair. Quickly looking down, he saw the tapering fingers and the small feet fitted like a glove in canvas shoes. Then slightly turning to his left, he saw Legaspi. There was nothing special or extraordinary about him, except his coffee-brown complexion. Legaspi was darker than the rest of them, even darker than the old man. Legaspi was daydreaming. He was still trying to remember the joke that had haunted him that evening. And Hassim wondered how his inconspicuous face could laugh so easily, how it could mask itself with a buoyancy of spirit in moments of despair. Is this the man who has a close fraternity with life? Hassim wondered. A sharp contradiction to that Dabu, who is the barbarous image of death? Life and death.

Hassim could not know. He would never know. They were all wearing masks, as he himself knew; one for the world, another for the idea. And between those two, so near to each other and yet very far apart, was the great loneliness. The world and the idea. Where had he heard that? Man is loneliness, he thought sadly. He made the world and yet does not own it. He conceived the idea and yet it eludes him. Only loneliness belongs to him, and he has so brief a time to know the reason for it.

Hassim's eyes did not stop at Linda Bie. They traveled swiftly to the old man.

Old Bio met his gaze and felt embarrassed. He thought Hassim was looking at his feet, and he was suddenly ashamed of their size. His were peasant feet, broad and thick-heeled. His were feet used to walking unreckonable distances on the rough surfaces of the earth. The underground had given him a precious gift when he joined – his first pair of shoes – which seemed awkward in the beginning. But the nail-like hardness of his soles had softened, and oftentimes he wondered if he could walk again without shoes. Now he turned sideways and hid his enormous feet behind Legaspi, away from the dark scrutiny of Hassim.

But Hassim was not interested in the old man's feet. He looked at Mameng's plain face. He wondered why she was sent along. Then he turned away from his companions and looked toward the wide valley below them. And suddenly the sun burst out of the mountains, casting long gray shadows upon the gray forest.

Old Bio glanced at Hassim, whose eyes, which had seemed lifeless a moment before, were now intensely alive and observing. The old man kept looking at Hassim. He was hoping Hassim would turn in his direction so he could tell him what was on his mind without saying a single word. And by some unexplainable coincidence, Old Bio's wish was gratified. Hassim suddenly turned in his direction and understood the pleading look in his eyes.

"All right, old one," Hassim told Him. "You can have a drink, but you should eat. We don't want to lose you on the way. You promised to carry the money."

Everybody laughed at the joke. But the old man took it as a serious matter.

"You understand the heart of an old man, Hassim," he said. "Yes, I will eat truly." He pulled at his knapsack and out came a drumstick that he had talked out of Mameng when they were in the cave. He took a big bite at the meat, and turning to Legaspi, who was in charge of the whiskey, he said, "Well, son?"

"You will be the death of the underground yet, old one." Legaspi warned him. But he took a bottle from the sack beside him and gave it to the old man. "Where did you learn to drink early in the morning?" he asked.

"When you are my age you are liable to learn anything," Old Bio said, lifting the bottle to his mouth.

"Take it easy," Dabu admonished him. "That bottle costs a fortune."

Old Bio swallowed a mouthful and looked at Dabu with resentment. "And my life does not cost a fortune?" he said.

"You have nothing to worry about, Dabu," Dante said. "He can't take more thana glassful on an empty stomach."

Dabu was not a heavy drinker. He looked at Dante for some explanation. Hassim knew that Dante interrupted to disrupt the strained conversation. He sat on a fallen tree and lit a cigarette.

"Drinking in the morning is a common practice in America," Dante explained. "Especially by those who are addicted to the habit. I almost became addicted to it when I was living with Felix Rivas in Seattle. That is in the State of Washington, Dabu."

The old man snorted. "So I am not the only one?" he said.

"No, Old Bio," Dante told him. "Today there are fifty million alcoholics in the United States. That is nearly three times the population of our country. The American people spend ten billion dollars a year on liquor alone. That amount could keep the government here for one hundred years of lavish spending."

"Are you pulling my leg, Dante?" Old Bio asked. He was about to put the bottle in his mouth. "I did not know there is that much money in the United States."

Linda Bie laughed.

"What are you laughing about?" Old Bio asked him.

"Even if you live a billion years and keep on counting the money in the United Stats every minute of your life," Linda Bie said, "you will not finish a fraction of it."

"Eh?"

"That is true," Dante Affirmed.

The old man smacked his lips.

"There is a man in Texas who owns a ranch as large as the island of Luzon," Dante said.

"No!"

"Yes!"

"Everybody has a big ranch in the United States?"

"Millions don't have any."

"How come one man owns an enormous land?"

"He has plenty of money."

"And millions don't have any?"

"Nothing to speak of."

Old Bio swore and said, "There must be something wrong in the United States. I won't live in a country like that. I would probably murder that fabulous Texas rancher."

"Somebody will probably do it for you, if he is not dead yet."

"He better not come near me."

"He is ten thousand miles away. You will never see him, Old Bio."

"Just the same," the old man said, his voice rising as though he were giving a warning to the world, "he and his kind better not come to our island. I am warning him wherever he is: *Don't come to our island!*"

The terror and magnificence of the old man's voice was felt by everybody. Even Mameng felt it. Hassim felt it, even as he had felt it early that evening when he and Old Bio were waiting for the other party.

Old Bio sucked the bottle and snorted angrily when the fumes of the whiskey seared his nostrils. Hassim was not interested in the old man's antics.

"Did you say Felix Rivas was a heavy drinker?" he asked Dante.

"He could put down the old man three days in a row. Yes, he was a heavy drinker when I was with him. That was seven years ago. He may have changed. A man of determination could change in that length of time. Felix is a determined person."

Hassim was still perturbed.

"You have nothing to worry about, Hassim," Dante said. "He can hold his liquor."

"I am glad to know that."

"What is in drinking anyway?" Dabu interrupted.

"Loveliness and paradise," Old Bio answered him.

Dabu looked sharply at the old man. He did not know how to interpret his definition.

"That is headache and remorse to you," Linda Bie said.

"Well said," Dante commented.

"By the way." Legaspi redirected the conversation, "What did Felix Rivas do when you were with him, Dante?"

Hassim was surprised. He thought he was the only one thinking seriously about Felix Rivas.

"I had known him for a long time and he had done many things," Dante said. "When I first met him in San Francisco in 1933, he was a professional gambler. We went to Portland, Oregon, the following year in a boxcar. There he worked on a celery farm. For his health, he told me. I left him that summer and went to Seattle. From there I went to Alaska and worked in the fish canneries. A year later, when I was in Alaska again, I found him in my cannery. After the canning season we pooled our money together and went to California, where we separated because he stayed in Los Angeles and I went to Imperial Valley. He was beginning to cough that winter."

Dante was talking quietly now. He looked at the faces of his companions and wondered if they understood what he was saying in a sketchy way. He was reliving the despairing years of the depression and the heartbreaking years after, when he was rehabilitating himself body and soul in another world, a world crippled and yet obstinate, bent on rolling into another decade of confusion and the long-awaited war that came to hurt everybody again, and the confounding years that threw him, Dante, back to the very soil where he had been born only to discover that his roots had been torn during the frantic years of his exile by the war that had come upon the world, and to find that everyone he had known in the long ago was gone. But he could not tell them the details, the days and weeks and months and years of anguish and pain and loneliness, because he was remembering only Felix Rivas for their information, and for the sake of the underground, because Felix Rivas had become important to them. And he almost broke into sudden laughter, knowing what a fool Felix Rivas was at times, remembering that mad spring when he had fallen in love with a Hollywood prostitute and when he found out that she was a lesbian, he almost took to drug addiction, so great was his disappointment. It was a shocking experience. He was twenty-four years old then, still a virgin, still hugging the wondrous illusions pertaining to women in his native land that had warmed him in a cruel and cynical country in moments of loneliness and despair and hunger. Should he tell them about these conflicts? Could they understand the dereliction of a complex country like the United States? Hassim could. Dante studied their faces.

Old Bio sighed ruefully when Dante mentioned that Felix Rivas was at one time a professional gambler. He violently despised gambling and other human frailties. In his peasant mind any form of vice or frailty belonged to the landlords and their blackguards and their spokesmen.

"It is their luxury," he had told a neighbor once, "and their death." He said to Dante, "That is bad."

"What is bad, old one?"

"You said Felix Rivas was a gambler."

"He was."

"I don't trust gamblers."

"Gambling to him was a means to an end. He took up gambling because it was the only way for him to make a living. As I was saying, he had lived many lives. Have you been following my story, old one?"

"Yes. But I still disapprove of gambling. Gamblers are liars, like politicians."

"There are many kinds of gamblers."

"They are all the same to me," Old Bio said with finality.

Dante wanted to tell the old man that even life was a gamble, and that there were several ways of betting on it. But he let it go, looking at the old man with a worldly condescension. He realized that the old man was too elemental and deeply rooted in old beliefs of morality. And looking at him condescendingly, forgiving the narrowness of his judgment but giving credence to his obstinacy to hold on to certain accepted concepts of life, Dante concluded that it was tragic that Old Bio was too old to readjust himself in a new world. It was true that the old man was with them and had been with them for some time, but his thoughts were back, almost a century back, where he had been nourished by different ideals and nurtured under different conditions. What a pity that he could not transfer the old man to the new world! Of course it was the whiskey that prompted Old Bio to pass a harsh judgment on Felix Rivas. Dante turned to Hassim and saw that he was writing his report to the Central Committee.

"Continue," Dabu said to Dante.

"Yes."

Old Bio got up and swayed like a thin reed under a heavy wind. They looked at him for a second, then to Hassim, then to Dante.

Only Mameng did not look up. Only she did not bother to see what was transpiring, for she knew it by instinct through her exclusive sex. Only she felt the temporary malignance in the atmosphere even without looking up, even in her silence. For even she had taken with her into the underground the silence and obedience and obeisance of her sex, where there was no need for them, where austerity of character and conformity to the rule were the fundamental principles, and where, above all, personality was dissolved in the general principles of the underground.

"Continue," Dabu said again.

"Well, from that time on," Dante continued, "for two years, Felix Rivas stayed in the hospital. He was sick with tuberculosis of the lungs. I did not see him for three years, but wrote to him when I had the opportunity. I kept moving around the country, up and down the Pacific Coast, following the crops and the seasons, and going to school when I had the money. Then I saw him again in 1939, in San Diego, California, where he was organizing the farm workers into an agricultural laborers' union. He was still very pale and weighed less than one hundred pounds, but he was entirely a different person mentally. I didn't know at the time that he had joined the labor movement, but he told me in confidence later. It seemed that when he was dying in the hospital some well-meaning Americans including two women got interested in him. It is easy to understand: he is a likable man, quick of laughter, perceiving and self-effacing when he knows you need sympathy. Well, these well-meaning people gave him books on general subjects to read. To refurbish his interrupted 'bourgeoisification,' he confided to me. Once, in a gay mood, I asked him about his 'proletarianization,' because he was neither one nor the other. What was his origin? That I've never found out. But as I was saying, these well-meaning people gave him books. When he was released from the hospital they gave him more books to read, but this time on trade unions and race relations in the United States. That was the beginning of the real Felix Rivas, the man whom we are going to meet. It is interesting to note in retrospect that he helped those people who had given him books that led him to the discovery of a world of unlimited intellectual possibilities, when he was out again, by giving them an unselfish friendship and sympathy and understanding."

Dante stopped and lit a cigarette. Hassim sat beside Mameng, who was busy scraping the dirt off her shoes: black canvas like the others, a man's shoes. But she was listening to Dante, trying to form a mental picture of Mabini. That was his name to her: that and no other: the other belonged to the confused long ago.

"He disappeared in 1940," Dante continued. "I saw him for the last time early in 1941. He was in a hospital in Stockton, California. He had an operation on the left knee. He had been beaten by vigilantes in San Jose, not far from Stockton, where he had gone to organize the fruit pickers. He was – " he stopped suddenly, looking sideways at Mameng.

"He was what?" Legaspi asked.

Dante hesitated.

"Go on," Old Bio urged him.

Dante's eyes became sad. And his sadness rode swiftly back on the turbulent crest of unforgotten years, unforgettable time. He bent his head away from Mameng, while his companions leaned close to him, trying to shut off Mameng from the long-awaited pronouncement.

"They crushed his testicles." Dante whispered.

There was silence for a full second. The impact of the revelation was so sharp that it violently jarred their thinking. They were not expecting a revelation such as what Dante told them, so unthinkable was it to them. But for a second only, because Linda Bie snapped his flute into two pieces, so great was his anger. Hassim closed his eyes and sighed. He felt dizzy.

"The bastards!" Dabu hissed, glancing swiftly at Hassim. He was thinking of Hassim, for he alone, he, Dabu, knew everything about Hassim, all, his political and private life.

"Goddamn it to hell!" Old Bio cursed for the first time in his life.

Legaspi almost fell on his face.

Hassim opened his eyes and said, "What a way to hurt a man."

Dante let the image of the atrocity done to Felix Rivas sink into their troubled minds, let the sadistic monstrosity seep into their disturbed consciousness. Then the sadness in his eyes was gone. It was in the eyes of his companions now. It was their sadness now. And it was for them now to remember always, if they wanted to consolidate the ashes of the past into a flaming phoenix of faith, to set afire the darkness of their own lives with it. It had been too heavy a burden for Dante to carry alone. Now they would carry it for him. They would carry it for him, now and forever. He had given it to them at last. And now it was up to them to give it another name for the world to remember. It was up to them now to besiege their individual lives with the sanguinary reality of that cruel image. And he, Dante, knew now that he had released a dark secret that was unbearable for him to remember alone through life. And his thirst for the remembrance of Felix Rivas was assuaged at last, here in the silence of the great forest.

Old Bio was the first to react. "There is nothing left?" he asked. He was thinking what a great waste that such a man could not bring forth children into the world. For that was always his first thought of men: their primal obligation to mankind. He himself had given the world several children with pride. "Then there is nothing left for him?" he repeated.

"There is something left," Dante said, fisting his right hand into a tight ball. Shaking his trembling fist under their noses and suddenly striking it sharply against the flat palm of his other hand, he whispered angrily, "The right ball is this size but soft as cotton. The left is gone: only a wrinkled bag is left."

Hassim turned his face away. Mameng closed her eyes, trying to forget what she had heard.

"The ruthless dogs." Old Bio exclaimed.

"Yes," Dante said softly.

Dabu snatched a stone off the ground and hurled it with all his might against a tree. He was trembling with rage, thinking of Hassim.

"I would rather lose my legs than that," Linda Bie said.

"Why, that is the most important thing in a man." Legaspi said.

"Are there such vicious men in the world?" Dabu asked. He had classified his viciousness as of another category, as justified viciousness. He was still looking at Hassim, still thinking of him. "Are there?"

"There are all kinds of men," Dante said. "Even among us there are all kinds of men."

Hassim turned to his companions. He knew that Dante was right. He looked at him and wondered why he was right.

"Now, what about the other thing?" Old Bio demanded.

"What other thing?" Dante said.

"He is no longer a man, is that right?"

Imcomprehension was in Dante's eyes. So Old Bio made his question more specific by drawing a phallic symbol in the air.

"Well – " Dante said.

"Will you tell me that without mincing words?"

"It is there, all right. But I don't know if it still works. That is for someone to find out."

"So that is it?" Hassim said, jumping to his feet. He looked at Mameng, thinking of Dimasalang. "What a clever man!"

Dante understood Hassim's comment. He looked at Mameng. Then the others followed his eyes.

Mameng sat quietly, her face blank; then, bending forward and covering her face with her hands, she began to cry.

Old Bio walked away. Legaspi wanted to comfort Mameng. Linda Bie wanted to play his flute, but Dabu stopped him with a movement of his hand. Dante looked at Hassim, who was wondering how to approach Mameng. Why didn't they send Luming? he asked himself. At least she is more attractive and experienced. There would be no pain and remorse for her. But Mameng? What does she know about these things? Perhaps she is still a virgin.

Hassim knew he had to carry out his orders. He knew that in the execution of this kind of order some defilement of human character was inevitable. Was there a way of consecrating it? He did not know. But his conscience told him that something human should be done to lead Mameng toward the execution of her specific task and make it less degrading and painful. And he was the one who would find the way. He turned to Mameng.

"May I speak to you, Mameng?" he said.

"Of course, Hassim," she said.

They watched her walk away with Hassim. Then they looked at each other and felt ashamed.

Hassim and Mameng stopped at a distance, behind a tree. Hassim hesitated. But the time had come for him to resolve the problem the best way he knew how. And he wondered how to begin.

"Well, Hassim?" Mameng said.

"It is this way, Mameng," Hassim apologized. "At first I did not realize why you were coming with us. It is difficult enough to creep through the jungles without a woman. And the fighting. Not that I don't like your company, remember that. It is a new experience to me. Now that I understand why you were sent with us – "

"Say it, Hassim."

"When Dante was talking about Felix Rivas, it suddenly came to me why Dimasalang sent you along. I understand it now and I am angry."

"I understand too, Hassim."

"I am glad. Now it is much easier for me to speak."

"I am listening."

"We have duties to perform."

"Yes."

"And your duty is a painful one."

"All our duties are painful."

"I – "

"Say it, Hassim,"

"I don't know how to begin."

"I can take it."

Hassim turned his face away.

Mameng touched his hand. "Say it now, Hassim," she said.

Hassim took off his cap. "Are you a virgin" he asked, trying to make it as informal as he could, reddening in the face when he spoke. "Are you, Mameng?"

Mameng took her hand away from him. Her mouth trembled. She looked downhill, thinking deeply. Should a woman lie to herself? Or was it better to tell the truth? What was compellingly secretive about virginity? Was it a throwback to the fantastic rituals of dead religions and the weird ceremonials of primitive races? A truth or a lie.

"Are you, Mameng?" Hassim asked again.

"Yes, Hassim," she said finally. She felt as though she had been released of a heavy burden, a burden that was conceived as truth but was actually a lie. "Yes," she repeated quietly.

"I thought so."

"I knew that you knew."

Hassim knew that it was like a death sentence. He knew that there were many death sentences in life, accumulating gradually as you live the years until there is no more left, the final curtain. Always around the corner of life is death rushing toward you, brandishing his merciless scythe, and one day when you are not looking he is upon you. And that is the end of your dreams. But Hassim felt that he had to hold on to the old verities a little longer. Was he wrong? Was this a challenge to his convictions? Did he still carry with him the hypocrisies of the world they were trying to destroy? Was he still heir to the schizophrenic attitudes toward the life of that world? He could be wrong.

"Then you know what you are supposed to do." he said.

"I do."

"You should experience it before we arrive at Rendezvous Seven."

"I was not thinking of that."

"It is my honest opinion. It is only to relieve you from mental and physical pain."

"I understand. But Mabini – ?"

"That is what I mean, Mameng. You should be prepared before we see him."

"I don't know."

"We are only trying to carry out our orders."

"I know."

"Who shall it be?"

Mameng looked at him, appealing to his manhood, pleading to his nobility. She knew that there would be no desecration of her virtue if she told the truth, if she followed her instincts as a woman. And knowing that, she would cast away all fears, all doubts, all shame. For there was no shame in it, if she followed her instincts as a woman in love. And she wanted to fall in love with Hassim. And that was the most important thing: the shame of it. And she would not be ashamed with Hassim. And now the shame of it was gone that she wanted to follow her instincts as a woman in love. Now she was giving herself to Hassim without shame.

"I would rather do it with you first, Hassim," she said finally.

Hassim shook his head.

"Why not?"

"I can't, Mameng."

"But why?"

"I would never forget it," he lied. "The shame of it."

"I have no shame with you, Hassim."

"I have," he lied again.

"I thought you had trampled it long ago."

"I thought I had." He went on lying.

"Let us teach each other not to be ashamed," Mameng pleaded. "Will you do it? I have confidence in you."

"It is no good."

"You don't want to help me?" It was like the cry of a wounded animal, before it dies in the wild thickets of the world.

Hassim could not tell her the truth. Only Dabu knew the truth. He had to live in lies forever now.

Mameng studied his face and wondered what the underground had done to him. She looked at his eyes and wondered if death was the only truth to him. She did not know. She would never know.

"I don't know what to say," she said.

"Why not Dante?" Hassim suggested. He had been thinking of Dante all the time. "He is probably very experienced. He is the man for you, Mameng."

"I guess that is best," she said, knowing somehow that Dante was the man for her. He was close to her and yet far away, so there would be profound mystery and unreserved familiarity. And she laughed a little, saying, "Yes, Dante is probably very experienced. I hope the American prostitutes did not ruin him."

"I will talk to him."

"It does not matter now. He probably understands the situation anyway."

"I think so."

"We must not speak about it anymore."

"Yes."

They went back to the others.

"I am in your hands now, Dante," Mameng said.

Dante looked at Mameng, then at Hassim. He understood. He put a hand on Mameng's shoulder and pressed it.

"I will guard you with my life," he said.

Old Bio tried to make light of it. "What, what?" he said.

Hassim looked at him and thought, He understands. He is an old man and he understands many things. But he would kill his own daughter rather than do what I have just done to Mameng.

"Nothing of importance," Hassim told the old man.

"Why don't you be more explicit?" Old Bio demanded. "I know your words, but I don't understand what you mean?"

"You will in time."

"In time. Always in time. And I am closer to the grave every day."

Dante knew that he had to say something. So he said, "I will take good care of Mameng."

"Thank you," Mameng said.

Dabu wanted to say something, but he decided against it. Legaspi had thoughts of his own. He looked at Mameng meaningfully. Even Linda Bie was speculating. But Dante was the man. Old Bio walked away.

"How about some breakfast?" Hassim asked Legaspi.

"It is about time," Dabu said, slapping his belly.

The tension was broken. Dabu and Legaspi opened canned sardines. Old Bio returned and watched them opening the cans. Legaspi gave him a can. Old Bio suspiciously smelled the fish and his nostrils flared up obscenely. Then he sneezed.

"You call this food, Legaspi?" Old Bio asked, shaking the can under Legaspi's nose.

Legaspi looked at the old man with a faint smile and said, "So you have acquired the expensive taste of the rich landlords?"

"Hogwash!" Old Bio said.

"Since when did you begin disliking this manna from heaven, old one?"

"Look, son." Old Bio said seriously. "I don't like fish in any form, understand? There was a time when I liked fish, understand? There was also a time when I liked rich landlords, understand? Now I don't like them both, understand? They both stink like hell, understand?" He stopped to control his sudden fury. He spoke aloud for the benefit of the others. "You speak of the expensive taste of the rich landlords, but do you know what you are talking about? You have to be born three times to put something over this old man. Look, son" he said, leaning over Legaspi. "Do you call this food? Is this the kind of hogwash that we are fighting for? Is It? Where is your tongue, peasant?"

Legaspi took the can away from the old man. He smelled the fish. He picked up a severed tail and ate it with relish. Then he picked up a head and ate it. He smacked his lips. Old Bio watched him with disgust.

"What is wrong with it?" Legaspi said. "It tastes very good to me. It probably came from the canneries where Dante and Felix Rivas had worked together. Don't you think this sardine is good and clean, Dante?"

"You bet your sweet life," Dante said. "Probably the cleanest thing you have ever seen in your peasant life."

"What, what?" old Bio said. "You call me a peasant?"

"He means me, old one," Legaspi pacified him.

"Well, I am not a peasant anymore." Old Bio looked at Linda Bie severely. "And I mean everybody! Including – "

"Me," Linda Bie said.

They were enjoying the repartee. Old Bio was both comical and serious. He did not know when he was comical or when he was serious. He had the forgivable innocence of the illiterate, but he also had the wisdom of the innately intelligent.

"Well, then," Old Bio concluded, "I am not a peasant anymore. I am now a first-class courier for the underground. Is that not so, Hassim?"

"That is so," Hassim agreed.

"Authority speaks," Old Bio said to Legaspi.

"I apologize," Legaspi said. "But this is probably the best can of sardines that you have ever seen."

"What, what?" Old Bio shouted. "young man, I have seen some good things in my life. Look, son," he said in a calm voice, pointing to the wide plain below. "That is my territory. I was born there. I grew rice there. I have a good piece of land there. I could take you to that place and show you things that would make your heart cry with envy. I know these hills, too. I used to hunt here as a young man. Do you know that these hills are a paradise of wild game?"

"You are right, old one," Legaspi said. "You have probably eaten black beetles and dog meat."

"What is wrong with dog meat, Hassim?" Old Bio asked. "You

said you have worked with the Igorots in the mountains. They consider dog meat a delicacy."

Everybody laughed.

"Will you tell this ignoramus here the truth, Hassim?" Old Bio pleaded.

"Dog meat is as good as any other meat if it is prepared right." Hassim said.

"Authority speaks again," Old Bio said with triumph, shaking a finger at Legaspi.

They were all eating now. Dabu scooped out the sardine with a hand, licking his fingers hungrily when the last morsel was gone. Linda Bie used a knife. He jabbed at the middle of the fish and ate the tail first, then the head, eating from one side to the other until the last piece was close to the blade; then he stuck the remaining portion in his mouth and wiped the knife on the grass. Legaspi drank the oil from the can. The old man watched him with disgust, then he turned to Dabu.

"You," he said. "How many children have you given to the world?"

Dabu was startled. He was putting a sardine in his mouth when the old man spoke to him, but the fish stopped in mid-air. He turned to Old Bio and narrowed his eyes on the old man's mouth, where two silvery threads of saliva were hanging from the black lips to the white beard. He put the fish back in the can and looked at the old man again.

"Children?" he said. "What children are you talking about?"

"Well, how many children have you made for the world?"

"What a foolish question!"

"Young man, there is nothing foolish in the fathering of children."

"I have never been married."

"Why?"

"I have no time to do it."

"Young man, there is always a time for it." There was a rising tone of anger in the old man's voice. "Suppose everybody makes excuses the way you excused yourself from this serious responsibility: what will become of the world?"

"Your universal patriotism is laudable."

"Don't evade the question. How many children have you given to the world?"

Now Dabu knew that he had to kid the old man. He picked up the fish head again and said, "None that I know of. But I am not sure. Are you sure yourself?" And he shoved the fish head in his mouth.

"Sure I am sure. Do you doubt my virility?"

"I am not talking about that, old one."

"Then what are you talking about?"

"About my children whose existence I am unaware of."

Everybody laughed.

The old man was flabbergasted. Knowing that Dabu had put something over on him, he changed the subject. "Did you bring cooked rice, Legaspi?" he asked.

"The old man wants to know if I brought cooked rice," Legaspi said.

Everybody laughed again.

"What is the laughing about?" Old Bio wanted to know. "Is rice to be laughed at nowadays?"

"It is about the food," Dante said.

"I don't want fish," Old Bio said with finality. "I will forage in the forest for something more digestible and healthy."

"Don't stay away too long," Hassim cautioned him. "We have something to do."

"Anything along the line of my work?"

"Yes,"

"I will not be gone long."

"Watch out."

"I know this country."

Hassim watched him walk downhill.

"What is he kicking about?" Linda Bie asked.

"He had a mouthful of whiskey on an empty stomach," Dante said.

"He will bring back worms and periwinkles to eat," Dabu concluded.

"He is all right." Legaspi said.

"It is his nearness to home," Hassim told them.

Dabu picked at his teeth thoughtfully. Hassim told him to bury the cans. Dabu gathered the cans and Linda Bie dug a hole with his knife. Dante lay down beside Mameng. A bird in a woodland glen nearby started singing.

Hassim walked to the edge of the hill and took the field glasses from his pocket. He adjusted the eyepieces and screwed up the lenses until the plain below him came into view. The sun was in the sky now and the visibility was good. He saw a thatched hut, but there was no activity in it. There was no smoke coming out of it and there were no animals in the yard. There was a footpath leading to the gate and the bermuda grass was lush and thick. He saw the bare earth where human feet had crossed it unnumbered times. He saw the brown earth further away, where the grass shone golden in the sunlight. He put the field glasses back in his pocket and returned to his companions.

"Have you decided on a plan?" Dabu asked.

"Yes," Hassim said.

"Are we to stay in the forest until night falls?" Linda Bie wanted to know.

Hassim nodded his head.

"If we travel only at night," Legaspi said, "how long will it take us to reach Rendezvous Seven?"

Mameng turned attentively to Hassim.

"Three weeks," Hassim said. "If we don't meet any challenge."

"Do you think there will be any?" Dante asked.

"If those brothers who came to the cave knew of our presence in this part of the country," Hassim explained, "then I expect some kind of challenge along the way."

"Are we safe in this forest?"

"Quite safe."

"Come on, Mameng," Dante said. "Let's take a little walk down the hill."

Mameng followed Dante down the hill and into a patch of tall grass.

Linda Bie began fixing his broken flute. Legaspi sipped the whiskey from the bottle that the old man did not finish. Dabu tied the mouth of the food sack with a cord and lay on it.

Hassim returned to his observation post. The land below him was coming to life. He sat behind a boulder and took the field glasses from his pocket again. He adjusted the eyepieces and screwed down the lenses until another part of the plain came into view. He saw animals moving about in the fields and a few farmers wearing palm hats. And farther away, he saw smoke coming out of a farmhouse. He saw chickens and goats in the yard. He turned to the other side of the plain. He was still studying the land when he saw the old man standing beside him.

"The land is barren," Hassim said.

"Yes," the old man answered in a sad voice.

## CHAPTER FIVE

. . . . . . . . . . . . . . . . . . . . . . . . . . . . . . . . . . . .

**D**ante and Mameng sat in the tall grass, thinking of Hassim.

"Here we are," Dante said.

"Yes," she said.

"Duty and pleasure."

Mameng looked at Dante and wondered if she would laugh or cry. Then she said, "Mostly duty."

"Mostly pleasure," he said.

They laughed, and the tension was broken. But it was only partially broken by their forced laughter. Creeping behind their evading eyes were unshed tears, prompted by a sad but necessary duty that they would have to perform. And behind their tears, lurking stealthily like a wild animal in his lair, was the shame of it, which was made more horrible by the lack of sentimentality and tenderness of the duty that they would eventually perform. It also lacked meaning and significance, however perfectly they would perform it. The performance of course was the main thing, because it was a vital part of their duty; it would lead them to the wholeness of it, the knowing of themselves finally. And the finality of the performance would resolve itself into a duty achieved, not without delicacy and nearness, not without meaning and significance. It would unmask them to each other and thereby conquer their fear.

They were sitting in the tall grass and looking down the hill through the trees. They were not looking at anything in particular, although nature's pleasant surprises were in great abundance. The woodland below them was trilling with the throaty songs of morning birds, some sweet and high and enchanting to the heart, others low and monotonous and ominous to the mind. And nameless wild vines crowned with multicolored flowers were creeping profusely on the hillside and hanging imperially on the branches of the trees.

They were neither listening to the birds' trilling songs nor admiring the flowers. They were outside that world, from which they had emerged with a nebulous dream of the future and to which they would eventually return with the dream crystallized though unfulfilled, if they ever returned to discover that the dream was achievable only in that world, where they had seen the first light of day and had felt the first darkness of night, and where, if they ever returned, the dream would finally vanish forever in the rimless darkness of the eternal night. They were in another world, drawing them magically to its depthless bright pools so they could see the reflections of their real identities in the formless water, so they would know before it was too late how to span a bridge of unchallengeable truth between the two worlds; for it was their only way to perfection, if they were made human enough to seek it.

The sun was high above them now and it mercilessly smote their bare heads. They could seek the dappled shade of the trees and the ponderous protection of the forest. They could sit on the thick carpet of the pine needles and feel the cool breeze on their faces. They could walk in the glades where butterflies were melting. But that seemed to them hiding from a sin that could not be hidden now that it had become a fact before the act, a fact forgivable now in view of the unintentional sin that was betrayable only by making shame of it. And the shame of it was bound up with their capacities to consummate the act, toward complete realization of self or toward complete failure of enthrallment. The betrayal would ruthlessly annihilate the very idea of it, even before the unescapable fact was accomplished.

They knew the act would be accomplished in terror and shame if they failed to realize themselves. They would have to dig deep into the well of loneliness and fear, deep into a depth no one had ever reached, deeper than the deepest depth ever imagined by anyone, so they could look at each other again without shame. And accomplishing it truly without shame, the shame would be given another name. It would become truth and beauty, and they could face each other again because of that impervious achievement. And they would be made human, far and above humanity, for the revocation of an inadequate term through the sufficiency of an old language made new by the fact of their impervious achievement, they could face each other and the world; and the loneliness and fear would be vanquished forever.

There was a rise on the hillside below them where a tuft of grass was like rice heavy with grain. They were looking at it now by coincidence, and in the mystery of that coincidence, focused on the gravitating rise, the symbol resolved itself into a phallic truth. For the rise became a woman in repose, undinal and containing the orgiastic truth of life, an antiphonal truth contending against a world of lies. The woman in repose ululant now and vibrant with life, breathing truths and suspiring half-truths on the hillside below them, suddenly became the inspiring magnificence of all that they had been resolving, the femaleness of it, the fecundity of it all. And every blade of the grass on the rise became germinal with their secret resolution, purged now to the very core of all the blackness of lies.

Then it was that their two worlds were joined together, spanned by a truth refurbished by their knowledge of it. The time had come for them to act against the flotsam of a submerged sea of shame, which was now bright with the phosphorescence of their acceptance. Now it had come, now truth reigned, and they were joined together by the finality of their resolution.

Because it was Dante who had seen other lands and years, it was through him that the expression of the resolution would be realized, then to be poured warmly upon Mameng, who was the denuded landscape on a prudish island. It would be through him that the sweet currents of experience would be siphoned into the very depths of her, to make her reach the stars with her hands and feel the world move under her body, now that the time had come for them to act. The time had come truly for them to act.

"Tell me," Dante said, not looking at Mameng, not even touching her hand, "did you ever have a pleasant experience that you can't forget?"

Mameng was startled. Dante's question was so sudden and out of place that she had no answer for a full minute. And when she finally had an answer, for it came slowly to her peasant mind, she laughed. Yes, she actually laughed. For even she, bewildered but obedient peasant woman that she was, could laugh like a little girl. And laughing, Dante was partially answered without the baffling encumbrance of language. But when the words came from her, they were even sweeter and more picturesque than her laughter. They revealed a world fully illustrated with the bright concordance of its newness.

"Yes, Dante," she said. "I have had a wonderful experience. It has followed me everywhere. It is with me this very moment."

"Tell me about it."

"It happened when I was sixteen," she began. "It was before the war. There was a high school boy that I liked very much in our neighborhood. He was quiet and shy. I used to embroider handkerchiefs for him, before he went away to school. He came home every Christmas and we used to have picnics in a banana grove, where the rice fields began. There was a river there which was a sort of meeting place among neighbors, where tantalizing gossips and the latest news were either whispered or spoken aloud, depending on who was listening or talking. There was really no need for a newspaper because the grapevine was faster in reaching the people. Well, I did not realize it at first, and neither did he. As time went by something definite was happening to both of us, which was then unexplainable to me. It happened actually when I was sixteen. It was the year of his graduation from high school. We went to the banana grove as usual one afternoon to celebrate his graduation and also to discuss our plans for the future. He was to follow in the footsteps of his father, who was a lawyer. He was preparing to go to college that year. His father did not kowtow to the rich landlord and influential politicians of the town, but he made a modest living from those who could afford to pay him. His clients were mostly tenant farmers who were overcharged on their rents and field workers who were so underpaid that they would have indentured themselves as slaves to the landlords had it not been for him. And also the victims of usury, because the moneylenders were always increasing the rate of interest. His father was responsible for the passage of certain provincial laws pertaining to an equitable arrangement between tenant farmers and landlord, between field workers and *hacenderos*, and between moneylenders and the borrowers of money. These laws were passed and acclaimed by the press. But they were only a fact on paper. The landlords and *hacenderos* and moneylenders violated them flagrantly. The government agencies responsible for the application of these laws did not move a finger. The agrarian tension was greater than ever.

"Well, he idolized his father even though his ideas were not applied. Perhaps his idolatry made him quiet and shy. That afternoon we stayed in the banana grove because it was a pleasant day in June, when the breeze from the plowed fields was filled with the fragrance of the new earth. We stayed on into the early twilight, when the cicadas began singing in the trees. We caught some of the cicadas, then threw them into the night. We were delighted when they were free to sing again. Then the moon appeared, but we stayed on into the night as though it were our last time together. Our lives seemed to stand still. It seemed as though there were no other lives outside our own lives. And our lives were not on this earth, but far away and untouchable, scintillating at the end of time. And from that unreckonable distance, coming closer to us as the hours passed, was the shining prism of our secret world, in which we saw ourselves and our future."

Mameng stopped, remembering that there was no future for her now. She put a finger in the corners of her eyes and flicked away the shining small tears. Then she continued in a voice that had become rich with remembrance. "So we stayed on into the night, when suddenly I felt him touching me, touching my arms warmly, caressingly, then up to my shoulders where his hands lingered like a bee lingering around a budding rose and sucking all the honey, and then up, up, up to my warming neck and face. And without knowing, I was doing the same thing to him. It was a wondrous submerging in each other: the annihilation of self when you finally discover that you have created a profound selfhood together, one and indivisible, complete in love. Then we were suddenly and miraculously divesting our clothes, as though our nudity were the ultimate realization of ourselves. Standing naked in the crystalline moonlight, it came to me that I would let him do anything to me. It came to me that he could overpower me, and I would let him; that he could annihilate me, and I would let him; that he could fling me into the night, and I would let him. But suddenly he said, 'No, Mameng.' Because I was still entranced, I asked, 'Why, Fedilio?' That was his name. Fedilio Reyes. 'Because,' he said sadly, 'it is all wrong. It is all wrong because we are not married. It should be done as the culmination of our marriage.' So when I finally understood what he meant, and realized that I had forgotten it for a moment of wild ecstasy, I began to weep. I wept copiously, not knowing how to cleanse myself of the shame. Finally he said, 'Let's just look at each other, Mameng.' And I said, 'Yes, Fedilio.' So we stood naked in the clear moonlight looking at each other, each turning around twice for the other to see; and in that act I felt cleansed and purified. I can still see the dancing shadows on his body and the deep hollows sloping down where the young flesh tautly receded into his underbelly and the mass of enticing darkness there where life stirred and raised its proud head in the moonlight. Oh, I was not always unbeautiful. Those ugly disfigurements came later, when the Japanese soldiers dragged me into one of their houses of pleasure." She pointed a finger to her broken nose. "I scarred myself when the soldiers caught me on my way to church. I cut myself with a broken glass and poured salt on the fresh wounds. It was the greatest pain I ever suffered, but it was the only way I knew how to save myself. When they came and stripped me and saw the bleeding sores, they thought I had been infected by a horrible disease. They did not even touch me with their rifles. They told me to leave. And they took another girl, who was so proud of her beauty. You should see what they had done to her. She lost her mind before they were through with her. Well, I went to the priest and told him what I had done and the circumstances surrounding it. He kept me in the church. He nursed me back to health. When I was well enough to travel, I left my hometown and joined the underground."

She stopped again, but there was no pride in her face. "Well," she continued, "Fedilio and I walked home in silence that night. The following week he went away to college. I never saw him again because the war came not long afterward. When I heard that he had been killed, I did not cry. I knew it had to come. I knew that he could not live in a country where there was no freedom. He talked almost all the time about freedom in those days: about civil rights and liberties, security of labor and the dignity of man. He was ahead of his father. His father grew up in another period, a period that historians call peace since there is no actual military conflict. Of course I understand now that there is no real peace at any period of history: the imitations of peace between wars are merely periods of preparation for the actual armed conflict and the eventual ruthless violations of those principles that Fedilio had firmly believed to be our great heritage. Well, he died gloriously and not vainly. The enemy beheaded him and cast his body to the dogs. There were dogs in those early days of the war that grew fat on human flesh, dogs that were also eaten by both sides when food became scarce. Fedilio's head was taken to the Japanese headquarters for identification. He was a courier for the first underground unit in the city. Well, I promised that I will never submit myself to anyone, not even to Fedilio had he lived. He had given me a beauty of self more beautiful that I have ever known. I did not want it to be violated, even by Fedilio had he lived to prove the true measure of himself. The marvelous essence of it was lost in the banana grove, when I was sixteen and I surrendered my self completely to Fedilio. It hung in the trembling moonlight and floated away from my life forever. And even if I went back to the old banana grove, I would never recapture the beauty of it. Never again. For it belongs to a time far away, when everything was new and clean and true. It is gone forever. And Fedilio is gone forever. Oh, there was a young man who could have given me the whole world! But now this business – "

Dante looked at her. He expected her to cry out her sorrow, her helplessness, her fate. But there were no tears in her eyes. The weeping was done in her voice, controlled at times and breaking loose at others. There was only a faint shadow of sadness in her face, remembering a grandiose dream that had sustained her since she was sixteen. Now that dream was revealed. Now she was exposed to the naked eyes of men.

But her role was prepared for her and the play was a tragedy. She would play her part heroically. She would forget the past and the voices of the past. She would be another woman now that she was twenty-three. She was no longer sixteen. She would never be young again. She who had wept when she saw living blood flow from the maimed limbs of young men would be another woman, since from now on blood would flow from her into the world of ungentle men; but somehow she knew that she would inundate with all her fertility the sterility of the world they were remaking, the world of their enemies. So she could do it now. She was ready now. Any other time would be too late. Now.

And Dante? Dante knew that the responsibility rested on it. It had always been men's responsibility to seek a new depth of life, giving it broadness and height; but it had always been women who gave a name to and a meaning for it, fueling it with men's knowledge of its depth. And yet, knowing what he had experienced in that land he could not forget, in love regretted or in love auctioned, in love stolen or in love given free to assuage someone's agonizing hunger for it: would there now be completion in a belated resolution that was made possible by a tragic drama?

So it seemed to Dante, looking back on the years and searching for a key to all that he had known, that there was no need to dramatize an organic fact that had so tenuous a relation with the intangibles of the mind. For these intangibles were born of the time and place you lived in, conditioned into flowering or deformation by the resiliency of tradition. And it seemed to him that there was no need to moralize on something that could not be moralized, for it was so common a denominator that even animals lived by it. Would that there were enough subtleties of the mind to categorize man as separate from animals in the realization of this common denominator! But there were none. There was only the ugliness or the beauty that you put on it.

Dante had resolved his side of the problem. There was no need for meandering, for seeking new definitions and sanctimonies. He had accepted what had been known by everyone since the dawn of man. Yes, that was it truly.

"Are you ready?" Dante asked.

"I am ready," she said.

"I want you to know that I have done this many times before."

"American prostitutes?"

"Some."

"Good ones, too?"

He nodded his head reluctantly.

"Have you ever been sick?"

"I have."

"I heard these women are very dirty."

"The filth comes from the business."

"I hope you will not hurt me."

"I have been well for years."

"I don't mean that."

"I will be gentle."

They were talking quietly now. They were holding each other now.

"Was there no affection at all?" she asked. "I mean between you and those women?"

"If there was I can't remember it."

"How could you do it without real feeling?"

"It was merely a business arrangement."

"Even with the good ones?"

"Sometimes. Sometimes it was the hunger for it."

"It was the same with them?"

"I suppose so. I suppose it was also out of curiosity."

"I can never do that."

"Of course not."

"I heard American wives are very unfaithful to their husbands."

"I guess so."

"Have you ever done it with an American wife?"

"Yes."

"Was it out of curiosity on her part?"

"She needed it. Her husband was impotent."

"She was faithful in her own fashion."

"She was."

"Did you have another experience with another married woman?"

Dante did not resent the cross-examination. He knew that she was fortifying herself against the act that they would perform. And he knew that he had to be honest with her.

"Yes," he said.

"Her reason or excuse?"

"She didn't love her husband anymore. They had been married for ten years."

"Time is not the element of love," she said reproachfully. "Did they have any children?"

"Two. A boy and a girl."

"She was an unfaithful wife and a bad mother."

"Marriages don't last long in the United States."

"My marriage would last even if I lived there."

"Not this woman's marriage."

"Why?"

"She suspected her husband of bisexuality."

"It was merely a suspicion. She was probably justifying her bad conduct."

"It was enough to upset her."

"They are a decadent people."

"I guess they are."

"Have you ever done it with our own kind?"

"No."

"Why?"

"I feel differently about it."

"What do you mean?"

"If I did it," Dante explained, "it would be for always."

"I did not know you felt that way."

"I do."

"How do you feel about this?"

"You know."

"I do. And I am glad."

"I am glad you understand."

"Yes, I understand. Tell me, Dante. If it had been the way you said it, between you and the American women, you must have lived in great loneliness?"

"I did. Terrible loneliness. There was no human affection or warmth in any of those arrangements."

"What do you mean?"

"I was like a piece of furniture, lifeless and dreamless."

"But you had to do it?"

"When the opportunity came. And I had the means."

"Money?"

"Of course."

"It must be an awfully unhappy country."

"I guess it is."

"I would not live in it."

"I wouldn't have if I knew."

"But you still think of that land?"

"Always."

"Why?"

"For reasons of my own."

"I don't understand."

"You would if you had lived there."

"Is it that bad?"

"Yes."

"You must have been hurt."

Dante nodded his head sadly.

"Still, you had to do it." Mameng said.

"I had to do it."

"There is no escape for anyone?"

"There is escape for some."

"What is that?"

"Death."

Mameng did not expect it. She closed her eyes and shook her head.

Dante touched her face. "Are you ready?" he asked again.

"I am ready."

"There is no escape from this."

"I have nothing to regret, either."

"If that is the case," she said, unstrapping the knapsack slung on her back, "let us go on with it."

"Let me say for the sake of something that I can't at the moment give a name that I love you?"

"Thank you."

"Now?"

"Wait. I want to tell you that I am a virgin."

"I know. Hassim told me."

"Now."

"I love you," he whispered, not knowing why he said it.

She lay on the grass and watched him fold his arms around her. Then she cried, "No. No. No." Then she sobbed, "Yes, Yes, Yes." Then closed her eyes. And the last thing she saw when he came upon her was the blazing sun that blinded her with its terrible heat. And the heat spread rapidly throughout her body, as he came again upon her, dispelling the sun's piercing heat. Suddenly, she moaned in agony. The heat became pain stabbing her everywhere, hacking mercilessly at her body. Then she heard the infernal grinding of rocks, as though there were a terrific convulsion of the earth and she was thrown into space, where burning lava and flaming trees filled the smoke-smothered air. And for a moment there was silence. Then, suddenly, roaring worlds below the infernal grinding noise, where everything was shaking and thundering and clamoring for life to remake itself in a frantic second of calling for help, calling, calling, calling until a serpentlike lightning from an unknown horizon burst frighteningly, until that fearful flight of terrible light was followed by a deafening thunderclap from underneath it, as though the whole world were blown to pieces and scattered in a bottomless cavern no one knew – no one would ever know – and there was the earth again and the flower-strewn month of June and the redolent hillside trilling with morning bird-songs. Then there was no more pain, there was no more heat, there was no more consciousness. There was only her body floating now, round and round the shores of the world, above mountains and seas and oceans, flying up, up, up into the whispering sky and among the singing stars, sailing there selfless now like a glowing vessel of majestic lights, hearing noteless music and passing through confounding silence, then back to that music; then she suddenly came down space, down, down, down to the earth again where there was only the proud thrusting and pulling out of a sharp column of light, now weakening and weakening in the overpowering floodtide of dikes bursting everywhere and rushing wildly to the four corners of the world; and then she could hear rivers cascading down to the murmurous sea, then the mournful voices of humanity shouting to the threatening winds as it walked across the troubled earth; and then she was reaching for nothing since there was nothing in her mind and hands now, not even the familiar voices of the living because it was done from nothing to nothing, knowing nothing, and in the end there was only the nothingness of it all. And running darkness. It was then that she realized its complete nothingness. She moaned again and opened her eyes. And the first things she saw was his face thickly bearded with beads of perspiration and slowly withdrawing away from her, the eyes lost and the corners of the mouth tired, the whole face suddenly sad and unlonging. He sat on the grass beside her, breathing hard and waiting for the weariness to disappear from his body. She was still lying on the crumpled grass, watching him. But when he did not turn to look at her, she closed her eyes to hide them from the ferocious sunlight.

Mameng was satisfied and gentle now. It seemed as though she had submerged herself in a shaded brook and emerged with long tendrils of underwater grass, cool and soothing to the caressing touch. Now there was neither pain nor heat in her body. There was that vessel of unbearable pain a moment before, but it was now vibrant with new desire. And vibrant with new desires, she touched the small of his back. The bewildering sensation of touching him thawed the hotness of the day. All reason was reduced to nothingness in the surging new desires, completely overpowering her. She reached for his neck and rubbed it ever so gently.

"Let us do it again," she whispered.

Dante shook his head.

"Why?"

He laughed at her innocence. "Don't you know why?" he asked.
"No."

"It can't be done."

"I still don't understand."

He rumpled her short straight hair. "Love is not a mechanical robot that you can move him anytime you want," he explained. "He is not a faucet either where you can draw water anytime you feel like doing it. Didn't you know that, Mameng?"

"I did not know that."

"Of course you don't."

"Now I know."

What had he done? But it was her duty and her calling. And now it was done. The fulfillment was complete, as he himself knew. Was that why she wanted it again, to fulfill herself? Was that a feminine instinct? Were women different from men who did it only to release themselves of pent-up desires or the excess of energies? Of course she was unacquainted with the facts of the fulfillment: that it had to be done time and again to give it human satisfaction, and even to sanctify it, if that was what she wanted to do. He had to make some explanation for her to believe that he was not dissatisfied with her.

"In another hour, maybe," he said.

"You will be ready then?"

"I hope so."

"I will wait."

"You are a whore."

She laughed.

"You are like the others."

"Am I?"

"I am afraid so."

"But I am not dirty like them."

"Yes."

"Were they good?"

"You are a bitch."

She laughed again.

"You are a good bitch."

"Were they big?"

"What are you talking about?"

"The American women you have known."

"You are a bitch and a whore."

She was looking tauntingly at him. What was it? Curiosity? No. Jealousy? Perhaps both. Yes, that was it. Both.

"I don't know what you mean," he said.

She smiled. She knew that he did not want to talk about it. She knew that she might drive him away from her. She did not want to do that now that it had been done. She did not want to lose him now that she had given herself to him. That she could not do now. She felt close to him, closer than she had ever been to anyone including Fedilio of long ago. And instinctively she felt that he was her man now and no other. She knew now that she would not give herself to anyone. The Mabini affair was her duty.

"Kiss me," she said.

He kissed her.

"Tell me you love me."

"I love you."

"Say it once more."

He hesitated.

"Say it!"

"I love you."

She put his hand on her hot breasts.

"Come," she said.

He lay down beside her. They talked for some time. Then sleep came, as sleep always comes after loving. It was a dreamless and an untroubled sleep.

Two yellow butterflies sprang from somewhere and hovered above them, flitting from grass to grass, and mated. Then they winged their way to the trees.

When they opened their eyes, Dabu was standing beside them.

"Well?" Dabu greeted them.

Dante rose to his feet and helped Mameng. They looked at each other with secret understanding. They brushed off the fringes of dead grass on their clothes.

"We had fallen asleep," Dante said.

"I thought you had been lost."

"What is up?"

"You could have been shot for all I know. Who will take care of Mameng if you are not careful? And you asked me what is up!"

"I knew you would be watching out for us."

"Is everything all right?"

Dante did not answer him. Mameng looked searchingly at Dante's glittering eyes. She knew that he knew. She did not say anything. She busied herself with her knapsack.

"You must have forgotten the passage of time," Dabu said insinuatingly.

"We surely have," Dante said.

"We have been waiting for you."

"Is that right?"

"The old man is drunk as hell."

"It is bad."

"I know the old man."

"Is this not his territory?"

"It is."

"That is the reason for it. Memories."

"He will sleep it off. Hassim and the old man will go down to the plain soon."

"Are you sure?"

"I think they will."

"Why?"

"It is part of our mission."

"I understand now. Legaspi will be next, then you – "

"You should watch out for yourself. Eh, Mameng?"

"Enough of that now," she said.

Dabu's face changed. He laughed and took their arms. They started climbing uphill through the tall grass. Their shirts were soaked through with perspiration. Dante wanted to look back to where they had lain, but Dabu was holding him tightly. Dabu was climbing uphill with his head down, as though he were carrying a heavy load on his back. They stopped when they reached the top. And they looked back. They stood side by side and looked down the hillside, thinking of what had been done. Then they turned around and walked to their companions, thinking of the vanquishment of shame, of the birth of dignity.

They ate in silence. When they were through and had buried the empty cans in the hillside, Hassim told Dabu to find out if there was a stream in the hills. The water bags were empty and the old man who knew the place was still asleep. Dabu discarded his knapsack and put the automatic pistol in his belt, took the field glasses from Hassim, and left. They watched him walk down the hill under the trees and disappear in the thick underbrush at the edge of the great forest.

They were in the last great forest. Between them and their destination was a wide rolling plain of corn and sugarcane, and some hills with scarcely any trees for protection, just before the descent to the city. Of course there were rivers with tall reeds and swamplands where nipa grew. These the peasants cut and dried in the sun for the roofs and walls of their thatched huts. The rice had been harvested some months before, and now the unplanted fields were parched and broken in squares and circles where the last moisture had been sucked dry. But when the rains came to soften and enrich the dry land, the peasants sowed the rice seedlings and transplanted them to the waiting land, when the heavy rains came from the sea across the mountains.

Hassim contemplated the coming green land. The peasants would be scattered in the fields, bending under the heavy rains and shoving the rice seedlings in the soft sod with their strong, thick fingers. He knew they had to go on making the earth green with their staple food despite danger. He knew as his father and grandfather before him that life would go on, be the time dark with terror and scarcity or bright with neighborliness and abundance. It was his only hope and guiding star: the undying light that shone brightly in the darkness of his life: the only truth in the crucible of his heart that urged them not to remain unresisting and afraid.

Hassim was watching the underbrush where Dabu had disappeared when he sensed that his companions had been silent for so long. He turned around to see why. But there was nothing in their faces that he could seize in an instant of detection to give him a solid steppingstone toward understanding their silence. They were the same faces that he had known for years, sometimes gay and laugh- thinking if it was possible to remake their country with motley crowds such as the one under him. He frowned as the doubt came to him. It came to him that bigger things had been accomplished in the world by more beggarly crowds. And he realized, not suddenly but gradually, that it was the degree of dedication that you put in a cause that determined its rugged course and final achievement.

Take Linda Bie. He was fiddling with his reed flute, which he had repaired with bandages and strings. The sound that came out of the instrument was unmelodious, for the broken section was loosely covered and a pinch of his wind was seeping out of it like a subdued whistle. There was a slight trace of concern in his face, but it was not for the world or what they would accomplish in it. It was a deep personal concern for the flute, as though the instrument were the only audible mechanism that could bring back what he had lost and forgotten. For he had forgotten or tried to forget a part of his early life. For that life belonged to his rich father and gregarious brothers. He blew hard at the flute and frowned. Then he started to cough, turning aside to spew the gray phlegm in his mouth. His face was red when his fit of coughing stopped. He looked up at Hassim to see if he knew.

Hassim knew. He had noticed Linda Bie coughing some months back. It was last year's rainy season and they had gone to the plain with forty men. They had been sent to requisition rice and corn, which were in the safekeeping of friendly farmers. On the way back to their camp, crawling through swamps and jungles at night, Linda Bie started to cough. Hassim thought at first that he had a severe cold, but as they progressed toward their destination and Linda Bie's coughing became more frequent and spasmodic, he knew that it was tuberculosis. And he felt unhappy for what had happened to Linda Bie: living in the mountains and hills without the comfort that he had known in a well-provided home was too much for him: and eating when there was something to eat or time to eat it contributed greatly to his discomfort and disease. But he had chosen a cause, and he was not easy to dissuade once he had committed himself. His was not the stubbornness of the peasants but the dedication of an intellectual middle class who found that he could not live in a country where there was no freedom, where atrocity and misery reigned supreme. He had not spoken about his illness because everyone had his own personal problem. He knew the big problem was what confronted them all: the destruction of tyranny and the liberation of their people. This was Linda Bie: perhaps he would cough out his life on this journey. And be it so: he had given more than his share to the underground and now he was tired. It was only his music that gave him a sense of freedom at times, as it was doing now; with it he was trying to recapture a lost melody that he had put aside somewhere in his happier days, but lost forever and forever now.

Hassim turned to Legaspi. Legaspi had dismembered his gun. He was absorbed in oiling the separate parts. He was sitting beside his knapsack, where he had neatly arranged the various parts. He was a peasant like Hassim, but mostly like Dabu. Legaspi and Dabu carried with them the trademarks of the real peasants: superstitious when confronted by a dilemma beyond their intellectual under-standing, ferocious when challenged to defend their beliefs. Hassim ratiocinated when challenged or confronted by a problem; but he was also ferocious once he had made his decision, and he seldom made a mistake in his decisions.

Hassim studied Legaspi. Legaspi's commonplace and insensitive face revealed nothing about his private thoughts. It was like thou-sands of faces you could forget once you saw it. For it was a face that saw things only within the range of his eyes. It was a visual face, without inward vision. Legaspi was remarkably perceptive in that limited scope of sight, but completely helpless beyond it.

Hassim watched him dexterously cleaning the parts of his pistol. He thought as he had already thought a hundred times before that Legaspi was not altogether unthinking and unresponsive to the inner chords of life, even though his main preoccupation was an intense cleavage with things within the reach of his long and powerful arms. Beyond this reach was a no-man's-land, an utterly defenseless void, that he had never given the slightest thought because it was nonexistent to him. But let the devil himself come within his reach, and you would know how he could fight to make his way in that narrow, visual world. This was Legaspi, the laughing fool when perturbed or challenged, but innocuous and simple when in repose.

Hassim studied Dante. He was sitting against a tree trunk and smoking a cigarette. His eyes were partly closed, but he was not sleepy. He had an unusual way of partially closing his eyes when thinking of the past and of that land that he could never forget, where he had spent fifteen years of his early life in another kind of terror and violence. The scars from that struggle were written in his face and prematurely gray hair. He was a thinking man. He had to raise a defiant fist against fate. He had grappled violently with the world in order to keep his dignity. And in that fight, begun when he was orphaned at seven and went on down the years in his native land and in that other land and back to his own land, he had sharpened his personality to a sharp and luminous degree that made him a scintillating nimbus of light around which other personalities revolved, projecting all that he had learned against the disordered world.

And Hassim, studying him, wondered what was going on in his head. He was curious to know because Dante had never spoken about his personal past, but only about the past as a part of a world he never made. It was the past that conspired to disenchant the dreams of men, the past that he, Dante, knew but would not tell. He would never, never tell. And that was what made him so detached and far away, so mysterious and unassailable, even in actual combat. That proud head of his, gray now beyond his years, held in captivity that unrevealed world. Only when that proud head crumbled would that world come to light, if ever. But even then, even when you hacked that proud head to pieces, that world would also be hacked to pieces. No one would ever know it. Only Dante knew it. But it was his personal world and he had the privilege to keep or destroy it.

And Mameng? Hassim watched Mameng patching her peasant trousers. The tiny black needle was disappearing and quickly reappearing in the streak of sunlight coming down between the trees.

She, too, was a quiet one. Why are our peasant women so quiet? Hassim thought. Is it because of the heavy burdens they have been carrying for generations? Is it because of the difficult tasks they have to perform in order to maintain their families and homes? Perhaps that is what differentiates them from the pampered wives of the landlords and rich politicians. Their wives are always talking and laughing and gambling. But the hollowness of their laughter echoes vainly in these hills. Oh, Mameng! We can't easily give a better world. We will make one, but it belongs to the children after us. We have seen the future, and it is good. So we will prepare that world for the children of the future. Through the preparation we will become an integral part of that world. This hope is the only truth that sustains us.

Hassim turned away from Mameng when she suddenly looked up at him. She noticed his contemplating look. She averted her gaze and fumbled with the needle. Hassim looked at the old man. Old Bio was dead to all the world. Hassim walked up to the old man and bent over him. He hesitated for a moment, then shook him lightly. The old man scrambled to his feet. He reached for his carbine.

"Eh, eh?" he said, putting the gun in position.

Legaspi leaped to action. He grabbed the gun away and said, "What are you doing?"

Old Bio's eyes were open, but he was still in the deep ocean of sleep. Then wakefulness came to him, and he apologized when he realized what he had almost done, "I was dreaming of an enemy attack."

"You surely have been dreaming," Legaspi said. The terror in his eyes was gone. He gave the gun back to the old man and said, "Keep it away. Some day you will shoot the wrong person."

"It was a bad dream," Old Bio explained, disregarding Legaspi's dark implication. "I have been dreaming bad dreams lately. Maybe it is the heat."

"You ate too much raw goat meat last night," Legaspi said.

Old Bio looked sharply at him. Hassim only smiled when he saw the guilty look in the old man's eyes. Dante threw his cigarette away and looked at the old man with amusement, but he did not say anything.

"Well, is that not so, old one?" Legaspi asked. His tone of voice was a direct challenge. He wanted Old Bio to admit his guilt. "Well?"

Mameng suddenly giggled, covering her unlovely mouth with her hand.

Old Bio suddenly turned to her. "What is the joke?" he asked her.

"The joke is on you," Legaspi said.

Old Bio grunted. He walked stumblingly to the sack where Legaspi kept the whiskey. Legaspi looked at Hassim inquiringly, then at Dabu. Hassim nodded, but Dabu did not bat an eye. Legaspi frowned and continued oiling his pistol. The old man untied the rope at the sack mouth and pulled out a bottle. He sat against a tree trunk and uncorked the bottle.

"What are you trying to forget?" Linda Bie suddenly asked the old man.

Old Bio stopped the bottle in mid-air and looked in the direction of Linda Bie. His deep-seated eyes seemed to pop out of their dark hollows, but he did not answer Linda Bie. The thin ends of his mouth curled upward, showing the ugly rotten teeth prominently, obscenely. He was about to say something contemptuous, but held it back and put the bottle in his mouth. He sighed lingeringly after the big drink and wiped his mouth with a sleeve. Then he looked in the direction of Linda Bie again, the popping eyes glassy and rapidly filming.

"Keep your thoughts in your mind, young man," he said calmly. "What I do is my own business, not yours by a long shot."

Linda Bie glanced at Hassim to see if he would intervene, but when he saw that Hassim was impassive, he repressed his reprimanding thoughts. Hassim had the authority to watch over the conduct of his men, Linda Bie thought, if he did not raise a finger at the old man, then it was none of his business. He changed his tone when he answered the old man.

"I am only trying to make conversation," he said. "It is too quiet here."

Old Bio spat noisily against the tree and said, "Well, converse with yourself. You are an educated one. All you educated ones are very complicated in the head and have two heads. Bad one, good one. But the bad one dominates. So you should be able to converse with yourself splendidly. Januses!"

Linda Bie was not slighted. He knew the old man's attitude toward him. Those who represented wealth were Old Bio's enemies irrespective of their political convictions. He felt some kind of enjoyment in titillating the old man's nasty sense of humor and sudden bursts of fury.

"Whiskey is not good for the head," he told the old man.

This was what the old man was waiting for, the first dent in Linda Bie's line of defense. He jumped to his feet, almost dropping the bottle. He ran to Linda Bie and shook the bottle under his nose.

"What, what?" he said, and there was genuine anger in his voice. "Is drinking only for the idle rich, eh? Is drinking the best brand of whiskey not good enough for a first-class underground courier like Old Bio, eh? Only the idle rich have good heads, eh?"

Linda Bie suddenly guffawed. He had succeeded in rousing Old Bio's pent-up hatred for the rich. He leaped to his feet and stepped backward, away from the old man's reach. Shaking the broken flute the way the old man had shaken the bottle under his nose, he imitated Old Bio's screeching voice, "Is drinking only for the idle rich, eh? Is drinking the best brand of whiskey not good enough for a first-class underground courier like Old Bio, eh? Only the rich have good heads, eh?"

Old Bio jumped at him. Linda Bie ran to a tree for protection. The old man tried to hit him with the bottle, but he slipped away to another tree. Old Bio was furious. Linda Bie ran from tree to tree, trying to tire the old man. And once behind the protection of a tree, he imitated Old Bio's voice.

Hassim watched them with some kind of boyish interest for a moment, then he sat on a fallen tree and looked in the direction where Dabu had disappeared. He was looking over Legaspi's head. He was sitting on a higher level, near Mameng, who was patching another section of her trousers. Finally, he saw the old man give up the chase. Old Bio sat near Dante and asked for a cigarette. Linda Bie walked past Hassim, playing his flute.

Silence returned. Always there were silences in Hassim's life, some deadly and confounding, others comforting and secure. There had been a long silence across the darkness of his life – when was that? Oh, a long time ago – there in that cigar factory where he had worked as a boy – broken only by the gliding presence of Consuelo, a timid young girl he had known in the long ago. Long ago? Did six years belong to the long ago? Yes, his heart cried out. Yes, so long, long ago. Then there were shorter silences that crossed his path from one jungle to another. There were silences that conspired against him, that besieged him with their deadly weapons of fear and sudden ambush, the bullet striking from some hidden enemy. And there were silences that struck him to the very soul, confounding even the imperious knowledge that he had acquired in all his living. Silences. Silences of truth and silences of lie. Silences of life and death. Could these silences ever be conquered? Deep silences.

Hassim rubbed his throbbing forehead. It was the long waiting that made him restless. Yes, the long waiting. You had to wait for the rain so you could plow the land for the rice. You had to wait for the hot months of April and May to pass, sitting patiently under your house where the plowshares were scraped clean and honed sharp for the plowing. You had to wait there splitting bamboo to tie the rice stalks in bundles the size of your arm so they would be easy to spread in the sun for drying. You had to wait there talking with your neighbors around an earthen jug of red wine until the first rains came and you watched the water pouring from the grass eaves, the warm rain falling on the ground near your feet and creeping away like snakes to the four corners of your yard and into the footpath farther down where it eventually rushed to the swelling river and from there, when the dikes were in good condition, the angry water burst upon the waiting rice land. And then, when the rice seedlings were finally planted so that your land looked like the pastures of heaven, you had to wait for the rain to stop, otherwise it would flood the field and ruin the seedlings. You had to wait in terror for about a month, although you knew it would stop somehow, as it had always stopped in the years before. Still, you had to wait because sometimes it did not stop, as it did not stop some time back and ruined your field. And when the rice was ruined by the rain, you had to wait another year in hunger and desperation. But you had waited patiently that year because you were used to waiting and had planted another crop and it had been all right that time because the rain had stopped when it was supposed to stop and the crop had been good, so you and your family had been well supplied with grain and had been happy and in good health again.

Yes, the long waiting. The waiting for daylight so you could start mending the fence around your vegetable garden. You rose from your mat at early dawn and looked out the east window to calculate the coming of the sun, and as you stood there looking and calculating, your wife was by the lighted stove preparing the morning meal because it was her duty to do it and to serve you as you prepared to go out of the house. You had to wait for the morning sun, and when it came bursting out of the horizon in its full glory, your heart almost jumped out of your mouth, so great and beautiful was your happiness.

And you had to wait for the night. You stopped at your work and looked at what you had done. You smiled with satisfaction because you knew you had done more than enough for the day. You had to wait there in the murmurous field with your faithful animal, and when nightfall came at last and the first stars appeared in the heavens, you started on your homeward journey because there, at the end, which seemed incredibly far at times and heartwarmingly near at other times, was your closely knitted lovely family. Your wife and children had been waiting, too. Your children had been waiting for you to give them assurance that they could live in the world and not be afraid. And your wife had been waiting for you because she wanted to tell you that the seed of your fertile manhood had grown big inside her again, making her a living part of you always, for that seed would grow slowly inside her and out in the world where men had been waiting for time immemorial. But you had to wait several months for that seed of yours to grow comfortably in the warm darkness of her world, then you had to wait many long years to see the slow growth of your seed in the world of waiting men. And when the time came for you to see that the fruit of your seed was not cankered but lush with the fertility of your manhood, you made your final deposition for all the world to corroborate when you were gone.

Yes, the long waiting. And you had to wait always. You had to wait until you die. But even for that you had to wait, even for death. So was all your long waiting for nothing? Could death be the ultimate of all your waiting? Death, then, was all you had waited for in the world? But you would not believe that death was all that you had waited for when you were alive. You would not believe that all that long waiting was only for death. For there in the wide world of waiting men, on the rough or smooth surfaces of your field, were durable fragments of your life that had been dropped when you worked in the rain or under the hot sun and became indigenous with the soil, making it rich beyond your knowing of it. There were drops of your precious blood, sucked by the soil, made new and fertile because of your living blood. So the long waiting was for all that, for all that and your children, who took over when you were gone, never to return. You were gone, but you had left your manhood in your children and part of yourself in the field that they worked after you; and they were assured that they could live in the world and not be afraid.

Yes, the long waiting. And you had to wait always. You had to wait for the night so you could continue your journey. The enemy would be sleeping in the night and you would be unseen and undetected in the darkness. Journey to what? Journey to paradise? Journey to the stars? Would that it were to the stars! But you knew it was not so. Perhaps journey to power? To fame? To fortune? But you would not believe that all the waiting was for these transitory things that foolish men had coveted since time began. You would not believe that all the waiting was for these ugly playthings of madmen. You had to wait for the night because there at the end of the journey was your just reward – not a personal one because it belonged to all of you – a collective reward that was the fruit of all your long waiting. That was the truth of all your waiting. So you had to wait with that fierce bullet of truth at your side, because somewhere, across some barricade of reckoning, was the enemy waiting too with his gigantic scaffolding of falsehood, ready to challenge the integrity of your truth and the durability of your world. So, now, you had to wait for the night, the way you had waited for the rain, because with your fierce bullets of truth you could seize the enemy and the world.

Hassim was distracted from his meditations when he saw Dabu coming up the hill with the water bags. He was carrying something alive and kicking that Hassim could not readily identify. But when he approached them, Hassim knew it was a kid. Anger shot through him. Did this damn fool risk everything for a stinking little goat? He rose with indignation and walked briskly to meet him.

The others left their preoccupations and watched in silence. Legaspi tickled the old man's leg with a twig so he would see what was transpiring or about to transpire. Old Bio bolted upright and rubbed his eyes. Then he saw Dabu hugging the struggling kid and Hassim walking toward him with a shadow of anger streaking his face.

Dabu saw the anger in Hassim's face. He waved it away with a slight movement of his chin and said, "No need to fear about anything."

"I don't mean the fear," Hassim said solemnly. "You could be trusted with that. But – " he looked at the goat.

Dabu smiled. "This?" he said, thrusting the goat to Hassim as though it were a newborn baby that Dabu would like to inspect with pride. "It is a wild mountain goat."

Hassim studied the animal and knew Dabu was right. He knew enough of wild game to be sure, but he had already showed a bad disposition that was beyond him to remedy. Old Bio came to his rescue. He went to Dabu and felt the goat's legs.

"It is a mountain goat, all right," he said. "I know these hills. Didn't I tell you I used to hunt for wild game here as a young man?"

"I am sorry," Hassim apologized to Dabu. "I was worried over nothing."

Dabu laughed softly. The others relaxed. Legaspi wanted to laugh too, but yawned loudly instead, suppressing his desire to brighten the charged atmosphere. They all knew Hassim was very strict about taking things from people, and Dabu was very indiscriminate about it.

"It must be about five months old," Old Bio said.

"Young and tender," Dabu announced.

Because Legaspi was more indiscriminate than Dabu about taking things from people, he did not say anything. He left his pistol cleaning and went to examine the kid. He slapped the animal's belly and said, "Ah!"

"What did you do that for?" Old Bio asked him with a frown.

"I wanted to see if it is fat enough for my taste," he explained.

"Young man," Old Bio said, "this kid is fatter than the fattest landlord!"

Dabu and Legaspi laughed at the joke. Old Bio had it on the rich all the time. Even he laughed at his own joke.

"Well, all right," Hassim stopped them. "Don't let it make any unnecessary noise."

There was no need for the admonition. Dabu was gripping the kid's mouth with a steel-like hand, while the others held the four legs tightly, so that the pitiful animal seemed dead except for its strangled breathing.

"We have time enough to prepare some of its meat," Old Bio said.

"Slaughter it where there is water," Hassim advised them.

"Where is the stream?" Legaspi asked Dabu.

"It is down the hill," he said. "On the right. You will not miss it."

"Is it safe?" Hassim asked.

"As safe as my grandmother's womb."

Legaspi laughed.

"Go to it," Hassim said.

"Give me that bundle of joy," Old Bio said.

Dabu gave it to him. Hassim nodded to Linda Bie and Legaspi.

"Go with the old man," he told them. Then, looking at his watch, he said to Old Bio, "Don't stay away too long, old one. We are going down to your village."

The old man looked at him sharply and wanted to protest, but at the same time he felt a longing to see his house and the people he had known, those who were still alive, if they had returned from the hills. He had not expected this as a part of their assignment to the city, but now he was beginning to understand the setup. He had almost lost interest in the kid. He wanted to go down to the village right away, but on second thought he needed some time to prepare himself emotionally, if his house was not there anymore and the people he had known had not returned from the hills. Or if they were all dead. "I will be back in a short while," he told Hassim.

"I will wait."

They went silently down the hill, the old man between Linda Bie and Legaspi, as though they were protecting him from all the world. Linda Bie was swatting at the grass with a big knife. The empty sack for the meat was flapping at Legaspi's shoulder. They disappeared behind a high scaffolding of rocks and fossilized earth.

Dabu hung the filled water bags on a limb and sat on the fallen tree near Mameng, facing her and the space of earth where he had disappeared awhile back. Hassim sat beside him, looking in the other direction.

"How did you catch the animal?" he asked. He noticed that there was no bullet wound or signs of strangulation.

"I saw it drinking thirstily at the edge of the stream," Dabu said. "It did not see me, so I crept up slowly to a huge boulder and jumped. It was a sudden surprise. It did not even move."

Hassim slapped him on the back. "Then the meat will be good," he said.

Dabu laughed lightly. He knew it was both a compliment for his ability and the truth. Animals were always good to eat when they were caught without wounds.

The noonday sun was blazing in the valley below them. The trembling haze was so strong it hurt Hassim's eyes. He turned in the direction where the three men had disappeared, in the direction where Dabu was looking. There was a screen of tall trees there and the lingering breeze that was deflected from it toward them caressed the pain away from Hassim's eyes. Then he looked at Dabu and noticed that his shirt was soaked through with perspiration.

"Mameng," he said, "why don't you wash Dabu's shirt where they went to slaughter the goat?"

Mameng rose without comment and went to Dabu, who was already taking off his shirt.

"Be very careful with it," he said, giving the soiled shirt to her. "It is my only shirt and I have to look clean in the city of fair women."

"Don't worry," she said. "I washed the clothes of eight brothers."

"No sisters?" Dabu asked, his face breaking with a sly smile.

Mameng could not tell whether he was kidding or serious. Dabu probed deeper, openly showing a concupiscent twinkle in his eyes now. "Are you sure you have no sisters?"

"You!" Mameng said, striking angrily across the bare breast with her palm. There was an obscene noise in the contact, like two naked bodies pulling away from each other and suddenly coming together in the intensity of maddening desires; so giving her an instantaneous delight, she struck him again and said, "You dirty-minded dog!"

Dabu was taken completely defenseless. But he managed to repeat, "Well, don't you have any sisters?"

Mameng looked at him quizzically for a moment, then turned around and started down the hill.

Dante leaped to his feet and said, "Wait, Mameng! I will go with you!"

Mameng looked back and stopped. She waited for him. Then they walked hand in hand down the hill.

Now they were alone. Hassim felt more at ease with Dabu than with any of the others, or when they were all together. Dabu had been with him in every major mission that he had undertaken. Dabu had some faults, like his overdaring, but it was due to his inadequate political training. The Political Committee had reprimanded him many a time, for his boldness not only foolishly exposed him but also endangered the safety of the whole organization. He took a boyish delight in openly challenging the enemy, sometimes exposing himself at a great disadvantage and running precariously into hiding, trapping the pursuing enemy with his men who had been previously entrenched along the getaway position for a sudden ambuscade.

Once, Hassim remembered, he and Dabu and twenty men attacked a trainload of ammunition and other equipment of war. Dabu entered one end of the train with ten men and Hassim and his ten men entered the other end, surprising the enemy soldiers at their eating tables and card games and sleeping quarters. Working furiously, they met in the middle of the train with their loot; then, throwing overboard all that they had taken, they jumped through the windows and escaped to the hills. When they reached their rendezvous, Hassim discovered that Dabu was missing. For a moment he felt the dark gloom of sadness, but in another moment he heard firing coming nearer. He and Legaspi ran down the hill. Then they saw Dabu running toward them. He was carrying a samisen with one hand, which he was holding high up in the air for fear of breaking it if he stumbled, the blazing gun in the other hand, held low, just above the knee so he could shoot freely and downward, which he did every five long strides or so, zigzagging as he ran up the hill toward them, a dozen enemy soldiers firing at him. He and Legaspi challenged them behind the trees, and they fled back to the train shouting curses. Then Dabu was with them, safe and unscratched, and laughing. Hassim remembered that when he saw what Dabu risked his life for – a strange musical instrument – he almost lost his temper. But how could you lose your temper with a man like Dabu? The laughing fool! Dabu was only eighteen then, new in the underground but well recommended by his activities against the enemy during the early stages of the war. He could still see Dabu holding the samisen high up in the air and running toward them, and he felt close to him now that they were alone. The resurrection of that day in the long ago surged in his being. And he put a hand on Dabu's shoulder, for he, too, was silent and evidently remembering that day or some other day that starred their lives forever.

Hassim rose and took three steps. Then he looked back at Dabu, who had also risen from the tree. They stood looking at each other, not knowing what to say. They had known many things together and words did not mean much unless they came from the heart. And words, too, did not mean much unless they were relevant to their plans. So their silence spoke louder than words, meant more than words, for it was the tranquil silence of conspirators against a world they did not make. That world was a parabola of despair and anguish and suffering. For what? Was that all there was left for men to do – suffer and despair? Was there no beauty left for those who appreciated it or for those who could be taught to appreciate it?

They were facing each other and yet they were far apart, pulled together only by the aura of a dream world – a nebulous world they were making, a world where beauty and dignity and truth could shine on a continuing plethora of living.

Suddenly Dabu stirred and looked downhill. "They are coming back," he said, breaking the great enchantment.

Hassim turned and saw them coming uphill. Legaspi was carrying the bulging sack. Behind him was Old Bio, who had big chunks of the meat in his hands. Linda Bie came next with a looped vine strung with smaller pieces of the meat. Then Dante appeared with a load in his arms. Perhaps the guts, Hassim thought. And the last was Mameng, wringing Dabu's shirt as she came up the hill.

Hassim watched them come up the hill like mountain climbers who are strung together by a stout rope, each bearing his own world of hope, yet each world revolved in itself and with the others; for all their worlds were animated by the same grand hope, like the stars in the galaxies that are animated by one sun. Hassim watched them and saw how humanity had to climb the limitless hill of life, clinging on ponderous scrubs of truth and resting under the bright petals of beauty; then, climbing again with heads and hearts singing gloriously from having reached the middle ascent to the hilltop of hope, the night slowly came on to hide them forever in its endless dark folds of sleep. And as he watched them approaching he thought, *Was that all there was in the sacrifice? That the perpetual night would come when they made part of the way? That the existence of that fabulous hope was made incontrovertible only in their daring to reach it? And could that hope ever be reached by someone more courageous and indefatigable than others? Or was it all for nothing?*

Hassim stirred when they approached him. They put the pieces of meat on the grass and leaves. He told them to prepare the pieces that were easy to spoil and took the field glasses from Dabu. Then he walked over to the old man and touched his shoulder.

"Let us go," he said.

## CHAPTER SEVEN

. . . . . . . . . . . . . . . . . . . . . . . . . . . . . . . . . . . . . .

**H**assim silently followed the old man down the hill through the diminishing underbrush. They stopped at the base awhile, before the final descent to the wide pastureland at the edge of a meadow. There were a few carabaos and cows and horses grazing lackadaisically in the pasture, but their fleshless flanks revealed they had been recently let loose there to take the place of a less fortunate herd of animals, which was possibly requisitioned by the enemy to feed his hungry soldiers. So they surveyed the pitiful animals in the pasture, knowing secretly that these too would be requisitioned in a few months, when they were fat enough to be slaughtered; and knowing, in their heart of hearts, that the peasants who owned the requisitioned animals did not give in to the enemy without some kind of resistance or plan of resistance. And knowing that heightened their courage to investigate the village.

Then they went on, walking abreast now, crossing the wide pastureland where the bermuda grass was as fragrant and juicy as the tall ferns in the great forest, and as thick as the carpet of pine needles there; and when they came to the meadow where the stubble of the harvested rice spread out before them like millions of crawling locusts rushing a cornfield, they stopped again to contemplate the distance between them and the first farmhouse at the edge of the village. The farmhouse was a kilometer away, and isolated on an eminence, and protected by a brown picket fence. They studied it silently but saw no sign of activity. And in silence they looked at each other with concern and premonition, tightening their belts where their guns were hidden under the sweat-soaked khaki shirts; and half aware now of the inactivity of the village, they walked on silently across the meadow to face the calamity.

Hassim noticed that the old man's jocularity disappeared suddenly when they started going down the hill. Now there was a spreading softening in his face, and the sunken dark eyes were wistful, and the thin dry lips were trembling slightly. For this was his territory, this was his land, this was his country. All his years were spent here until he joined the underground three years before. All the people he knew lived here or had lived here. He knew this part of the world like the palm of his hand. And even the very earth where he was standing now was a part of his youth, and manhood, and old age. He had played in this meadow as a little boy, and he had fattened his animals in that pasture as a dreaming young man, and he had worked in those sunlit fields as the years piled on and his hair started to turn gray; knowing that the little boy was borne gently through time by the dream of the young that was finally fulfilled in the old man, here in the village that was his own world. This was all the world he knew, and standing there with a long train of memories he suddenly knelt on the grass and dug his hand into the earth and grabbed a fistful of familiar soil that had given him a wondrous feeling of belonging to the place in the long ago. And Hassim, watching him kneading the fistful of earth with loving fingers that only a peasant could have after many years of tilling the fields, that only he, Old Bio, could have to express a secret language of great intimacy with the soil, wanted to say a prayer of consecration for the old man now that he understood how a peasant felt about his land. But even that was taken away from him, even that was destroyed by the enemy forever. So he silently watched the old man lovingly kneading and rekneading the fistful of earth as though it were a sick woman, as though she were the only woman in all the world for him, and as though she had been violated by some men through their impatience to fertilize her. He saw two tiny shining tears fall on the fistful of kneaded earth and disappear when it was rekneaded by the caressing peasant hand. For in these fields were fragments of the old man's life that had become indigenous with the soil. For in these fields were glittering drops of his precious blood, sucked dry by the hungry soil, but made new and fertile because of his living blood. So Hassim, watching the old man caressing and blessing his land, found the comforting truth of all his living: that these peasants who lived close to the soil would never be conquered because they were constant to the earth and to women; and through this unaffected constancy was revealed their deep attachment and fidelity to both lifegiving vessels of truth, as he himself knew.

Old Bio finally rose and brushed the earth-encrusted hand on his trousers. "It was good land," he said.

"It still is, old one," Hassim told him.

"This property," Old Bio said, indicating the ground where they were standing and the surrounding field to the pasture with a wide sweep of his hand, "is owned by one of my *compadres*.* Mariano Nunes. I wonder if he is still alive."

"We will find out."

"He was stubborn enough to stay behind when almost everybody was leaving for the hills."

"Some of them would rather die than leave their homes."

"It seems very foolish, but that is true. Yet, if they escaped to the hills, the land is here when they return."

"They can burn their houses, but they can't take the land away," Hassim said, thinking of the enemy soldiers.

"Always, and to the end of time."

They continued walking to the farmhouse. The dry rice stubble made a crushing noise as they stepped on it with their canvas shoes. Old Bio pulled down his cap to hide his face from the strong sunlight. Hassim stuffed his cap in his trouser pocket. They scared a field lark from its shade. It shot through the air straight as an arrow and landed on the other side of the meadow, where it started singing its vibrant sunlight song. Then they saw a fat green grasshopper jump from its shaded nook and hop into a crevice. But it was too late. Old Bio paused a moment and picked it up; then, tearing off the spiked legs, he stuffed it in his mouth. There was a sudden splash of juice as the grasshopper was crushed between the old man's sharp teeth. Hassim did not stop to see Old Bio eat the unfortunate creature of the field, but the old man caught up with him and touched his shoulder.

"Did you bring any of that whiskey?" he asked.

Hassim smiled and said, "No."

"I need something to wash down that slimy grasshopper."

"We will find some wine in the village."

"Ah, yes," Old Bio said, remembering one of his cronies in the village. "There was always a jug buried under Tiburcio's house. One of my friends."

"If he is still alive," Hassim said.

"I am sure he is still alive. He knows how to palsy-walsy with the enemy. He acts a fool and a fawning charlatan to them. But that is

*Godfathers; ritual coparents.

only a mask to hide the man. Behind it is the real man, unrelenting and unbreakable. Yes, he probably bowed his knees to save his precious jugs. He makes the best wine in this part of the country."

"We will locate him first."

"He lives on the other side of the village."

"We will see him later, then."

Old Bio nodded his head.

"Do you know who lives in that farmhouse?" Hassim asked, indicating the place they were approaching.

"Yes. Lucas Stopo. A young man with five children, the last time I saw him. Probably six by now, counting one for each year that I have been away." He laughed. "His wife is very fertile, like most women in this village."

"Is he friendly to our cause?"

"That I am not sure."

"We will find out."

"And risk our lives?"

"I don't believe he will do any informing on us, if you are not sure of his allegiance. At least he will not do that to you."

"I suppose not."

They approached the house and stopped at the gate. The house was quiet and all the windows and the door were closed tight. They looked at each other.

"It seems nobody is home," Hassim commented.

"Let us investigate," Old Bio said.

Hassim kicked the gate open and walked into the yard. Old Bio followed him to the bamboo ladder, where they paused to see if someone would appear at the door. There was a rusting plowshare under the house, beside a huge rice bin covered with wire screen. A pile of assorted firewood was in one corner and in another was a mother cat with her litter of six kittens. When they saw the cat and her kittens, they looked at each other again with secret understanding. There was somebody in the house.

Then Old Bio called, "Lucas! Lucas Stopo!"

Silence.

"This is Old Bio, son," he identified himself.

There was a whispering patter of bare feet on the split bamboo floor. The palm door opened slightly and a woman furtively peeked out. They both saw the fear-stricken face withdraw and the door

close. But there was no movement in the house. There was a deadly silence. They looked at each other for some kind of explanation. Then the door opened again and the same face leaned out far enough for the old man to recognize it.

"Pasiang," he called, "it is Old Bio. Don't you remember me, daughter?"

Pasiang remained silent.

"We are only passing through, Pasiang," Old Bio explained. "And we would like to have a few words with your husband."

"He is not here, Old Bio."

"Ah, you remember me at last?"

"Yes." She looked at Hassim and quickly turned her face away.

"And where is Lucas?"

"I don't know."

"You must have an idea where he went."

"Try Mariano Nunes."

Old Bio looked at Hassim. Then he turned to Pasiang and said, "We will do that, daughter. Good day."

"Good day."

The door closed. Hassim and Old Bio walked back to the gate and stopped.

"Something must have happened in the village recently," Hassim said.

"Do you think the enemy was here?"

"I have no doubt about it."

"Let us go to my *compadre* and find out what happened."

They walked across the unplowed fields, through a grove of banana trees, and came to a little stream, where they stopped and threw water on their faces and heads. Then they waded across the stream to the path that led to the village road, where they stopped again and cast doubtful glances at the houses. They seemed deserted. Only cats and dogs were lolling in the shade of the trees. They followed the path and walked on the road. Old Bio's face was crisscrossed with worry. He looked on both sides of the street at the deserted houses.

"Do you know where your *compadre* lives?" Hassim asked.

"We are approaching it now." He pointed to a bend of the road. "If he still lives there. We could find out for sure if we saw someone."

"Take this side of the road," Hassim said. "I will take the other. In case – "

Old Bio nodded his head. Hassim crossed the road and walked on, the old man keeping pace with him. When they came to the bend, Old Bio motioned to the right. So they turned right, each following his side of the road cautiously. Old Bio stopped when they came to a clump of trees on his side of the road and pointed to the house behind the trees.

It was a thatched house like all the houses they had passed by. There were two wooden benches in the yard and in a corner was an old pig tied to the fence. Hassim crossed the road over to Old Bio, and they stood at the gate looking up at the house. All the windows were closed.

"There is somebody inside," Hassim whispered.

"This looks bad."

"You go in first since they know you. But be careful."

Old Bio knew it was a command. His hands suddenly became clammy and he pulled at his beard to control himself. Then he put his right hand inside the shirt where the gun was hidden and kicked the gate open. He approached the house slowly, looking at the windows. Then there was a shot. He darted behind a tree and crouched low. The gun was aimed now, his eyes racing from one window to another. He looked sideways quickly to see the fence where the bullet had struck, then in the direction where he had left Hassim, who had disappeared when he heard the shot. Old Bio looked at the windows again and began to perspire.

When the shot rang out, Hassim ducked behind the fence and ran toward the other side of the fence, half crouching as he ran to the point where he was exactly opposite the old man. They were about twenty-five yards apart, and between was the house. He wedged himself between two trees and looked at the windows. He knew they had been seen approaching. Then he searched the yard where the old man had disappeared, and when he saw him crouching behind the tree, he smiled because, as he waited, he knew that the old man was still quick as lightning. He waited.

But the long interval of silence was making Old Bio uneasy. He did not want Hassim to be exposed. He had to know who was in the house. He could not hide behind the tree forever. He had to get away from there before nightfall. Then he made a bold decision. He aimed skyward and fired.

Hassim was watching him. He saw the tongue of fire streak through the branches of the trees and smiled again. The old man knew what he was doing.

Then a booming voice rang out of the house: "Who is there?"

Old Bio could not recognize the voice. Was it possible that his *compadre's* voice had changed in three years? The voice that he could identify from a kilometer away in the long ago when his *compadre* shouted on the back of the wind? He was not sure, so he kept silence.

Then another voice asked: "Who is there?"

That he recognized.

"*Compadre* Mariano Nunes," he shouted. "It is Old Bio."

A window opened slightly and a sunburned face appeared.

"Old Bio?"

"Yes." Old Bio recognized his *compadre.*

"Show yourself."

Old Bio came out of his hiding and showed himself.

"It is Old Bio, all right!"

Mariano Nunes came down from the house and greeted Old Bio. Hassim watched them from his hiding place but could not hear their conversation. Then he jumped over the fence and joined them. Mariano Nunes eyed him, not without suspicion. Old Bio noticed it.

"My traveling companion," Old Bio introduced Hassim.

Hassim and Mariano Nunes shook hands.

"What is going on here?" Old Bio asked.

"We are having a meeting."

Hassim and Old Bio exchanged glances.

"Let us go upstairs," Mariano Nunes said.

They followed him up the house. Hassim was struck by the sudden darkness, and for a second he saw nothing in the house. Automatically his hand went inside the shirt where the gun was hidden, for he felt that there were people in the darkness. Somebody took him by the arm and led him into the lean-to, a small subdivision of the house. He let himself be led, but he was not sure if it was the old man or Mariano Nunes. Standing inside the door of the lean-to now, he was sure that there were other men. A flint suddenly flickered in a corner, and in the sudden faint light Hassim saw that there were four men sitting on the floor. And in that brief moment of light, he saw Old Bio's apprehensive look, before the lean-to was plunged into darkness again.

The light was so brief that Old Bio did not have enough time to recognize all the faces, although he, like Hassim, was used to darkness and the sudden flash of light. However, he had a quick glimpse of Lucas Stopo, who was sitting near one of the two windows of the lean-to. He nodded to him. Even as the light faded, he heard a voice that seemed strange and far away.

"Welcome, Old Bio."

"Greetings," he answered.

"And who is with you?"

Old Bio felt Hassim's hand tug at his elbow, so he hesitated to answer the unknown voice. Then he knew what to say, having understood Hassim's warning touch.

"A friend."

"What kind of friend?"

Old Bio knew where the voice came from, but he was not sure at first. He faced the man directly, though they were five yards apart.

"A friend on our side," he answered.

"What side are you on?"

Old Bio was taken off guard. He threw back the question. "What side are you on?" he asked.

Now his hand was on the butt of the hidden automatic, and in the silence that followed one of the men shifted positions. Hassim pushed the old man back, near the door to the main part of the house. They both had their guns out. They were standing near the door almost back to back, so they could maneuver their automatics in case something was wrong.

Is this a trap? Old Bio asked himself. What happened to my *compadre?* But he repeated his question, "What side are you on?"

But there was no answer. Even Mariano Nunes, who was standing close to his *compadre* at the beginning of the inquiry, had moved noiselessly away. And Lucas Stopo, Old Bio knew, was the man who had shifted position. He was not afraid but somehow his hand with the gun trembled a little. He was at home at last – if it was a home – and yet death was so close and imminent. And he felt a pang of regret that he had to come home and kill some of his friends, if there had been a change since he was away. Maybe he would be killed, too.

But Hassim broke the silence. "Tell me," he challenged the unknown voice, "what side are you on?" His voice was commanding now; it streaked the darkness with its fierceness. "And who are you?"

And the old man, alert to the signs of violence, thought: *This is it, this is the real Hassim. But damn it, why didn't the son of a whore keep quiet? What luck I have to fire point-blank among my friends.*

"Well?" Hassim demanded.

"Well what?"

"I asked what side are you on and who are you?"

"I asked you first."

Old Bio felt Hassim half crouched, left foot forward, aiming directly at the unknown voice. He did the same, his left hand groping for the door.

Mariano Nunes cut the silence short.

"We all know Old Bio," he said. "He is on our side. I am sure the man with him is on our side, too."

"I can vouch for Old Bio," Lucas Stopo seconded Mariano Nunes. "I am sure he does not travel with our enemies."

"I will say the same for myself," another man said.

"Same here," still another voice said.

There, Old Bio thought, four against one. Who could the other two be? I don't seem to recognize their voices.

"You told me you have not seen Old Bio for three years," the unknown voice said. "There have been many changes of allegiance since he left."

"True enough," Lucas Stopo said. "But we have heard good things about Old Bio and the men he is working with."

"It is true that my *compadre* left three years ago," Mariano Nunes said. "But I know my *compadre* like I know myself. There is no doubt that he is on our side. And his friend, too."

"That is also my opinion," another voice said.

"Not on our side," the unknown voice said.

Old Bio trembled with rage. He hoped Hassim would not lose his temper. Hassim would not, he knew on second thought. And he was glad Dabu did not come along. Or else . . .

"What side are we on, then?" he asked.

It was like a shot in the dark, for the magnificence of his old voice came back. And his friends knew.

"The communist side!" the unknown voice cut the darkness with its deadly fieriness.

Old Bio's finger trembled at the trigger. Tragedy was saved by a split second.

"Wait a minute!" Mariano Nunes called out from his corner. He knew somehow that Hassim was an important man in the underground, because he knew that Old Bio was only a courier. And a courier, he concluded, would not venture to this village with another courier, or something less than a courier, whatever that was. And since it was the first time that the underground invaded their village since its organization, a big man must have come with his *compadre*. He knew he was right. So he said pacifically, "At present we are not concerned with political allegiances. We are concerned with the organization of the peasants in our part of the country. Is that right, Patricio?"

"I understand," the unknown voice conceded. "But we don't want any foreign elements in our midst."

So that is his name, Old Bio thought. Where did this rascal come from? I have never seen him before. Or even heard of him. But he asked, "Who is a foreigner among us?"

"We all know you, Old Bio," four men answered.

"I know you would not turn against me."

"That may be true," Patricio said. "But what about your friend? Nobody knows him here. Maybe he is one of those – " But there was already a note of defeat in his voice.

"Look here, son," Old Bio said. His patience was nearing its end.

94
..........
*The Cry
and the
Dedication*

"I don't know you, either. And if you were not in my *compadre's* house – Maybe you are on their – "

Patricio knew the implication. "Who are you to say that about me?"

"Who are you to question my supposition? I have never heard of you before, and we have a large organization. I don't know where you came from."

"So you doubt my – ?"

"Look here," Mariano Nunes intervened again. "We are not going any place. If you don't mind, Patricio – "

"Wait." Hassim stopped him. He knew now that he had to probe deeper into the psychology of Patricio, because he was sure of the others, the old friends of Old Bio. He would have to use the old tactics, to get this man Patricio. "Since Patricio is reluctant to identify himself except in a vague way, and since he is with you and therefore I can have his confidence because he is with you, I will say this – "

Old Bio touched him. Hassim, in the darkness, pressed the old man's hand to tell him that he knew what to do.

"It is better that everybody should know who I am," Hassim said. "I am just one of the men in the underground that don't go out much. I am in the educational side of our organization – but just a small cog in the wheel – some kind of clerk, you might say. We have a big organization, and even the educational department is so big that I seldom see the top man, whose name is Dante."

"I have heard of Dante," Patricio said. "Is he the man from America?"

"Yes."

"You have a man from America?" Mariano Nunes was interested.

"We have. But he is our countryman who had lived there for fifteen years. He is head of the department where I work."

"I have a brother in America," Lucas Stopo intervened. "Maybe he knows him."

"Maybe he does," Hassim said. "But he is in our camp."

Old Bio thought, If they only knew that Dante is only four kilometers from here.

"So that is what I am," Hassim concluded. "When I was informed that Old Bio wanted to visit his village, I came along for my department in the underground. They could have sent a bigger man, but they were all occupied at the time we left. Besides, I speak more of our dialects than most of them. That is why I came with Old Bio: to be informed of the conditions of this village. That and nothing else."

"Welcome, then," Patricio said.

"Welcome, friend," the other men said.

"I know my *compadre* is traveling with good company," Mariano Nunes said.

"So you have all those things?" Lucas Stopo said. "Educational, political, organization, and so forth."

"We have," Hassim said. "To run an effective campaign against the enemy."

"I am sorry I doubted you," Patricio apologized. "I am the partisan leader here." He lighted a flint and when he saw Hassim's gun he pushed it aside and said, "Please . . ."

Mariano Nunes, who was almost as old as his *compadre*, was struck by Hassim's youthfulness. He looked at the young man in silent admiration.

"You came from Alipato?" Patricio asked Old Bio.

"From Hassim," he answered.

"Hassim?"

"I work for him."

Mariano Nunes rushed to Old Bio. "*Compadre*," he whispered, "what kind of a man is he? I understand he is just a boy."

Old Bio's eyes gleamed in the darkness. And he thought, If he only knows that he is looking at Hassim he will crawl on his kness. But he whispered back, "Yes, he is only twenty-one years old."

"That young? And I have heard he has been in the underground for five years?"

How he wished to tell his *compadre* the truth! But he would tell him someday.

"Let us sit down and talk quietly," Lucas Stopo suggested.

They spread out in the lean-to and found their places, sitting against the four walls. Hassim sat between Old Bio and Mariano Nunes, who was eagerly waiting for Hassim to say something.

"It is a great privilege," Mariano Nunes whispered to Old Bio.

"It is for me, too," he said.

Old Bio almost revealed the secret to his *compadre*. But he said, "We call him Mabini."

"I have never heard of him."

"He is just one of the men in the educational department of the underground, as he said. But he can explain many things to us. He is educated by the underground." And he smiled in the darkness.

"Ay." Mariano Nunes sighed. "They educated you, too?"

"Of course."

His *compadre* sighed again.

Then Hassim spoke up. "Old Bio's visit to his village is the important thing," he said. "I just went along to learn a few things from you. That is of great importance to our organization."

"That is so," Old Bio said.

"Now tell me," Hassim addressed Patricio. "What has transpired in here for the last few months?"

"The enemy came and took away our animals," Lucas Stopo said sadly.

"We surmised that on our way down the hills," Hassim said.

"And they threatened to come back to take the scraggly animals we have in the pasture now."

"They will never stop taking things from you," Hassim said.

"But the worst is yet to come," Mariano Nunes intervened.

"Eh?" Old Bio said.

"They will come at harvest time and take away our grain."

"They will do that for sure," Hassim said.

"What are we going to do?"

Hassim was about to answer when there was a loud drone of planes in the sky. They listened in the darkness until the throbbing sky was clear again. Hassim knew there were three planes passing by. He knew they were American planes.

"I wonder what it means," Lucas Stopo said when the planes were gone.

"They are just reconnoitering," Hassim said. "Americans. But they don't have very many now in this country."

"A warning," Patricio said.

Hassim did not share the pessimism. "Now tell me," he addressed them all, "what have you been doing down here?"

"We have been organizing what are left of the men," Patricio said. "We heard of the underground as organized by Alipato. That is a good thing for the peasants, who are our people. We are fighting the same enemy, but as I understand it we have several differences in organizational methods and operations. For one specific thing, we are not a political unit but a peasant group dedicated to warding off the enemy."

"Ward off?" Hassim said. "Just ward off?"

"What else is there to do? The enemy has many soldiers and they are well armed. They can crush us in one blow."

"I can see the futility of your organizational methods. There are millions of us and this is our country and we know every mountain and river and hill in it. They can't crush us in a million years."

"Why do you say that?"

"You have to join us to see the effectiveness of our struggle."

Old Bio nudged his *compadre*. The urge to reveal Hassim's identity was overpowering. But he kept silent.

"The freedom of our country can be achieved only through a united front under the leadership of the underground, where Alipato commands. That is the only way now and always, if we organize ourselves properly and conduct our struggle scientifically. We can surely destroy the enemy that way."

"With what?"

"With endurance and our numbers. With new tactics, insubordination, striking at night, withholding food. In one phrase: terrorize the enemy where he is weakest."

"We don't have men to do those things."

"You have. You have always had them."

"They are afraid."

"Afraid? Who is afraid among us in the service of freedom?" Hassim stopped, remembering one important detail that he and Old Bio had noticed on descending into the plain. "Are you afraid when they take away all your animals?"

"They took away our animals," Lucas Stopo commented. "And now we have those carcasses in the pasture to work our lands. Lucky the planting is still several months off."

"They will take those away too when they have fattened enough," Hassim said.

"What?" Mariano Nunes said.

Lucas Stopo answered for Hassim. He said, "I was not fooled by them. I know they will come back and take these animals away."

"And your next harvest," Hassim said.

"Our harvest?" Patricio said. "Then how are we going to live? How are we going to work?"

"That was why a moment ago," Hassim emphasized his words, "I told you you that I saw the futility of your organizational methods."

There was a momentary silence. Hassim, even in the darkness, saw their heads turn in the direction of Patricio. He knew now that Patricio was not a peasant. He spoke with the aggressive authority of an educated man from the lower middle class. Evidently, Hassim thought, he has some severe disagreements with his class that drove him to the cause of the peasants. To fight the enemy without a political setup in view was disastrous and fatal, Hassim knew. He understood without listening too carefully to Patricio's train of words. It was his responsibility to explain the principles of the underground, of which he was one of the leaders; for it was also his responsibility to draw the separate groups of fighters into the underground, under a conclave of leadership. It was, he knew, their responsibility to politically educate them so that they would understand that the national liberation movement was national in scope. Now he seized his opportunity.

"All over the country," Hassim said, "there are groups like what you have here, and it is a good thing, as you say. But you can't fight the enemy effectively in your separate ways. That would be like fighting a storm with a grass coat, or a catastrophic fire with a bucket of water. The enemy is tightly organized into one gigantic body of phalanxes, composed of military units and an intelligence corps. To deal the enemy with a deadly blow needs, on our part, a strictly coordinated national organization with the view to organizing the peasants as a mass base for the underground. But that is only the first move. The second move is to politicize them so that, when a change of government comes, we will be ready to form one and operate it successfully. We of the underground mutually agreed on this point to prevent chaos and anarchy."

"Wait a minute," Patricio interrupted. "You have brought up several points and I would like to take them one by one for clarity. For instance, do you think the enemy will be vanquished?"

What a fool, Hassim thought. And he almost shouted the word. But he answered him, "If you think otherwise, what are you organizing yourselves for?"

"For mutual protection."

Undoubtedly a careerist, Hassim thought. And as it dawned on him, he felt Old Bio groping for his elbow. Aware, perhaps, that Patricio prolonged the silence, Old Bio, when he found Hassim's elbow, pressed it hard, urging him to say something. Hassim was not one to be pushed, for he always took his time in injecting his ideas in other people's minds.

Then he said, "The enemy will be vanquished."

Mariano Nunes, sitting beside him, sighed loudly. He was waiting for this moment. Old Bio took his hand away from Hassim's elbow and relaxed against the wall.

"And how?" Patricio shot back.

"By a united front of all partisan organizations."

"That was what I thought. I knew you would say that. And it comes to me, now. What would be our status if we joined the underground under the leadership of Alipato?"

"If you join the underground," Hassim said, "you will have the unit you have now, your own men, under your own leadership."

Patricio scowled in the darkness.

"Is that true?" Lucas Stopo asked.

"It is true," Old Bio answered for Hassim.

Mariano Nunes sighed again. He was eagerly waiting for his chance to join the conversation.

But after a brief pause, Patricio took up his quelling challenge. "With no obligations to anyone?"

"One obligation for all units within the framework of the national liberation movement," Hassim said. "And that is the cause of our people. That and nothing else."

"Of course," Old Bio said.

"And no ramifications of that one obligation in the interlocking status of the separate groups?"

"There are various ramifications, but they are simple," Hassim said. "These ramifications are relevant only to our successful struggle against the enemy. In order to effectuate a successful operation, we are all governed by a set of principles covering the whole movement and another set of principles governing our obligations to each other as separate groups in the national liberation movement and to the masses of our people, but mostly to the peasants and the unorganized workers in the towns and cities. And all these could be ironed out at a conference of the various leaders from the groups or units, if these leaders are elected democratically by the members."

"Then we can keep our separate status if we join you?" Mariano Nunes finally interjected.

"That is what I have been trying to say," Hassim answered him. "For if you fight as a separate group, like the scores of others fighting separately, you will come to disaster. How would you sustain your men if you fought separately? Where would you get food, clothing, medicine, and arms? How about your communication lines? How would you establish them? And your intelligence corps? How could you watch the movements of the enemy?"

"And you have all these things?" Mariano Nunes asked.

"We have, surely. And we are expanding every day."

"It seems to me that you have the right program," an unknown voice said. "There is no reason why we should not join you, unless Patricio decides to fight the enemy singlehanded."

The unknown voice disenchanted the atmosphere of enmity. There was a chorus of approval, but mostly from those who had not participated in the discussion. Old Bio beamed in the darkness, and his *compadre* leaned against him.

"Do you have a gun, *compadre*?" he whispered.

"Naturally."

"Do you have quite enough over there?"

"Certainly. And – " he cut himself short when he realized that he was about to divulge the nature of their mission to the city, thinking of what Dimasalang had said about Mabini and the possibility of having a shipload of ammunition and medicines from the United States.

"And what?"

"Well, we have quite enough to arm those who will join us."

"And money?"

"That, too."

"Where do you get these things?"

"We have friends everywhere."

"Everywhere?"

"Yes."

Mariano Nunes relaxed and leaned against the wall. Of course, Old Bio congratulated himself, I have not told him that Mabini is bringing five million dollars from the United States. Then he heard Hassim's voice. He was asking questions now and confining the interrogation to the local situation. The men answered him, even those who had not spoken before. There was a general agreement now, and Old Bio became impatient. He wanted to ask his *compadre* about something.

But Hassim was saying, "If you want to join us it is not absolutely necessary for you to leave your village en masse. It is good strategy for your future operations that some of your best men remain here and work anonymously among those who have not yet joined with us."

"How could we find your leaders?" Patricio asked.

"You know the great forest above the pasture?"

"Yes."

"In three weeks send four of your men there to meet us. We will take them to the Central Committee for a conference."

"And where is this Central Committee?"

"We will take your men to it."

"That is reasonable enough," Lucas Stopo said.

"In three weeks, then," Patricio concluded.

There was a silent agreement. They began to stir. Old Bio groped his way to Lucas Stopo who, he noticed when the flint was lighted, was sitting near one of the two windows. He almost collided with him, but Old Bio, because his eyes were focused on him, sidestepped and grabbed his arm.

"Lucas?"

"Yes."

"Old Bio."

They shook hands heartily.

"You heard him?"

"Every word of it."

"Are you with us?"

"Wholeheartedly."

"That is the way to feel."

"You have good leaders."

"That is so."

"You know them all?"

"Nearly all the living ones."

"I have heard of Hassim. What does he look like?"

Old Bio bit his lower lip. "I have not seen him yet."

"No?"

"He is always on the go."

"A brave young man, I heard."

But Old Bio did not want to pursue the subject. So he asked, "What happened to Tiburcio?"

"The winemaker?"

"They finally got him."

"How?"

"Hanged."

"May he rest in peace."

"Amen."

"Son," Old Bio said, "I have something to tell you."

"I am listening."

Old Bio pulled him to a corner. He whispered something in his ear and strode across the lean-to to the main part of the house. Hassim went out first. Old Bio, following him, stopped at the door.

"By the way, son," he said to Lucas Stopo, who had followed, "how many children have you got now?"

"Six, old man."

"Ay," Old Bio said with satisfaction. "That is the way it should be. And where are they now?"

"They are with my mother – where they are safe. Pasiang will join them tonight. They will be safe there."

"That is good. We will see you in three weeks, son."

Lucas Stopo nodded. Old Bio shook hands with his *compadre* and went out of the house. Hassim was waiting for him at the gate. They stood there and looked back at the house, but it was as silent as when they had first seen it. The door and all the windows were closed, but they knew that six men were watching them depart. Then, without saying a word, they walked down the village road and back to the unplowed fields and the meadow and then the pastureland, where they stopped to look at the animals grazing there. After a while they continued their way back to the hills, and at the foot of the trail to the great forest they stopped again and looked back to the deserted village.

"Do you think there will be any trouble from Patricio?" Old Bio asked slyly.

"I don't think so," Hassim said. "Your friends will take good care of him."

Old Bio turned to Hassim and looked at him with incredulity. "So you know?"

Hassim looked at the old man and said, "Didn't you know my name is Hassim?"

Old Bio's eyes flickered, then a genuine smile spread in his face, and he bent over and slapped his thigh laughing. He was still laughing when they started climbing up the hill to their friends in the great forest.

# CHAPTER EIGHT

As soon as Hassim and Old Bio were gone, Dabu built a fire in the nook of a big tree trunk. He gathered an armful of dry leaves on the hillside and put it in the nook, covered it with dead twigs that he had broken into short pieces, and on top of the mound he placed, in crisscross fashion, large pieces from the branches of the fallen tree. Then he scratched a match on the tree trunk and set the dry leaves underneath on fire; half-crouching, he watched with fascination the fire spreading and leaping like hundreds of fiery snakes to the twigs and branches. When he was satisfied with the dexterity of his work (the fire built in the nook so that it would not reveal their presence), he looked in the direction of Legaspi, who was cutting the goat meat and impaling the pieces with a sapling with a pointed end, and nodded with great satisfaction.

Legaspi arose and walked over to Dabu with two pointed saplings impaled with meat from end to end. Dabu took the saplings from Legaspi and neatly leaned them against the tree trunk near the fire, waiting for the blue smoke to disappear and for the red coals of the large branches to appear. Meanwhile, Legaspi returned to his chore. He squatted on his legs and worked in earnest, the blood of the animal smeared all over his hands. He looked up from his work and saw that Dabu was placing the two saplings alongside each other on the crisscrossed branches, which were now beginning to glisten with the bright luster of red coals. When he had impaled all the meat in several saplings, he walked over again to Dabu and leaned his handiwork against the tree trunk the way Dabu had done it. Then he wiped his hands with leaves and joined Dante, who was sitting on the fallen tree and smoking a cigarette.

Dabu sat on the ground finally and far enough from the fire so that he could turn the meat without changing position. He picked up a pebble and threw it at Linda Bie, who was stretched on the grass near Mameng.

"Linda Bie!"

Dabu's call was so sudden that Legaspi, Dante, and Mameng, who was cleaning her canvas shoes, leaped to their feet and looked in his direction. Linda Bie was half awake, so when he heard his name called and at the same time felt the pebble drop on his stomach, he rolled over on his side quickly and knelt on the grass, also looking in Dabu's direction. All had their guns ready. But Dabu slapped his knees and started to laugh loudly. When they realized that he was only playing to break the long silence, they put back their guns and returned to their former places, except Linda Bie, who was still kneeling on the grass with the gun in his hand.

"Don't do that again, Dabu," he complained.

Dabu laughed louder than ever, slapping his knees and bending double. Then Dante and Legaspi began to laugh too, but not as heartily as Dabu because they were smoking cigarettes. Even Mameng, who seldom laughed, joined the chorus of laughter. Linda Bie looked at them and felt like a fool because he could not take the joke. Finally, however, he put back his gun and relaxed. He scrambled to his feet and walked to the fire.

"Were you dreaming of fair women?" Dabu asked him.

"I was not asleep."

"Then you were thinking of fair women?"

Linda Bie looked at him seriously. He did not know how to take Dabu when he was in this mood.

"I was not even thinking," he said.

"You were not dreaming, you were not thinking, you were not sleeping. So what were you doing?"

"I was resting."

"From what?"

"From the agony of waiting."

"Waiting for what?"

"Nightfall."

"What goes on when nighfall – "

It was then that they all heard the shot from the village where Hassim and the old man had gone. The clownish look on Dabu's face suddenly disappeared, and he jumped to his feet. With a wave of his hand he motioned to the others to hide behind the tree trunks and ran downhill, his right hand holding the gun and the left adjusting the eyepieces of the field glasses. He jumped behind the underbrush and put the field glasses to his eyes, adjusted the eyepieces hastily, and pointed it to the village.

Legaspi followed him and dropped beside him.

"Do you think they are in trouble?" he asked.

Dabu did not answer him. He was scouring the houses and the village.

"I can't see anything," he said finally.

"That was a gunshot, all right."

"I know."

"Linda Bie and I should go down."

Dabu turned to him with a scowling face.

Legaspi understood his refusal. "Something should be done!" he protested. "We can't let them alone in a village full of men!"

"There is nothing that could be done."

Linda Bie crept silently to the underbrush where they were hiding. He was about to say something to Dabu when the second shot rang out and echoed in the hills. The second shot made Dabu unsure of what decision to make. He screwed and unscrewed the eyepieces feverishly. But the trees in the village obstructed his view, and he saw nothing except smokeless grass huts and the animals in the pastureland. He knew that if he went down to the village with his companions, their mission to the city would be curtailed. If something fatal happened to Hassim and Old Bio, there were still five of them left to accomplish it. But his heart ached with terror, thinking of Hassim and Old Bio. He was breathing hard now and his face was thick with perspiration, as though he had run a long distance to reach a safe place.

"There were two shots," he murmured.

"Could it be – " Linda Bie did not finish the sentence.

"I am not sure."

"I insist that Linda Bie should go down," Legaspi said.

Dabu scowled at him again. "There is nothing that could be done, now."

"But it is Hassim and the old man."

"We have something to do," he said; and even as he said it, his heart cried out to Hassim and Old Bio. "That is more important, now. And above all, there is nothing we could do now if – "

"I am thinking of reprisal."

"We can do that later, if something happened to them."

"We will wait and see," Linda Bie suggested.

Legaspi twisted his face in agony. But they waited, half-crouching behind the underbrush. They waited half an hour, but when they saw no sign of activity in the whole village, they gave up and returned to the campfire. Dante and Mameng came out of hiding and met them with inquiring faces. Dabu looked at them in silence and turned his face away. When he smelled the burning meat on the coals, he snatched the saplings and flung them down the hill. His anger was so great that he had to unleash it on something; then, having flung the meat, and knowing the futility of his action, he beat the tree trunk with his fists until his knuckles started to bleed. He stopped and looked at his bruised hands. He sucked the blood to stop the bleeding and tears appeared in his eyes.

Legaspi opened a bottle and poured the whiskey on Dabu's hand. But he did not even feel the sting of the alcohol. He did not even know what he was doing. It was only when Mameng started bandaging his hands with pieces of cloth that she had torn from her shirt that sanity came back to him and made him realize the weight of his responsibility now that Hassim was –

"Watch the meat," he said to Legaspi. "And please start packing," he said to the others. "I will go down again and watch the village. Don't do anything else until you hear from me."

They watched him go down the hill with the field glasses in his hand. They knew he was in command now. But they also knew that he was not a disciplinarian. He was not stern in his judgments when one of them unwittingly and unknowingly committed an act that was detrimental to their plan. He was a genial and easygoing man between bursts of fury. He would have been a successful officer had he joined the regular army of the enemy. There the soldiers would have found in him a man who would not take advantage of his rank for personal gain or self-immolation. Fortunately for them, he had fought his way into the underground where the relationship between commander and the men was emphasized on the principles of equality, since they were all fighters for freedom.

Legaspi put the meat on the burning coals. Now and then he turned it over, or cut a slice with a knife and ate it; and when it was evely browned, he wrapped the meat with fresh leaves and put it in the sack. Then he put another on the fire, browning and turning it at intervals. But even as he worked seriously, he was thinking of Hassim and the old man. Sometimes his hand stopped in mid-air when he was about to put a piece of the meat in his mouth and looked at his companions, wanting to communicate what he was thinking.

But Dante and Mameng were suddenly busy. They were furiously packing their knapsacks, throwing away unnecessary things and keeping those that were essential on their trip. For that was their only preoccupation now: their mission to the city. When they were through with their knapsack, and Dabu's and Legaspi's, they looked at each other wordlessly when they came to Hassim's and Old Bio's knapsacks. They did not know what to do with them, and Legaspi noticed their indecision.

"Keep them in order just in case," Legaspi said to them.

"Well, I can always carry two of those," Linda Bie said, pointing to Hassim's knapsack. He had just come from downhill where he went to search for the pieces of meat that Dabu had flung there in anger a moment before. "And Dabu can carry the other – "

Dante looked at Linda Bie with a blank face. Then he bent over Hassim's knapsack and started discarding what seemed to him unnecessary, keeping only a few canned foods, a map of the city, and a water bag. When he came to the shirt at the bottom of the knapsack, he picked it up and studied it. It was a blue shirt, unironed but clean; and a sad thought came to him suddenly, knowing that Hassim had saved it to wear when they reached the city. Carefully he refolded the shirt and put it back in the knapsack, feeling low and sad about the whole affair.

Mameng started cleaning Old Bio's knapsack. She found a pair of peasant trousers, old and unpressed but clean; and it struck her that even the old man was saving something to wear when they reached the city, a place he had never seen. She herself had a clean pair of trousers and a white blouse in her knapsack that she was saving for the same purpose; and as she pondered over the purpose of all these unpressed but clean clothes, her unlovely mouth twisted in anguish. Then she found a piece of roasted meat carefully wrapped in banana leaves; and she sighed, because it was the meat she had given him at the cave. He was saving it too for future emergency. A real peasant, Mameng thought. Always saving something for the future. Always afraid of the future because he has known the pangs of hunger, the terror of deprivation. She brushed the mist from her eyes and tied the knapsack with a cord, then put it beside Hassim's knapsack and looked in the direction of Dabu. She was speechless because her heart ached so; and when Dante put his hand on her shoulder, she almost cried out her sorrow. But she did not. She would not. She could not. For she was taught to check her emotions, to hold her tongue, to keep her thoughts. So she stood straight, trembling.

And Dante, knowing what was going on in her mind, stood beside her in silence. When her body stopped shaking, she turned to him and gently stroked his chin.

"It is all over now," she said.

"It is better that way," he consoled her.

"Let us help Legaspi with the meat."

Dante nodded. But their help was unnecessary. Linda Bie was helping Legaspi, not only in turning the meat over the coals but also eating some of the choicest pieces. Linda Bie had long ago learned to eat anything, anything at all, because they were always on the run and they picked up anything to quench their hunger and thirst. So as he ate the pieces of goat meat with relish, he thought of his family and rich friends gorging themselves with beef and pork and chicken, and champagne and rare wines and imported whiskey. And he laughed a little, knowing what his family and rich friends would say if they saw him now eating wild goat meat in the forest. He knew they would call him barbarian or cannibal. Or even Igorot, although Igorots did not eat goat; but they would not know the difference, for they even called the peasants peons or slaves.

Legaspi broke the sad mood. "Hey!" he said to Linda Bie. "Don't gorge yourself with the meat. There will be nothing left for Hassim and Old Bio."

"I am just pecking at it," Linda Bie protested.

"Pecking at it? Why, you just finished the liver and now you are at the ears! Watch out – when the old man comes back – "

"Wait a minute! You are accusing me of being a peasant, a goat eater, is that it?"

"You are worse than a peasant."

Dante laughed.

"What could be worse than a peasant?" Linda Bie wanted to know.

"A rich landlord!"

Dante laughed louder. Mameng joined the laughter. Legaspi

looked at Linda Bie amusingly. But Linda Bie caught the joke. They could not put anything over on him, like the old man for instance, so he stuffed a big piece of meat in his mouth and turned away.

"I don't like goat meat anyway," he said in a humorous tone of voice.

They all laughed. Then the sound of planes roared in the clear sky in the midst of their laughter. They suddenly stopped laughing and looked up. It was Linda Bie who first saw the three planes flying northward in a V-formation. The planes gleamed whitely in the hot afternoon sun. They watched them come overhead and their thundering noise echoed in the forest and down the hills into the ravines and onto the plateaus. They saw the planes disappear behind the tall mountains in the north.

"Americans?" Legaspi asked.

"Yes," Dante said.

"I wonder what is going on up north." Linda Bie wanted to know.

"They went in the direction of our camps," Mameng answered him.

"I hope they will not spot Dimasalang and his men," Legaspi said.

"They should be at our camps by now," Linda Bie told him.

"Almost," Dante said.

Dabu came running up the hill. His eyes were very red from watching the blistering village. His agitation was apparent.

"Did you see them?" he asked.

They nodded.

"Americans," Dante told him.

"I thought they had gone back a long time ago."

"Some of them are still here to watch over their investments."

"This is a bad sign. Something is bound to break out somewhere."

"They are probably trying to locate our camps and photographing the whole terrain for future destruction."

They looked at each other in silence. Legaspi went back to his work, and when the last piece of meat was put in the sack of food, he tied the sack mouth with a rope and laid it beside their knapsacks. Dabu returned to the underbrush down the hill and kept his vigil, screwing and unscrewing the eyepieces of the field glass to get a better view of the village. But he saw nothing. Linda Bie, to break the anguish of waiting, began playing on his flute. He had carefully fixed it, and now it sounded good and new. He was playing a lively dance tune. Legaspi jerked his head and looked at Dante and Mameng.

"Well, what are you doing?" he said to them.

"What is there to do?" Dante answered in anger.

Linda Bie's eyes twinkled. He knew what Legaspi meant. He blew at his flute stronger and the lively melody trailed under the trees and down the hillside. Legaspi approached Mameng and put his arms around her.

"This is what you should do, Dante," he said gaily.

Now Mameng knew what Legaspi meant, too. She took Legaspi's arms without protest and started to dance with him. At first she was stiff and clumsy, for the grass got in her way. Linda Bie winked at Dante as he played the tune, waving the flute slightly like a baton. And Dante, having understood at last, wiped off the anger on his face and smiled approvingly.

Meanwhile, Mameng was beginning to enjoy the dance. She whirled and whirled like a dervish, laughing when she bumped against Legaspi's big shoulders. Linda Bie repeated the song three times. He was enjoying the song and the scene. This was his forte: to make people dance. It was reminiscent of his younger days, when he was still with his family. But then, he had a violin and a piano, and he was an accomplished player in both. The rugged life he lived in the underground had driven him to seek a less cumbersome instrument, and it was then that he thought of a flute. So he cut a tall reed one night when they were passing through a swampland and dried it in the sun when day came. He dried it for three days successively, and when it was ready, he started boring holes with a burning nail. It took him several hours to make the instrument, cutting here and there slowly and painstakingly; and when it was finished, he admired his handiwork with such enthusiasm that even his companions were moved by it. But it took him several weeks to learn to play to his satisfaction, until finally, some months later, he could play it easily the way he used to play the violin and piano at home. So as he ended the lively tune he felt as though he had found some lost threads of his life. He tapped the flute on his knee to emit his saliva in it.

"How do you like it?" Linda Bie asked Mameng.

"Very good," she said. She really enjoyed it. "What is it?"

"South America," Dante said. "It is called samba."

Legaspi was puffing hard and grinning at Mameng.

"Boy, what I could do with that tune if we were in a house!" he exclaimed.

"I will play it again when we get to a house," Linda Bie assured him.

Legaspi slapped his knees. "Why don't you play something for Dante?"

"I have not danced for years," Dante protested. But he really wanted to dance with Mameng.

"Why not try a folk dance?" Legaspi suggested.

Linda Bie nodded and blew at his flute. Legaspi listened and screwed up his eyes disapprovingly.

"No, no," he said, shaking his head. "Try this. Listen – " He closed his eyes, put the tip of his tongue between his lips, and whistled a folksong that was popular in the northern part of the island. He was not a whistler for his lips were thick and so was his tongue, but he was trying his best to give Linda Bie an idea of what he wanted his flute to play for Dante and Mameng. There were several false notes in his whistling, but Linda Bie seemed to get it. When he ran out of breath, Legaspi stopped and opened his eyes. "Do you get it now?" he asked.

"I guess I get it," Linda Bie said. He whistled a few notes, and Legaspi nodded his head. Then he tried it on the flute, and Legaspi smiled. "Is that it?" Linda Bie asked.

"Yes!"

"What is it called?"

" 'The Lady Dayang-Dayang.' "

"Igorot folksong?"

"Originally. It is Ilocano now."

"Ah."

"Try it, Linda Bie," Mameng suggested.

Linda Bie tried it.

"That is better," Legaspi approved.

"It sounds good," Dante said.

"It is good," Legaspi bragged. "I used to play it on a *cutibeng*\* when I was a little boy. Linda Bie, play and I will sing the words. And you two," he said to Dante and Mameng, "dance!"

Linda Bie started the song on his flute. Dante approached Mameng, who curtsied in the manner of a princess in the presence of a king; then, when Legaspi raised both hands and tapped a foot on the grass, held hands and started to swing round and round. And Legaspi sang happily:

> *When the Lady Dayang-Dayang opens her door,*
> *The sun comes down the weeping sky*
> *And the whole world smiles even to the poor.*
> *Ay-yay-yay! Ay-yay-yay! Ay-ay!*
>
> *When the Lady Dayang-Dayang closes her door,*
> *The sun withdraws from the weeping sky*
> *And the whole world frowns even to the poor.*
> *Ay-yay-yay! Ay-yay-yay! Ay-ay!*

Again and again Linda Bie played the rollicking folksong, and Legaspi sang it at the top of his lungs. Their merriment filled the air. Birds fluttered above them with envy. A wild goat crawled up the hill to see them, hiding behind a tree and watching them with dull eyes. Farther down the glade was a shoat, its black ears flipping in accompaniment to the song.

Mameng was a real woman now. The distracted look in her face was gone. Her eyes were soft and caressing, and even her unlovely mouth was lovely now. Dante, too, had lost his faraway look. He was of this earth now, of this air, of this hill. His gray hair glistened in the sunlight as he swung around and jumped. He was even smiling. And Linda Bie, watching them dancing above the length of his reed flute, was touched beyond words. Where had he seen such happiness last? In what house, in what village, in what town? This was the life he knew and would like to know again. He suddenly rose and started tapping his left foot on the grass the way Legaspi was doing it.

At this instant Dabu came running up the hill, calling to them.

---

\*A musical instrument.

"They are coming back!" he called. "Hassim and Old Bio are coming back!"

They abruptly stopped their merriment.

"Nobody is hurt?" Legaspi asked.

"No."

"Somebody must be hurt," Linda Bie said.

"It is not Hassim or Old Bio," Dabu affirmed.

"Where are they now?" Dante asked.

"They are at the foot of the hill. They will be here soon."

Mameng sighed. "I am so glad," she said.

They were all relieved.

"Well, what was it you were playing?" Dabu asked Linda Bie.

"It is Legaspi's folksong. It is called "The Lady Dayang-Dayang." "

"Well, play it again. I like to dance."

Linda Bie started the song. Legaspi raised both hands again and tapped his left foot on the grass. Then Dabu grabbed Mameng and whirled her around, shouting with happiness.

"Louder!" he called to Linda Bie. "And you two," he said to Dante and Legaspi, "dance to a glorious day!"

Legaspi and Dante could not resist the contagion of Dabu's happiness. They kicked the knapsacks away and held each other, Legaspi taking the part of a woman. And Linda Bie played on, trying hard not to sob; his heart was aching so.

It was thus that Hassim and Old Bio found them when they came to the crest of the hill, where they stood watching them with amusement, not knowing what had transpired in their hearts when they were gone.

## CHAPTER NINE

. . . . . . . . . . . . . . . . . . . . . . . . . . . . . . . . . . . . . .

**H**assim and Old Bio approached them. Old Bio, trailing behind Hassim, cocked his head left and right, wondering at the meaning of their merriment. Hassim's amusement had already left him.

"You have quite a gay party here," he greeted them.

They all laughed, including Mameng, but with tears.

"Somebody's birthday party?" Old Bio asked. Then he noticed Mameng; so slow to catch on as usual, he asked further, "Is it hers?"

They all turned to her. But quick to tears like most women, and also quick to anger like most of her companions, she abruptly brushed away her few tears and smiled at Hassim and Old Bio. Hassim was doubtful, whereas Old Bio began to believe that it was her birthday. To clarify Mameng's momentary tears and their sudden gaity, Dabu volunteered to explain. He explained the two shots in the village that they had heard, the three planes that went north, and their anxiety over the welfare of Hassim and Old Bio. When he was finished, Hassim and Old Bio suddenly understood their feelings. And Hassim especially, who understood the deeper implications of their sentiments, felt an aching compassion for them; for he would have done the same thing.

Old Bio, however, took it lightly. But he explained their side of the story. "It was just my *compadre*," he said. "He had not recognized me when we approached his house, so he fired between my legs to make me identify myself."

"Is that all?" Legaspi asked.

"How about the second shot?" Dabu wanted to know.

"It came from my gun," Old Bio said, smiling a little. "It was just a warning that Old Bio was coming home."

"That was all," Hassim concluded. "Of course we had some kind of argument with his old friends."

"And quite an argument, too," Old Bio said.

"Are you ready?" Hassim asked them.

"Yes," Mameng said. "Everything is ready."

"You can have your drink now, Old Bio," Hassim said. "We will move on in an hour."

The sun was nearing the rim of the western horizon. Birds began to fly to their roosts. Down below, where the stream was darkening under the trees, wild animals were drinking their fill. In the ravines and on the plateaus the shadows of the trees were lengthening. Now everywhere in the great forest life stirred, asserting its presence in the coming twilight.

Hassim sat on the fallen tree and started to write his report. Old Bio, having found the sack where the whiskey was kept by Legaspi, opened a bottle and sat against a tree trunk to enjoy his drink. Linda Bie went back to his flute and played "The Lady Dayang-Dayang." Dabu was cleaning his gun. Dante and Mameng walked down the hill to the underbrush, where they sat down facing the sinking sun.

"What is wrong with Hassim?" Mameng asked.

"What do you mean?"

"He seems without feeling for women."

"You are wrong."

"You mean he has feelings for women?"

"Yes."

"I asked him to do it to me."

"And – ?"

"He did not want it. He suggested you."

Dante looked at her. "He did?"

"He did."

"He is a wise young man."

"But why didn't he want it?"

"You really don't know?"

She shook her head.

"Of course," Dante said. "Something happened to him before you came to the underground."

"What is it?"

"You will find out someday."

"I hope it is not what I think."

"Maybe it is."

"The Japanese did it?"

"No," Dante said and looked away. "Our own people."

"And yet he does not hate."

"No."

She touched his hand. "Do you love me?"

He looked at her again. "What a silly question."

"But you do?"

He did not answer her.

"A little?"

He laughed.

"You must love me a little."

"Why?"

"Because I love you."

He did not laugh. He studied her ugly face and frowned.

"Well," she said, "love has no place in our work?"

"It definitely has – it's what we are fighting for – so that love ..."
But he could not finish what he wanted to tell her. So moved was he
by her feelings for him, that he could not tell her the truth.

"Why are you all like that?" she asked.

"Like what?"

"So indifferent to women, to love – "

"I am not." But he was. Love had long ago died in him, and she
knew it. The desire in him was merely physical. He repeated his lie.
"I am not at all like that."

Mameng knew he lied. But it did not matter to her now.

"Tell me, Dante," she said. "What happened to you in that land
you can't forget?"

"Nothing much."

"There must be something important." She knew, all right.
"Otherwise you wouldn't act the way you do."

He looked at her and did not know what to say.

"Tell me a little something to hold on to, because I really love
you." She was pleading to him, begging him to share her love for
him. "It is the only thing I have now. In two days we will be passing
through Dabu's territory."

"I know."

"There are unfriendly people there. I think we will have a little
trouble, if Hassim and Dabu are going into the place to investigate.
Maybe I – "

"Nothing will happen to you."

"I hope not."

There was doubt in his face.

"So you must tell me something to remember. What have they
done to you there?"

"Who?"

"The American women."

Now he knew. But he could not tell her. Not now. Not ever. But he had to fabricate another lie to ease her mind, to betray himself to the world. But even now that he knew he had to lie to her, he felt ashamed of the thought of it. He felt a great sense of guilt, that he had to lie to one who had given herself completely to him. What great lie could he tell her now?

"They destroyed my humanity," he said. But he was unaware that he was telling the truth; that he had said exactly the opposite of what he had wanted to say. "They did that, but completely – "

"The women too?"

"All of them."

"I am sorry to know that. You must have been hurt."

"I was."

"Poor Dante."

He turned his face away from her.

"I am not asking too much," she said.

"No."

"Somewhere, not in your heart but in your mind, there must be a little place for me. If you don't have it now, please make one for me. That is all I am asking, Dante."

He did not answer her. From between the trees he heard Linda Bie's flute. He looked up suddenly and saw that the sun had already sunk; the violet twilight was creeping on the hillside below them. He knew it was time to go. He leaned against Mameng and kissed her broken nose.

"Let's go now," he said.

She got up to her feet. "Thank you for the kiss," she said. "I wanted something else, but I will keep it for some other time."

He grinned at her. He took her hand and together they walked to their companions. Hassim was still writing his report. Dante noticed the seriousness in his face. He strode over to Hassim and touched him on the shoulder.

"It is getting dark, Hassim," he said.

Hassim looked up at him and around the hillside. He had been unaware of the time, but now he saw that darkness had fallen.

"I will be through in a minute," he said.

Dante went to Dabu. "How is your hand?" he asked.

"It hurts me a little."

"Let Mameng dress it again."

Mameng took a bottle of whiskey from the sack. Hassim told her
to tear off a piece from the clean shirt in his knapsack.

"You won't be able to use it for a few days," Dante told Dabu.

Dabu frowned. He flexed his forefinger, as though he were
pressing a gun trigger.

"It works," he said.

"You will miss it," Dante told him.

"We will see."

"Can't you use your left hand?" Dante asked, thinking of Hassim, who could fire a gun with either hand.

"I don't want to waste bullets."

"There now," Mameng said, finishing the last bandage.

Dabu tussled her short hair. Mameng looked at him a moment
and walked over to Dante.

"You were trying to tell me something a moment ago," she said.
"What is it?"

"Nothing."

She looked at him with uncertainty and walked over to the
knapsacks. She picked up her knapsack and strapped it around her
shoulders. Then she walked back to Dante and told him to do the
same. He walked to the knapsack without looking at her. Linda Bie
followed Dante, then the old man and Legapi. Dabu was the last; he
picked up his knapsack and Hassim's. He carried Hassim's knapsack
to him and dropped it on the fallen log. Then he joined the group;
they were all looking at the darkening sky except Mameng, who was
watching Dante's face to see the answer to what she had asked him
a moment before. But Dante evaded her eyes and lit a cigarette to
hide his nervousness.

Hassim finished his report. He folded the notepaper and put it in
the canvas bag he had taken out of the knapsack. Then he put back
the bag and tied the knapsack; jumping off the log, he swung the
knapsack to his back and joined his companions.

"I hope we will make sixty kilometers tonight," he said.

"Where is our next stop?" Dabu asked.

"Rendezvous Two."

Dabu understood it, but the others did not. Hassim saw their ignorance.

"Legaspi's territory," he explained.

Legaspi's face lit up. He had not seen his town for five years, and now he was finally going to see it. He did not know what was left of the place and of the people he knew. Still, he felt elated to see it again. He tightened the straps of his knapsack and turned away to hide his emotions.

Old Bio watched him walking away. He saw Legaspi stop a few yards away and light a cigarette. He stood there unmoving, looking southward to his own territory. Old Bio knew what Legaspi felt, because he had felt the same when he and Hassim went down to his village. He too did not know when he would see his village again, but it lifted up his spirit when he saw it after many years of absence; and especially when he saw his old friends and understood what they were doing.

Ashamed to have peeked into Legaspi's privacy, Old Bio turned to his companions. "Legaspi can't take it," he murmured.

"He was engaged to be married when he was driven away from his town," Hassim explained. "That is enough for a man to cry over. But he will get over it."

They all turned toward Legaspi.

"He will be all right," Hassim told them.

When they saw that Legaspi was about to turn toward them, they quickly turned away from him so he would not be embarrassed. Linda Bie lighted a cigarette, while Dabu picked a stone and threw it down the hill. Old Bio coughed behind his hand. Dante grinned at Mameng, who grinned back. But Hassim met Legaspi halfway and put his arm around his shoulder.

"I feel all right," Legaspi said.

"Good." Hassim looked at his watch. "We will be there in ten hours. Maybe less."

"It is good to see the old place again."

"I know how you feel."

They approached the others.

"We will leave at exactly six," Hassim said.

They all looked at their watches. It was twenty-five minutes to six.

"There will still be a little light when we cross the valley," Dabu said.

"Old Bio has taken care of that place," Hassim explained. "There will be no more light when we have crossed it."

Dabu and Dante looked at Old Bio, who challenged their puzzled eyes. When Linda Bie and Mameng looked at him, he grinned and his large black teeth showed. From Dabu's angle the old man appeared as though he were snarling at the world, so it was he who understood Hassim's comment before any of the others understood it. Then he looked at Hassim, but his face was expressionless. When they all understood it, they looked at Old Bio for a moment and turned away with their separate private thoughts. Old Bio came to them then, but he had stopped grinning. In his face now was the sign of a repressed anger.

"May I have another sniff before we go, Hassim?" he asked.

Hassim nodded his head without interest. Legaspi frowned, but he opened the sack and gave the old man a bottle. Old Bio drank the whiskey like water and gave back the bottle to Legaspi.

"Thank you, son," he said.

Legaspi did not answer him. He put the bottle back in the sack and tied the mouth. Now the sun was gone and darkness was falling upon the land.

Hassim stirred. "Help Legaspi carry the food sack, Dabu," he said.

Dabu picked up the food sack and swung it across his left shoulder. Legaspi did the same thing with the sack of whiskey. Dante carried two of the water bags and Linda Bie carried the other two.

"Let us go," Hassim said.

Old Bio led the way down the hill. Hassim walked close behind him. They climbed down single file. Dabu was at the end; he was peering down the valley above the heads of his companions, through the spreading darkness. When they reached the base of the hill, Old Bio and Hassim stopped and waited for the others. Then they walked in twos across the field: Hassim and Old Bio together,

Dante and Mameng, Legaspi and Linda Bie. Dabu was still at the end, alone. He adjusted his knapsack and shifted the water bags in such a way that his right hand was free of movement. He cocked his head from left to right as though he were expecting something to happen.

They skirted the edge of Old Bio's village, evading the houses that were now flaring in the night. They walked in the shadow of the trees, alert to dogs and other animals. When they passed Lucas Stopo's house, Old Bio and Hassim stopped again and looked in the direction of the village center. There was no light in Lucas Stopo's house, but farther away they saw five houses with light. Mariano Nunes's house was also in darkness.

The others also stopped and looked in the direction of the village. Dabu bent over to light a cigarette. Then the shot rang out in the village. Hassim looked at Old Bio, but he could not see his face. He saw only the white fringes of his beard. But Dabu, who was about to strike a match on his shoe, dropped quickly to the ground to prepare himself for the fight.

"What is that?" he whispered.

Hassim saw him. "It is nothing," he said.

"So that is the end of Patricio?" Old Bio commented.

Dabu got up to his feet and said, "Patricio?"

"It is nothing," Hassim said. "Let us go."

## CHAPTER TEN

. . . . . . . . . . . . . . . . . . . . . . . . . . . . . . . . . . . .

**A**ll night long they passed through the sleeping villages. Once they came to a village where a wedding was going on, and for a moment they stopped under cover of the trees and listened to the loud music. But when they seemed fascinated and intended to stay awhile, Hassim told them to go on with the journey.

So they marched again, skirting the towns, following winding rivers and crossing fields cooling with the coming dew. Now they

walked in two groups, three persons to each group. Dabu was the leader of the first group; Old Bio on his left, Dante on his right. Legaspi was the leader of the second group; Mameng was on his left,
Linda Bie on his right. Hassim was the last, a group all by himself, following them with easy steps. They were walking ten feet apart, sometimes a little closer, sometimes a little farther. But they never faltered or lost sight of each other.

They walked silently until midnight, when they stopped at the edge of a village for some rest. They found a bamboo grove near a river, so they sat under the protection of the trees. The houses on either side of the river were a kilometer away and in darkness. They sat on the soft bamboo leaves and smoked, careful not to set the trees afire. They smoked their cigarettes to a finger and crushed the butts with their shoes, except the old man, who saved the shreds of tobacco in a small pouch and chewed a mouthful when it was inconvenient to smoke.

They had to stop because of Mameng. An hour of rest would give her enough strength for the next rendezvous. They had five more hours to go, then it would be another morning.

"Are you tired, Mameng?" Hassim asked her.

"Yes. But I will be all right after a little rest."

"Good. How about you, Old Bio?"

The old man laughed. "Me tired? I can walk to the end of the world." He spat the tobacco juice in his mouth, making an obscene noise. He laughed again. "You better ask Linda Bie. He is the soft one in this crowd."

Linda Bie knew that the old man was always chiding him, but not with malice. And he always gave it back to Old Bio without hurting him, to let the old man know that he could use his own weapon against him. So now he said, imitating the old man's voice, "Me tired? I can walk to the end of the world." Then he said to the old man in his own voice, "I can walk to the end of time. Can you beat that, Old Bio?"

"To the end of time, he says," Old Bio said, spitting brown spittle again. "He is panting like a schoolboy now and the goal is still far away. Young man, you should have been with me when I went north to locate Hassim. You should have seen me climb those rugged mountains and brushy hills. You should have seen me penetrate those dangerous jungles and the villages of wild people. Only a real man can do that. You probably can walk across a dance floor with grace. But I doubt even that; I was not quite stupid when I was your age. Listen, son. The women proposed to me, and I proposed to nine. It takes a real man to do that. And even now – "

"How come you married only one woman?" Linda Bie interrupted him.

"How come you married only one woman, he says," Old Bio said with great sarcasm. "Since when is it moral to marry two, not to speak of three, women in our country? I don't even want to argue with you about it. Now it seems to me that your education and money have made you lose track of the traditions of our country, which are moral no matter from what viewpoint you look at them. And it seems to me – "

The others were listening with some interest, but Dabu interrupted the old man again.

"Tell me," he said, "did you ever dance the fandango?"

"Did I ever dance the fandango?" Old Bio said. He tapped Dabu on the shoulder. "Listen. I was not a peacock like some of you young people nowadays, but I will tell you that I was a man in my own fashion. A real man, understand? A man who can stand on his feet against other men, against storm and wind, against animals and other ferocious things. Not a mouse, or a snake. Once when I was young and villagers saw me coming everybody cried with joy and made way for me, as though I were a general or a king. Listen: when I walked across the dance floor ladies fainted upon my approach and men popped out their eyes with envy. Ten women proposed to me, and I proposed to them; but I married one because I was ever with man in my morals, unlike other men in my time. Now you think that monkey-jumping that you boys pass your time with is called dancing, eh? In my time we really danced with the ladies, easy and smooth and gentle. We were not wrestlers on the dance floor like you boys today. Look at a real man even in old age!"

"Wrestlers," Linda Bie said.

"Monkey-jumping," Legaspi said.

"Peacock," Dabu said.

"A real man," Dante said.

But they were talking quietly. They were trying to provoke the old man into some exhibition. Hassim and Mameng were silent, but they were watching the game with interest.

"Do you think I am boasting, eh?" Old Bio asked. "Blow at that flute of yours, Linda Bie. I will show you how a real man dances."

"It is all right," Hassim said. "Play low. The houses are far enough. I don't think anybody can hear us. This is a friendly village."

"Well?" Old Bio said.

Linda Bie tried a snatch of fandango music. "That one?" he asked.

"A little softer and slower," Old Bio said.

Linda Bie tried again. Old Bio nodded. He took off his canvas cap and gave it to Dabu. He poised for the fandango dance: both arms lifted high above his head, the right foot raised six inches above the ground, and eyes screwed up as he clucked his tongue and started to dance toward Mameng.

They all watched the old man with fascination. Old Bio's feet were as nimble as a young man's. He was so caught up in the rhapsody of his own dancing that he seemed to have forgotten where they were at the moment. Now there was a quick twinkling in his feet and eyes, for he was back in time fifty years in some village of his youth, where ladies were fainting upon his approach and men were popping their eyes out with envy. He was a young man again, and he was free again, and he was striding gracefully across some dance floor in the long ago, when he was twenty and ladies fainted upon his approach and men popped out their eyes with envy. He was not a peacock, and he was no wrestler, even though he was dancing on rough ground under a bamboo grove. He was a real man, he was dancing with great dignity. They watched him, and they were carried away by the gracefulness of the man who was no longer young, yet still young enough in heart and spirit to be their companion.

Then Old Bio glided toward Mameng, took her hands, and in another moment they were dancing. The darkness of the night had shrouded them, but they were visible enough in the faint light that filtered between the trees.

Dabu leaned against Hassim. "The old man surely has something," he whispered.

"He was quite a man in his day, I heard."

"I can see it."

"If you can do that at seventy, you are something."

"You are telling me! I can't even do it at twenty-three."

They looked at each other.

Legaspi walked over to Dante and touched his arm. "The old men really have something over us," Legaspi said.

"They are the real stock of our heritage."

"Yes."

"This old man is probably the last of the great generation that produced the best of our revolutionary leaders. He will outlive us all."

Legaspi nodded without comment. Linda Bie's flute floated softly in the still air. And the night seemed enchanted, seemed fraught with faraway, delightful things, creeping quietly into their minds and hearts with all the wonder that each and every one of them could assimilate and integrate in their separate lives. So enthralled were they with the music, and the old man, and the still night, that when the flute stopped they seemed to be lost for a moment; and then, realizing that the enchantment was over, that they were again conspirators in the night, hiding from the suspicious and watchful eyes of the world, they sighed and congratulated the old man. And the old man, content with his marvelous performance, chuckled without embarrassment.

"You believe me now?" Old Bio asked Linda Bie.

"With all my heart and eyes," he answered, meaning it. Then he gave his hand to the old man saying, "Here is my hand, Old Bio. I believe you sincerely. When we come to my province, we will drop at my father's house and I will play the piano or violin for you. I am sure you can dance better with the piano accompanying you. Is that a date?"

"I am glad you approve of me now. Sure it is a date."

"Good." He turned to Dabu and said, "How about you, wrestler on dance floors?"

Dabu laughed. "I believe you, too."

Old Bio turned to Legaspi. "You?"

"Same here," Legaspi said.

"I don't have to ask the opinion of Dante," Old Bio said humbly.

"He understands this thing. I know he has seen other lands and known other peoples. I am humble to him."

Dante was moved by the old man's humility. He said, "I didn't see much, old man. I've seen a little here and there, but in sum they will not measure up to what you have known in your long life."

"Thank you."

"I'll remember your performance tonight," Dante said with sincerity. "When we get back to the camp I'll write something about it for the convenience of our young men. How do you like this for a title: 'Night of the Peasants'?"

"Eh?"

"It is honorable to be a peasant," Dante explained, sensing the old man's volatile pride.

"Well, yes! I like the title. Go to it."

Old Bio turned to Mameng. "And you, young woman?"

"I have never enjoyed dancing before," she said. "You are marvelous. Truly. I don't mind dancing all night with a man such as you."

Old Bio bowed to her without saying anything. He was so moved with the half flattery and half adulation that tears were about to choke him. He bowed twice to Mameng and withdrew. Then he took his hat from Dabu and whispered to Legaspi for some drink. His throat ached him so with happiness that he had to hold his emotions or burst into tears. Legaspi understood him. He fumbled for the sack in the darkness and uncorked the bottle for the old man. Then they sat in a circle and waited for the hour of one.

Old Bio did not have to ask for Hassim's opinion, for he knew that he approved of it. He knew that Hassim, of all the young men he had come in contact with in the last few years, understood many things but kept his own thoughts and opinions. He respected Hassim. And he wanted to venerate him, but he knew that Hassim would disapprove of it. Hassim was Hassim, a world by himself; and Old Bio knew that that world was complete, if not immortal. And he sighed deeply, thinking somewhat vaguely that such a great young man would have to waste his life fighting instead of creating beautiful things for others to admire or copy, that he would have to

perish without giving to others the very best in him. And following this sad train of thought, he suddenly could not hold his tongue any longer.

"Is this all there is in life, Hassim?" he asked.

As though he had been following the old man's thoughts, Hassim said, "This is not all, Old Bio. For us at this hour and place, yes. But life is not measured by moments, by months, not even years. It is measured by decades, by centuries. If at this hour and place there is one man like you, in a few years there will be five or ten. And when you are gone, the five or ten will be twenty or thirty. And it goes on like that, forever. In a hundred years, maybe two, you will have become millions. And then it will be a different world, entirely different, I can assure you."

Old Bio was listening attentively.

But Mameng was disturbed. "A hundred years, did you say?" she asked. "What about us today? Is there nothing for us but to wait for one hundred years, when we will have been dust and no one can remember us?"

"There is surely something for us, Mameng," Hassim said softly. "Nothing is lost that is achieved honorably. And we are doing an honorable task. Whoever will live a hundred years from today will look back to our time, to us, not without some pride. Of course they will smile, for they will be living in a world better than ours; pridefully they will smile because of the obsolescence of the weapons we have to fight with, compared with theirs, since everything we have will seem antiquated to them. But somehow we must keep believing that a better world will emerge from our chaotic and harsh one. Have not our ancestors lived in a more chaotic and harsher world than ours?"

"That is true," Old Bio said. "I remember when I was a young man that I had to fight barefoot and with a homemade gun that fired only once. Now I have an automatic garand, plus a pair of shoes, though of course it does not come up in quality with Linda Bie's father's shoes."

Hassim smiled at the old man. "That is only one example," he said. "But there other examples, and better ones too; and others so big they involve us all. So you see, Mameng?"

"Yes."

"Dante can tell you about other changes that will take place in the mind and the heart," Hassim said. "Those changes are very important in the development of society, which is the habitat of man. But it is about time for us to go. Some other time perhaps."

Dabu looked at his watch in the light of his cigarette. "You are right, Hassim. It is getting late."

"Are you ready, Mameng?" Hassim asked.

"I am ready."

"How about you, Old Bio?"

The old man laughed. "How about you, Old Bio?"

They all laughed and got up. Legaspi and Dante crushed their cigarettes. Linda Bie helped Mameng to her feet, putting the flute in his shirt pocket at the same time. Hassim tightened the straps of his knapsack.

"We should be in Legaspi's territory at six," he said.

"Seven at the most," Legaspi said.

"What is your hurry?" Dabu asked.

"Well – "

Old Bio patted his shoulder affectionately. "I understand, young man."

"Let's go then," Hassim said.

Now they walked double file. Dabu and Legaspi were ahead, followed by Linda Bie and Mameng. Then came Old Bio and Dante, followed by Hassim, who was by himself again.

Hassim looked up to see the nature of the sky. There were many stars and in their cool light he saw a chariotlike mass of clouds. The flash of recognition reminded him of a time when he was a little boy and his father took him to the province to visit his uncle. Now he could not remember how old he was at the time, but he remembered that one night they went to his uncle's farm to see the sugarcanes growing tall. They were sitting on the grass and talking about the prospect of the forthcoming harvest when suddenly Hassim looked up at the sky and saw masses of clouds sailing by. He saw several images then: dragons with fiery tongues, elephants with tusks as long as the length of his arms, rivers as wide as the world. So great was the fascination of the sky images that he did not hear his father calling him that it was time to go. And when he was finally jerked to reality, Hassim took his father's hand and got up. He walked silently between his father and uncle wondering about those people in the sky. He wondered about it for a long time afterward. But some years later he discovered that the only people were on this earth, that there were no others; but even if there were somewhere, in some place that he did not know, that did not matter to him then because they were unknown to him. And the only people known to him were on this earth, and that was all that mattered to him. And that was all ever since. Hassim smiled because of that remembrance.

Ahead, Dabu and Legaspi were talking about the latter's town. Their voices were low; Mameng and Linda Bie, who were following them, could not hear what the conversation was about no matter how hard they strained their ears.

But Legaspi was saying, "We have a grass house at the edge of town, five kilometers from the farm where I used to work with my father and two brothers. We worked on a share basis, fifty-fifty at first; that is when the old landlord was still alive, and he used to visit his tenants. Then one day we heard that he died, and his sons took over the hacienda. I never saw the sons; nobody ever saw them. An overseer was assigned to do all the transactions with the farmers. And that was when the trouble began."

"Well, what happened then?"

"The overseer gave us an ultimatum. Thirty-seventy, or leave the place. That is seventy percent of the harvest to the new land-lords. How could you live on thirty percent?"

"Well?"

"Some of the farmers left the hacienda and went to other hacien-das in other places. But the percentage was the same everywhere because it was the time when the landlords got hold of the national government and they had every big politician in their pockets. Our case seemed hopeless, but my oldest brother heard of the union of peasants in another province. He started organizing the peasants in the hacienda where we worked, then sent me to this province for information on the operation of a peasant union. And imagine my surprise!"

"You found me directing one union in a district of my province!"

"I am not laughing."

But they both laughed. Of course Dabu knew the story, but they were only making conversation. He knew how Legaspi went back to the hacienda where he worked with the detailed plan to organize the peasants. He knew how, months later, they struck against the landlord. He knew that the landlords brought the constabulary to the hacienda and arrested nearly two hundred peasants. He knew how they were put in the high school building because the local prison was too small to accommodate them all. He knew how over seven hundred peasants and their families paraded up and down the square demanding their release. He knew how they were released finally on condition that they would not strike anymore, except Legaspi, who demanded an unconditional release and stayed in jail until it was given to him. He knew how Legaspi, when he came out of prison, said to the big crowd of peasants awaiting him, "We lost materially but we won a moral victory. On with the strike!"

And the strike went on, and the constabulary came again and shot some of the peasants. Legaspi's oldest brother was captured and sent to prison, where he stayed until another national president was elected to the congress. He was released and exiled in another province. But his exile was not in vain, for he organized the peasants wherever he went. Upon the completion of his exile he returned to his town for a brief visit, then went to another province for other organizational work. Then the war came, and he was one of the first victims of the Japanese.

Where was Legaspi all this time? After the breakup of the second strike, he escaped. There was a price on his head. It seemed that a local official was killed during the strike, and the blame was put on Legaspi. The truth was never known because he never spoke about it. Whether he knew the guilty party or not, whether he did it or it was foul play, a frameup, he would never tell. But Legaspi went back once to his hometown, after years of hiding. By that time there was already a strong union working collectively with other locals throughout the nation. He tried to readjust himself to new conditions, but the war came; and believing that the time had come to have national unity against the invader, he joined the regular army and fought with it until it surrendered to the enemy. But not Legaspi. He escaped and joined the first units of the guerrillas who were operating in the fields and hills. But he found that there were many kinds of guerrillas: one for the landlords, another for the people, and still another for themselves. Those were bloody times, he remembered, when all these guerrillas were fighting each other instead of collectively fighting the enemy. He was confused. But he refused to be intimidated. When the liberation came and he once again discovered that there was a price on his head, Legaspi escaped and joined the newly formed underground.

"And imagine my surprise," he said again.

"You found me in the underground," Dabu said.

They laughed.

"It seems you are always ahead of me," Legaspi said.

"You are not behind me now."

They laughed once more.

Behind them, Linda Bie and Mameng heard their laughter. Mameng was looking down to see the path where her feet were going to avoid stumbling. She jerked her head straight ahead when she heard them laughing. She wanted to talk to Linda Bie, but he seemed to be absorbed in his private thoughts. So she looked down again, not thinking but merely to keep on walking. She had long ago given up thinking; there were others now who thought for her, who told her what to do and say. Yet there was an urge within her to speak, for she was used to speaking in the long ago. Did she speak every day when she was a schoolteacher? Was there a difference between children and grown-ups that she would not speak out her mind now?

Mameng glanced at Linda Bie again, but he was still absorbed in his private thoughts. She frowned.

Old Bio was in a talkative mood. He was chewing tobacco and spitting to the left and right of him. "Tell me," he said to Dante, "do you have a wife?"

"No."

"Not anywhere in the world?"

"Still no."

"It is too bad."

"I suppose so. I have no time for it."

"I understand the *now*. But I am speaking about the *then*."

"America? I had no opportunity."

"Why not?"

"For various reasons. For one thing, I was always moving around. For another, I never had money. It takes money to have a wife and raise children, if you want any."

"Money," Old Bio said contemptuously, spitting loudly.

"It is important in that country," Dante said. "You can't get a woman without money."

"Bah! Why not kidnap her, abduct her, seduce her?"

"There are laws against all those things. You could be in jail for life for any of those things."

"What a complicated country!"

"It is complicated."

Old Bio was silent for a moment. Then he leaned against Dante and whispered something to him.

"Of course I did, old man," Dante said quietly.

Old Bio slapped his thighs and said, "Then it is all right! I say that is more than having a wife and children."

Dante wondered about the old man's strange joy. But he also slapped his thighs and said, "I guess you are right, Old Bio."

The old man clicked his tongue and spat again.

Hassim was far away enough, otherwise he would have been soaked with the old man's brown spittle. He looked up at the sky again. There were very few stars left and even the moon was waning. It was the hour before dawn. He looked straight ahead and saw the town they were approaching flickering with few lighted houses. Suddenly he realized what they were approaching. He walked faster, passing all the others until he came to the head of the line; then he told Dabu to take his place while he retained Legaspi with him.

"I wanted to tell you something before," Hassim said to Legaspi. "I waited this long because it is imperative that you should know. We are now nearing your town and – "

"You don't have to tell me, Hassim. I know. It is about my other brother, who is working with the enemy."

"You know how to deal with him?"

Legaspi was silent. Finally he said, "Yes."

"That is all I want to know."

Legaspi's heart leaped and hurt him. Hassim glanced at him swiftly and saw that his face was contorted with pain.

"I will be with you," Hassim said.

"I will do it myself!" Legaspi cried.

Hassim grabbed his shoulder and steadied him. "Yes," he said.

## CHAPTER ELEVEN

Their lively conversation had increased their speed. They reached Rendezvous 2 sooner than they had expected, exactly an hour before their scheduled arrival. They reached the edge of the town at five in the morning; it was still quite dark because the nights were longer at this time of the year. The moon was gone; only the Morning Star and a few smaller ones were left in the brightening sky.

Legaspi led them across a wide bare field, veering straight to the west, then along a long column of leafless mango trees to a shallow river, which they crossed without wetting their faces or washing their legs, and up to another field dark and wide with lush corn. Here Legaspi told his companions to rest awhile, before Hassim decided what to do in the town.

They surveyed the cornfield that stretched southward as far as their eyes could see. The corn was over six feet tall and beginning to bend with its heavy load. Then they followed Legaspi into the cornfield, walking single file between the magnificent rows of cornstalks. They stopped now and then to touch the large ears hanging on the stalks, admiring the richness of the soil that produced such high-quality produce. When they came to what they approximated to be the center of the field, Legaspi stopped and unstrapped his knapsack and the sack of liqour. His companions followed his example. Then they sat down on the grass.

Old Bio was the first to speak. "Is this your town, Legaspi?" he asked.

Legaspi looked at the old man without expression and nodded.

"Is this the best hiding place that you know of?" Hassim asked.

"It is – on this side of the town."

Old Bio looked at Hassim inquiringly.

"Well," Hassim said, "it is a good place."

"There is no better place," Legaspi assured them. "This is a flat country. There are very few trees, and these are found only around the houses to protect the people from rain and the heat of the sun. There is no rice this time of the year where we could hide, but even if there was, it would not be as safe as this cornfield. As you can see for yourself – " He got up and measured his height with tall corn at his back, putting his hand on the level of his head palm down and squinting skyward to see the top of the corn, which was over a foot higher. And he said with satisfaction, "We are safe here."

Dabu had followed Legaspi's head when he got up, but he did not see the difference between his height and the corn, because the three big ears of corn behind his head attracted his attention. It was not so dark now among the rows of corn; the stars had vanished and the skylight had begun to penetrate the leaves, revealing the young ears of corn. Dabu smiled when Legaspi sat down and the three ears of corn appeared in full view.

"I see," he said.

The others nodded in approval of Legaspi's logic. But Dabu meant something else: he meant the inviting ears of corn. He was still looking at them with hunger when his companions began to busy themselves with other things, like smoking or scratching themselves. It was the old man who first noticed what he meant, so he followed Dabu's gaze and saw the three ears of corn.

"I see," Old Bio repeated.

Dabu looked at him and laughed.

"Quick, huh?" Dabu said.

"Ay."

They rose to their feet and plucked the three ears of corn. They shucked them hastily and when the white soft kernels appeared, Old Bio sank his teeth into the cob and the sweet juice trickled down his mouth.

"Young and sweet," he said.

"I wish there was a fire," Dabu complained. "It tastes better when roasted over a fire."

"Don't build any fire," Hassim reminded him.

"I was just dreaming."

"What about you, Legaspi?" Old Bio said. "Why don't you try your corn?"

"In a little while," he said.

Old Bio plucked some more of the corn and threw two ears into Mameng's lap. Mameng, however, was not in the mood for eating raw corn. She put the corn in her knapsack, after she had shucked them. Old Bio was disappointed. He gave two to Dante and another two to Linda Bie. These two were not hungry, but the contagious appetite of the old man and Dabu contaminated them. They ate the corn without relish.

"You should taste the sugarcane in my territory," Dabu said to the old man between mouthfuls. "As tender and sweet as a girl's first kiss."

"Huh?" Old Bio's lips curled upward, revealing his rotten teeth. "How could it be tender and sweet when rivers of human blood have been poured on the soil where the cane grows? When oceans of human tears make the cane juicy?"

"Those things make it tender and sweet."

"Human suffering never makes anything sweet. Anything at all."

"Blood does, though."

"What are you saying?" But Old Bio heard Dabu. Then with anguish in his face, he flung the cob of corn in his hand and stamped his foot. "You desecrate the sanctity and sweetness of the sugar-cane, Dabu!"

"Are you disgusted with me?"

"Why not? You talk like a barbarian."

But Dabu knew how to get the old man's goat. He wanted to go to the limit, to see if the old man was not only acting. It was still dawn, and Old Bio was already in a devilish mood. Dabu knew that the trip did not tire to exhaustion. Old Bio must be up to something. He had to find out.

"Well, is your rice any better?" he asked.

The old man was furious. "What is sugarcane compared to rice?" he said. "Rice fills your stomach and eases your hunger. Rice makes your body and mind grow. And sugarcane? You plant it with a starvation wage, then the rich landlords make wine out of it, and you buy it back for more than you can afford. So you buy the wine and your family starves to death, and your body becomes wracked with internal disorders, and your mind becomes weak and then it is paralyzed. So where is the comparison, eh?"

"I was not thinking of that."

"Then what were you thinking about?"

"Was not your rice planted too with human blood and tears?"

"I don't want to talk to you any longer. I refuse to accept your line of reasoning. I dislike your logic. Go away!"

Legaspi finally laughed. He was silent all the time that they were sitting in the cornfield. Now he was in his gay mood again. Old Bio looked at him to say something cruel, but he suddenly realized the significance of Legaspi's silence a moment ago. So he left Dabu and went over to Hassim. He sat beside him and threw a handful of tobacco pieces in his mouth, screwing up his eyes when the juice stung his tongue and the roof of his mouth. Then he spat in the direction of Dabu, who had to jump away from the blob of brown spittle.

Now the morning sun was peeping at the rim of the mountains. Birds and field animals began to stir. The first noise of the town reached them: the pounding of wooden mortars where the women-folk were threshing rice, the hammering on fence posts, the shrill cries of children. Then they heard herdboys calling to one another and men shouting to each other on their way to work.

The peasants rose before the sun, and they went their separate ways as soon as it was halfway between the sky and the mountains in the eastern horizon. They worked all day when there was work, in the heat of the sun or under heavy rain, stopping only briefly at noontime for a light lunch of rice and fish or just rice and salt. They went home only when the sun had set in the west, for they could not see what they were doing in the darkness. So it was already night when they reached their homes, where their wives and children were waiting for the evening meal to be spread out on the rough bamboo or wooden floor, depending on the prosperity of the family. But often it would be a bamboo floor; it would take years of austerity for a family to save enough money for the purchase of wood. And the night was short because they had to save the oil in the lamp for other nights. But seldom, when they had important matters to discuss, did they sit in the darkness and talk quietly and patiently. Of course the children would be in bed, for only the man and woman of the house were concerned.

Legaspi knew that this was the daily life of the peasants. Remembering it, he got to his feet and bent the cornstalks so that he could see through to the village. He saw some men walking the bare fields about half a kilometer away, but could not recognize them. The sun was in the way of his eyes and blinded him. Tense with emotion, he sat down and fiddled with his knapsack.

"Would you like to go now, Legaspi?" Hassim asked him.

"Any time you are ready."

"Won't you have a bite before we go?"

He shook his head. "There is always food at my mother's at this time of day."

Hassim got to his feet. "Dabu, I am not going to eat," he said. "Wait for us here, unless it is absolutely necessary."

"You may need us, in case – "

"I will give you the sign."

"Two shots in succession, followed by a third after a minute?"

"Yes." Hassim looked at the old man. He said, "Don't drink too much, old one. We might need your assistance. This is a bad country."

"You think there is trouble?"

"Maybe."

"In that case," Old Bio said seriously, "I will follow orders."

Hassim smiled with approval. "Let us go, Legaspi," he said.

They walked across the cornfield in the direction of the town. They walked slowly so as not to trample on the cornstalks. When they came to the edge of the cornfield, they stopped and peered between the stalks. They saw nobody. They looked at each other and nodded their heads.

When they came out of the cornfield, the sun was already above the mountains. Hassim looked quickly eastward and calculated the time, without bothering to look at his wristwatch. It was about seven o'clock, he knew. And knowing it, he began to arrange his mind; for Legaspi might become emotional, might inadvertently reveal their secret mission.

"Do you think your family is at home?" Hassim asked.

"I suppose so."

"And your youngest brother?"

"He is home, I am sure of that. He never wanted to leave the town because he had a hero complex. But I think my older brother is gone."

"We will have to be careful."

"I know. That is what makes it difficult."

"I hope your mother is still alive."

Legaspi did not answer him readily. "It is hard to know these days. There have been so many lives lost; any man's family is not invulnerable to the enemy."

"We hope for the best."

"Thanks, Hassim."

They walked on, Hassim trying to make conversation now and then. He was expecting the worst for Legaspi; perhaps Legaspi had a premonition of the tragedy that would befall him. That was why he was often quiet all the way to his town. He had been away from home for five years now; he was just past seventeen when he took up arms during the war against the enemy, but now he was twenty-three. And the five years that he had been away had aged him considerably, but they had also given him a wide scope of life. He knew his family would not be able to understand him anymore, he knew he had grown away from them forever. Still, he had to make some connection with them, to be with them although he would be far away. He brushed his forehead and sighed.

"Have you ever seen any member of your family since the war?" he asked Hassim.

"I have no one left."

"I did not know that."

"My brother, who was with us during the retreat to the mountains, was the last of my family."

Legaspi glanced at Hassim swiftly, but he noticed no sadness in his face. And there was no bitterness in his voice, and no anger either; it was a matter-of-fact explanation of events. Perhaps he has steeled himself against emotions, Legaspi thought. Is it possible that you can purge yourself completely of all sentimental attachments? Or is it because his intellectual capacities are above mine? Yet, though, he is also a human being. He must have feelings, thoughts, memories.

But he asked Hassim, "Have you ever gone back to your father's house?"

"We had no house. We never had a house. All my life we moved from one cheap apartment to another, all in the slum district. My father was a street sweeper. My mother – she did needlework until she lost her eyes. I went to work in a cigar factory when I was eleven."

"We have a house, at least," Legaspi said. "I should say we had one up to the war. It is only a small grass hut, but I hope it is still there. I hope."

"That is one advantage you peasants in the plains have over us city workers. Of course, we all work under terrible conditions and live miserably, but you have houses. When you have a house, and even if you have not eaten for two days, there is at least a place where you can lie down with an empty stomach and aching head. Did you ever wander in the streets at night during a storm because you had no place to go?"

"No."

"That is a difference between peasants and city workers."

"What a miserable life. At least in the plains we can always pull some herbs and roots or cut some grass and leaves of trees for a meal. We used to do that during drought and bad years. Once when I was a small boy – maybe I was seven at the time – there was a famine due to the drought in the previous year. I remember one evening when my father came home with a handful of corn kernels in the palm of his hand. My mother put the corn in a cup and divided the kernels among us; three to each person. We chewed the corn raw and drank plenty of water. But not my mother: she chewed her portion and then put it into the mouth of my young brother, who was not yet two at the time. My mother, however, did not masticate the corn thoroughly because in the middle of the night my brother became ill. He cried and cried, but my mother could not do anything. And my father just stood there watching the tragedy, angry but helpless. Once my brother stopped breathing, but my mother put her mouth on his mouth, breathed air into it, sucked the air out, then breathed in again. And his respiration came back, but slowly. The next morning he was well again, laughing and kicking his short legs. So that evening, when my father came home with a handful of beans, my mother boiled them with a potful of water. That was our dinner. But I saved my portion of the broth for my young brother, who subsisted on it the following day. Then I found out – to my amazement – that my older brother had saved his portion too for the young one. It was a terrible year, especially so because I was still a small boy and did not understand the nature of our deprivation. But my brother was saved from death or some deformation of body and eventually grew up to be a healthy boy."

"And that is the same brother who – ?"

"That is what I can't believe. He has seen poverty as I have, yet he turned out to be a different sort of person."

"There are many kinds of men in a family, Legaspi."

"That is just it. My father and mother are good people."

"Good parents are of course essential in the making of good children. But in the world outside the home are social forces operating to determine the eventual personality of the child, whether it is positive or negative. And there is education, or experience, or association. These are important too. And also the innate quality of the child, whether he will grow up to be a weakling or a courageous person, depending upon the quality of his resistance to adversities and temptations to an easy life."

"You have it there in a nutshell."

They were entering the town now. They saw a boy on the road playing with a dog, but he was too young for Legaspi to recognize him. The boy looked at them as they passed by with the same reaction. He was barely five. Still, Legaspi looked at him with an almost embarrassing scrutiny, thinking perhaps he might recognize in the small boy's face the features of some of the people he knew. He was disappointed.

They walked on into the town. They passed by a large wooden house, and Legaspi looked up at one of the windows and thought he recognized the face staring at them there, but it withdrew so quickly that he had no chance to see it again. When they were approaching the public market, Legaspi remembered that his mother used to sell a few farm products, such as eggplants, tomatoes, bitter melon, and sometimes a dozen eggs. He stopped, seized by terror.

"What day is it?" he asked Hassim.

"I don't know."

"I wish I knew."

"Why?"

"We are approaching the public market, and my mother used to sell a few things there. Maybe it is the day!"

"We should go straight ahead to your house, and if she is there she will come home eventually. I don't like too many people seeing us. They might recognize you."

"Then we have to avoid the public market."

"I will follow you."

They turned away from the road and followed an alley lined on either side with coconut trees. It was cooler in the shade, and they met nobody. Then they crossed the alley and entered a tall gate that opened into a field tall with yellowing okra. They waded their way through the okra field, behind the public market, and came out to the provincial highway. A bus was just passing by when they emerged, but it was speeding so fast that Legaspi had no chance to read the name of the company printed on its side. He was interested to know if there had been many changes since he left.

They crossed the highway and dropped into a hollow where an artesian well had been constructed since Legaspi had been away. They pumped the handle and drank the sweet water from twenty-five feet below, then wet their heads and continued on their way. They crossed the wide hollow diagonally and climbed up the high embankment of a corner and came out in a deserted lot where ylang-ylang trees were in full bloom.

They sniffed at the fragrant air simultaneously and glanced up at the trees. They saw the long-petaled flowers hanging on the stout branches, and somehow, without knowing it, they thought of the sweetness of women when they bathed naked in the rivers at dawn. It seemed strange to them both, thinking separately, that they thought of women at this particular moment when they had never had any experience with them. Then they reasoned, separately, that the fragrance of the ylang-ylang blossoms had always been identified with the bright innocence and fragility of the women they had known in the long ago.

Legaspi bent to the ground and scooped a handful of the fallen blossoms, smelled it with blissful contentment, then stuffed it in his shirt pocket. Hassim did the same, only he put the flowers in his cap; this proved to be exhilarating to him, because as they walked in the hot sun and the moisture on his head began to trickle down his face and neck, a slight distillation of the fragrance of the ylang-ylang went down with it, wrapping him with an aroma that commingled with the sweetness of the new grass spreading out like a huge carpet of green before them.

They picked up the flowers and walked on without exchanging words. Then they came to a footpath that led to the *presidencia*\* through the rosal and violet bushes, where curled bits of newspapers were thrown carelessly in the shade. Farther on their left, where the footpath ended, about five hundred yards away, was the old *presidencia*. It was a two-storey building, painted white on the outside and red on the inside; and in front of it, hanging on a pole fifteen feet above the ground, was the red, white, and blue flag of the Republic. And there was the spreading huge tree across from the *presidencia*, where automobiles and buses stopped to pick up new passengers. Built close to the trunk of the tree was a shack, with front and back awnings propped up by bamboo poles. This was the town cafeteria where coffee and sweet cakes were served. And farther away to the southward, between the *presidencia* and the

---

\*The town hall or municipal building.

schoolhouse, was the cement monument of Jose Rizal, the national hero.

When Hassim and Legaspi were in the protection of a patch of cactus plants, having crossed the vacant lot and away from the houses, they stopped on a rise and looked toward the *presidencia*. They saw the antiquated building, the national flag fluttering in the breeze, and the momument of Rizal. Then they saw a policeman coming out of the *presidencia*, followed by three peasants who were also followed by another policeman. They followed the procession with their eyes to the huge tree, where an army truck came dashing from the east and stopped. Four soldiers with fixed bayonets jumped out of the truck, corraled the peasants into it, and in another moment they were roaring back toward the east.

Hassim and Legaspi looked at each other.

Legaspi was nonplussed. "Prisoners?" he asked.

"It looks like it," Hassim said.

"I wonder where they are taking them."

"There is a company of them bivouacked east of town."

Legaspi frowned.

"Informers," Hassim told him.

"Here?"

Hassim nodded. Pain crossed Legaspi's face, and he turned away from Hassim to hide what he was thinking, as though his thoughts were so enormous that Hassim could see them. Then he started to go in the direction of his parents' house, and Hassim followed him silently.

They crept out of the cactus patch and came to another vacant lot where stray goats and sheep were grazing. Legaspi stopped, trying to decide which way to go. His parents' hut was not so far off, a walk of about ten minutes through closely packed houses of people he knew, there at the edge of the other side of town. Hassim stood beside him, and Legaspi looked to the left first where the provincial highway wound around groves of coconut and bananas, then to his right where a cornfield was shining resplendently under the boiling sun. He decided to take the right, where there would be little chance of meeting anybody he knew, and where, under cover of the corn, they could proceed to his parents' house easily and unseen.

They walked side by side toward the cornfield, but as they came to the pasture, a boy of ten leaped out from the shade of a tamarind tree.

"Uncle Fernacio!" the boy cried, running toward Hassim and Legaspi. "Uncle Fernacio, wait!"

They stopped and looked back to the running boy. But Legaspi had forgotten his real name, so long had he used another in the underground; it was only when the boy grabbed his hand and began to cry that he remembered that he was being addressed, that his real name was spoken, and he held the boy's head between his hands.

"Who are you, son?" he asked.

"Uncle Fernacio, don't you remember me?"

Legaspi tried to reach out to the past, but he could not place the boy. He shook his head, and the boy's face was broken with tears.

"I am Peping, Uncle Fernacio," he cried.

"Peping!" Legaspi said, for recognition had come to him. "But you are a big man now. You were only a baby when I left."

"I have grown up, all right," Peping said with a smile. He brushed away the tears from his eyes and said, "They always talk about you, especially my father."

"And how is my brother, Peping?"

"I don't know. He went away three days ago and he is not back yet."

"Where did he go?"

"I don't know."

Legaspi looked at Hassim.

"And my other brother – where is he, Peping?" he asked the boy.

"He is at home. He was sleeping when I left this morning to tend to the goats and sheep."

Legaspi looked back to the herd of animals.

"Are those yours?" he asked.

"They belong to my grandparents. They said I could have two of the first young ones. In three months, they told me."

"So my parents are at home?"

"Yes, Uncle Fernacio."

Legaspi knelt on the grass in front of his nephew so that he could look into his eyes.

"Listen, Peping," he said. "You are a man now and I want you to listen to me carefully."

"Yes, Uncle Fernacio."

"I don't have much time to visit, because I came only to see how all of you are getting along. Understand?"

Peping nodded.

"Don't let anybody know that I am in town. Not anyone. You understand that?"

"I understand, Uncle Fernacio. I understand."

"Good. Stay right here. I will talk to you again on our way back."

"Are you not going to stay even for one day?"

"No, Peping. Next time. There will be plenty of time for that, eh?"

The boy did not say anything.

"What is the matter now?" Legaspi asked.

"I would like to go with you, Uncle Fernacio."

"You are still too young, Peping."

"But you said I am already a man."

"Yes, you are. But I am going far away. Anyway, I will come back for you, nephew."

"You promise?"

"Yes."

Peping began to smile.

"That is the way," Legaspi said. "And by the way, you should meet my friend. His name is Manuel."

Hassim gave his hand to the boy. "I am glad to meet you, Peping," he said. "I will see you again soon, son."

"Yes, sir. But who are you?"

"I am a friend of your uncle's."

"Then you are my friend, too."

"Surely."

Legaspi laughed, followed by his nephew and Hassim. Peping was still laughing when they left him. They looked back to the boy before they entered the cluster of houses. But Peping was already running among his flock with a stick, for a dog had come into the pasture and had tried to molest a yearling.

Then they continued on their way. They walked cautiously

between the houses. They saw children playing in some of the yards, but they saw no grown-ups anywhere. They both had their hands inside their shirts where the guns were hidden. When they came to the last house, which was fenced with edible vines, Legaspi stopped and put his hand on Hassim's shoulder. Hassim looked at Legaspi, who nodded his head slightly.

Then they pushed the gate open and walked toward the house.

## CHAPTER TWELVE

Legaspi's mother was the first to see them. They were climbing up the last rung of the bamboo ladder when she turned around from the earthen stove where she was cooking something pungent in a clay pot and spotted them setting their feet on the landing, and her face was violently stricken with fear because she did not recognize her son in the darkness of the house. But when she finally recognized Legaspi, in an instant, when they stopped at the door to the small kitchen, she dropped the wooden ladle in her hand and rushed to him with a cry of motherly agony.

Legaspi grabbed his mother in his arms wordlessly; then, after a minute of painful silence, he began to rock her gently as though she were a sick child that he was trying to put to sleep after an hour of prolonged crying. When Hassim saw the tears in his eyes, he turned his face away from them and tried to look at nothing in particular. It was then that he saw the young woman in a corner of the kitchen who was nursing a baby of about eight months old. She was looking at Legaspi with a frightened face; so great was her fright that, for a moment, she had fortotten to attend to the baby, which began crying plaintively because she had accidentally withdrawn her large brown nipple from his hungry mouth. She turned to the baby, put its mouth to her nipple, and looked at Legaspi again, her mouth hanging open.

Hassim stepped into the kitchen and walked toward the woman, who withdrew closer into the dark corner as he approached her. She hugged the baby protectively with one hand and made a motion to ward off Hassim with the other, as though he had come to take it forcefully away from her. She emitted a pitiful whine when Hassim stood in front of her, looking down at the baby with a nameless feeling tormenting him. When she realized that Hassim did not come to molest her or take away the baby, she looked up at him with inquiring eyes.

"Yours?" he asked.

She nodded her head. Hassim cradled his arms toward her.

"May I?"

The shadow of a fear crossed her face.

"I will do no harm," he explained.

Mechanically she handed the baby over to Hassim, who took it with a smile.

"Boy?"

She nodded her head again.

"Don't be alarmed," he said. "I came with Legaspi. I am a friend of his." And gently he began swinging the baby back and forth, humming unashamedly snatches from a song that his own mother used to sing to him when he was a little boy. And humming that almost forgotten cradle song of long ago, he saw in memory an improvised cloth hammock hanging on a rope in a kitchen similar to this, where his mother was bent over a tubful of dirty clothes. His little brother was sleeping peacefully in the hammock, and he, Hassim, was watching at the doorway. His mother would stop her washing now and then and tug at the hammock to keep it perpetually in motion. Hassim would watch the swinging hammock with fascination for a few minutes, then go into the kitchen and take over the tugging so that his mother could go on with her work without interruption. And he would swing his little brother until his mother was through with the tub, and then performing her other domestic chores, Hassim would keep on his vigil until she was ready to feed the baby. He would then stand by to watch the baby suck at his mother's nipple, the way this baby was sucking his mother's nipple when he came into the kitchen. Where was that little brother now?

Had he come out into the world remembering the love that had been given him by his mother and Hassim? Had he given it to others, there in the wide world where he had ventured to find a place? Hassim shook his head slightly, remembering the little brother who was then a young man crouching with him behind a rock to protect himself from the heavy bombing of planes and artillery, there on that hapless hill when the enemy came on a punitive expedition; remembering how he was hit by shrapnel and died instantly, how he dug a hole furiously with a piece of wood so that the enemy could not desecrate his body, before he ran down the hill to safety. O lost, that little boy hugged with love into life, lost forever now. Hassim stopped swinging the baby in his arms and looked at it with sadness. Would it too grow up to be killed? Would it too venture into the world of plundering? Would there be nothing for him too but fear and want? O lost! Gently he gave back the baby to the mother and said, "Thank you. Yes, thank you ever so much."

Now the mother understood Hassim, and she felt ashamed for misinterpreting his intention. She knew that she had to make some kind of restitution.

"You have children?" she asked.

Hassim shook his head.

"Wife?"

"No."

"Why?"

"I have been away. I have been busy."

She got up to her feet and was bewildered to find Hassim so tall, for she was standing in front of him now, measuring his height from her smallness.

"I was afraid of you," she said.

"You didn't have to be afraid."

"I never saw you before. This baby – you see – "

Legaspi and his mother approached them.

"Manuel," Legaspi said to Hassim, who did not realize for a moment that he was being addressed, "this is my mother."

The young woman turned her face to them. Hassim followed her eyes, then he realized that Legaspi was addressing him. He took the old woman's hand and gripped it in his warmly. Now he could see the flat face, flatter even than Legaspi's, the dark skin pinched tight to the prominent cheekbones, the small eyes dull like a dead fish.

"I am glad to know you, Mother," Hassim said.

"Yes, yes," the old woman said. Then turning to Legaspi, who was staring at the young woman and her baby, she said, "This is Josefina, Fernacio. Your brother Francisco's – "

"Go ahead, Mother," the young woman interrupted. "Tell him. I am not ashamed."

The old woman could not explain.

"Francisco did not want to marry me," the young woman said to Legaspi. "I was already big with child and I did not know what to do, so I just packed up my clothes and came to this house. I waited patiently and when the child came he still did not want to marry me. I am still waiting for him."

Hassim looked at Legaspi for explanation.

"My young brother," Legaspi said to him.

Hassim did not say anything. He looked at the old woman, who had suddenly leaped to the stove to stir the boiling pot; then she turned to Legaspi, still stirring the pot.

"You have come from a very far place?" she asked.

"Yes, Mother," Legaspi said.

"You must be hungry."

"We did not eat breakfast."

"My son."

"It is nothing, Mother."

The old woman turned to the young woman and said, "Josefina, go to the neighbor and borrow a demijohn of red wine."

Josefina turned to go.

"May I hold the baby while you are gone?" Legaspi suggested.

She handed the baby to him and walked to the door. When she was gone, Legaspi looked at Hassim with a pained face.

"That brother of yours, Fernacio," the old woman said. "He brings nothing but trouble to this house."

"I heard about it, Mother."

"Nothing but trouble, I am telling you. He does nothing. He

sleeps all day and goes out at night to God knows where. He travels with a bad company."

"Where is he now?"

"He left an hour ago, but he said he will be back for breakfast. A friend of his came running and told him something important that they have to do. Something about a meeting. That Francisco, my son – "

Legaspi looked at Hassim's face, then down to the belt where the gun was hidden. Hassim nodded his head.

"Where is Father?" Legaspi asked.

"He is working in the field," his mother told him. "I will send Josefina to call when she gets back."

"I would like to see him before we go back."

"Are you going back today?"

"We are, Mother. We still have a long way to go."

"But you have just arrived?"

"I know. But we have things to do. And he – " he stopped abruptly, looking at Hassim's face. "Well, we – "

The old woman looked at Hassim. "He is one of them?" she asked.

Hassim stared at her without batting an eye.

"He is traveling with me, Mother," Legaspi explained. I hope it is not too late, he thought. I hope I can fool her. "You see, he is my assistant. He goes everywhere I go."

"Please," the old woman said to Hassim, "release my son. Let him stay. We have nobody to help his father in the field now that his brother Nicanor is dead."

"Dead?" Legaspi said

"They took him away and shot him in the back."

"But why?"

The old woman burst into tears. The muscles in Legaspi's mouth quivered, knowing the reason why his brother was killed. He suddenly turned to the wall, away from Hassim so that he could not see the anger in his face. His mother was still crying when Josefina came back with the wine. Josefina filled two cups with the wine and gave them to Legaspi and Hassim, then took the baby in her arms. Hassim and Legaspi picked up the cups and drank without looking at each other. The old woman stopped crying and looked at Hassim.

"You don't say much," she said.

Hassim shook his head.

"Josefina," she said to the young woman, "go to the field and tell your father-in-law to come home. Tell him Fernacio is home. But don't tell anybody else."

"Yes, Mother."

"Hurry!"

They watched her go out of the door. When she was gone, Legaspi's mother looked at Hassim again.

"I suspect who you are, son," she said. "You must be very careful in this house. And don't let anybody hurt Fernacio!"

"We all take good care of each other," Hassim said.

"How is your work?"

"Expanding rapidly."

"We have no one here – except Nicanor when he was alive. But he did not know how to go about it. He often wished Fernacio were here to help him. Now that he is here, it is too late."

"Nothing is too late, Mother," Legaspi said. "There must be someone in this town who could be taught to organize the dissident elements."

She looked at him and tried to search his face, as though she wanted to be sure if he could keep what she was about to impart. Then she said, "There is your cousin Armando, son. He is reliable."

"Armando? Where is he?"

"He is in town – perhaps in his field."

Hassim and Legaspi looked at each other. A clattering noise from the door made them turn suddenly, stepping quickly to the wall as they did, ready to challenge any emergency. Then they saw Peping appear at the door, pausing there for a moment while he looked inside the kitchen. Legaspi's mother stopped ladling the pot and ran up to the boy.

"What are you doing here?" she scolded the boy. "I told you to watch the herd, didn't I? I told you to stay there until sundown, didn't I?"

Peping looked at his grandmother unafraid, then to Legaspi, who walked across the threshold to the doorway.

"It is all right, Mother," he said. "Peping is eager to see me. We saw him in the field on our way here."

The old woman went back to the stove, murmuring something about insubordination. She continued ladling the bubbling pot. Hassim wondered what it was that she was cooking, for the smell disturbed him and was beginning to give him a headache.

"Peping," Legaspi said to the boy, "go look for Armando, my cousin. Tell him to come here. But remember, no word to anyone. Understand?"

Peping broke out with a smile and nodded his head. Then he climbed down the ladder and broke into a run when he reached the ground. Legaspi filled their glasses with the wine. The old woman filled a wooden platter with cooked rice and dished out what she was cooking in two coconut shells, which served as plates, and set them on the floor.

"You eat now that you still have peace," she told them.

"How about you, Mother?" Legaspi asked.

"I will eat later."

Legaspi looked at Hassim, squatting on the floor. "This is what I call home," he said.

"Yes," Hassim said, squatting beside Legaspi. Then he saw what the old woman had cooked. He tasted it. "Dried fish," he commented.

Legaspi nodded his head and began eating. But he had no appetite. Hassim, however, was hungry. He could not identify the leaves floating in the bowl, but it tasted good. Legaspi tried to swallow the food but could not, while his mother watched him with disatisfaction. He had another glass of wine; still the food would not go down his throat. He balled a handful of rice and swallowed it with the wine. Finally, he got up to his feet and and looked out the window. Hassim went on eating.

"What is the matter, son?" the old woman asked Legaspi.

"I am not hungry, Mother."

She looked at the food and seemed to apologize for the kind of fare she had to offer them. She sat down and ate Legaspi's untouched food. She and Hassim ate in silence. When they were through, Hassim helped her wash the dishes. Then he sat on the wooden bench near the door and lit a cigarette.

Legaspi was pouring wine into a glass when his father came into the house, followed by Josefina, who was trying to calm down the wailing baby in her arms. The old man stopped at the doorway, looked at his son for a second, then at Hassim, who had slowly risen from the bench and nudged Legaspi to attention. When he saw his father, Legaspi put down the cup and walked to him.

"Father."

They embraced each other.

"This is my friend Manuel, Father."

Hassim shook hands with the old man. Now Hassim could see that he was a small man with patches of gray hair and dark like his son. He was a silent man, Hassim knew, for the old man looked at him steadily without blinking an eye, then to his son, who was waiting for him to say something.

"Let us sit down," the old man suggested.

Josefina went into the kitchen and put the baby on a bundle of rags. She filled the cups with wine and served the men, while her mother-in-law went into the main part of the house and then down into the yard where she hung her washing.

"You have just come?" the old man asked Legaspi.

"Yes, Father."

"You are not going to stay, I know that much."

"We will leave right away. I just came to see how you are in the family, Father."

The old man nodded his head, finishing his drink. He looked at Hassim again. There was something that disturbed him about Hassim, who was very quiet; he had not even moved from the spot where he was standing when the old man came into the house. Hassim saw the beads of perspiration rolling from the old man's face and falling onto his sweat-soaked shirt, open wide at the neck and conspicuous with patches and repatches of different colors. His hands were large and veined. He was barefoot. Then he looked at his son again; he wanted to ask questions, but did not know how to begin or where to begin.

"How is everything, Father?" Legaspi asked.

The old man shook his head. "Bad. Very bad, son. The town is bad, especially to us. But we have no place to go. Your brother – "

Josefina looked at them.

"Well, is it hard over there? the old man asked, changing the subject abruptly. He was addressing Legaspi and Hassim; he was rapidly looking from one to the other, expecting a straight answer.

"Everything is hard," Legaspi said. "But we have good men. We have all kinds of people. We even have a seventy-year-old man who has a very dangerous job. He is a courier, and he travels long distances day and night. He is with us now."

"Is that right?" the old man asked Hassim.

"Yes."

"Of course he has no family responsibility," Legaspi explained. He noticed the pain in his father's eyes. "He is all alone."

"He is here?"

Legaspi nodded his head. Peping came back with Armando, who immediately went into the kitchen and grabbed Legaspi's hand. He nodded to Hassim. Legaspi took his arm and together they went down to the yard.

"I am glad you came," Armando said.

"How are you?" Legaspi asked.

"Like everybody else."

"We have very little time left," Legaspi explained. "I may not see you again, Armando. So let us go on with the business."

Armando nodded his head.

"Do you know that cornfield across the river?" Legaspi asked.

"Yes."

"Well, it is this way, Armando. I understand you know what I am doing."

"I am for it."

"Good. Now go to that cornfield. We have friends waiting there – in the middle of the field. Go to them and talk to a man named Dabu."

"Dabu?"

"I have heard of him."

"He will give you the kind of instruction you need for this town."

"What shall I say? Is there no password?"

"Tell him you are from Hassim."

"You mean – " Armando stopped and looked up toward the house. "You mean that is Hassim?"

Legaspi looked at his cousin silently, then nodded his head.

"My God!" Armando said. "They don't know it?"

"No." His name is Manuel here."

"I will go now. But let me go up and look at him again."

"And another thing: be very cautious going to the cornfield. Everything depends on your secrecy. This is not the end of our journey. We are going farther south – to the city."

"You can depend on me."

"Take Peping with you. I would like him to meet the others. He is a good boy."

"I will, Fernacio. And what are you called?"

"Legaspi."

Armando looked at his cousin with astonishment. "I should have known. Yes, I should have known. Let us go up now."

They went back to the house. Armando looked at Hassim, and he could not control his emotion. He rushed to Hassim and shook his hand. He was a small man like Legaspi; he gripped Hassim's hand and turned to Peping.

"Let us go, Peping," he said to the little boy.

Peping looked at Legaspi, who nodded to him. The old man watched them go out of the house, then turned to Hassim and Legaspi.

"You are not alone?" the old man asked his son.

Legaspi did not say anything. Josefina's baby started to wail again. They all looked at her.

"Take the baby out of the house, Josefina," the old man said.

Josefina obediently went out of the house. When she was gone, Legaspi looked at Hassim. The old man filled their cups with wine. They drank silently. Then they heard Josefina screaming in the yard and Legaspi's mother shouting to them in the house. There was a patter of feet climbing up the house, and Francisco appeared at the doorway. There was an obscene leer on his face. He looked at Legaspi, then to Hassim and back to Legaspi. He did not even bother to look at his father, who was staring at him with contempt. Josefina and the old woman appeared behind him, their faces wracked with fear.

"So you have come back," Francisco said to his brother.

Legaspi did not say anything.

"You were not brave enough to come alone," he sneered. "You had to bring a bodyguard with you." He glanced at Hassim. "And you brought along a big boy, too."

The old man approached the leering Francisco. "Son, please," he said.

"Let me alone, Father," Francisco said, pushing his father aside. "I want to see how brave these guys are. They seem to have lots of fun killing people and hiding in the mountains."

"You should not talk like that, Francisco," Legaspi admonished him.

"How should I talk?"

"Well, we did not come here to make enemies. In my case, I just came to see the family."

"You have no family here."

"You are wrong."

"Look, we were brothers once but not anymore. And if you don't get out of this house this minute, I will – "

"You will what – ?"

"I have friends in this town – "

"Son!" the old man reprimanded him.

"We are leaving in a minute," Legaspi told him. "I would like to talk to Father before we go."

"I will give you five minutes." He looked at his wristwatch. "No more. Then out you go."

Now Legaspi realized what kind of monster his brother had become. He looked at his parents and said, "I am sorry that you have to live with a beast. And you, Josefina – "

"Watch out for your tongue!" Francisco shouted to Legaspi.

"Listen, Francisco," Legaspi said, "you seem to have grown a pair of horns since I saw you last."

Francisco looked at his watch. "Your time is up. You better go now. Otherwise . . . "

"Otherwise what?"

"I will call my friends." Francisco moved to the door. "And we will see how brave you guys are."

The old man grabbed Francisco's hand. "Don't go, son!"

Francisco pushed his father aside. The old man fell against the wall. The two women rushed up to him and helped him to his feet. Legaspi ran to Francisco and grabbed his shirt.

"You did not have to do that, Francisco," he said.

Francisco swung viciously at Legaspi, who stepped aside quickly. Francisco tried to hit him again.

"You better stop this foolishness, Francisco," Legaspi warned him.

Francisco's hand leaped into his trouser pocket and came out with a gun. But he was too late; Hassim's gun was already cocked toward him.

"Drop it, Francisco," he commanded.

Francisco turned to him and fired. They fired at the same time. Francisco was hit in the stomach; he fell on his knees and looked at his father.

"You see . . . " he murmured, and dropped to the floor.

The old man turned to Hassim viciously, then reached for the sharp bolo on the wall.

"No, Father," Legaspi begged him. "You can't do that."

"He is my son."

"It is useless, Father."

"But he is my son."

"Father," Legaspi said, taking the old man's bolo away from him, "I might as well tell you the truth. You are looking at Hassim, Father."

The old man stared at Hassim and felt weak. He turned to the bench against the wall and sat down. The women knelt beside the dead body and started to cry. A neighbor went to their yard and called out to them.

"Anything wrong, Matias?" he called.

The old man went to the doorway. "Nothing, Porfirio," he said. "Just an accident. Go home, please."

They heard the neighbor go back to his house. The old man returned to the kitchen. He carried the dead body into the main part of the house, where the women attended to it. Then he went back to the kitchen and stood in front of Hassim.

"What can I say, son?" he said to him. "I am just an old man and I don't understand these things. He is my son, yet you are Hassim. Tell me what to do?"

"I am sorry," Hassim apologized. "I had to do it, you know that. It was not for Fernacio's safety alone. It is for our mission."

The old man nodded his head sorrowfully. "It is better that way, I suppose," he said.

"It is better," Hassim said.

"I don't know what to do."

"Do what you are doing," Hassim told the old man. "Plant things in your field. That is the way it should be, planting things for our people to eat. You must work and live, while we will do the fighting. That is all that we ask of you."

The old man looked at Hassim for a minute. "Is it true that you are the one called Hassim?"

"Yes."

"I did not know you are just a mere boy."

"War ages people."

"Is it true what they say – that you have killed lots of people?"

Hassim did not say anything. He put back the gun under his belt and went into the main house to look at the dead body. Legaspi touched his father's shoulder and shook him slightly.

"Is it true that they have an organization here, Father?" he asked.

"Not an organization, son. Just a group of town rascals and good-for-nothing boys. Stool pigeons, informers, thugs. They are paid by the police. Your brother was one of them."

"Who is their leader?"

"A man from somewhere – an ex-convict or something like that. I heard he has a long criminal record. He came here before the national election with money in his pocket and distributed it to the loafers who saw to it that the electors voted according to their instructions. Of course there were belligerents, but they were eventually cowed to submission. It was a farce: even I had to vote for their candidates. Dogs, cats, carabaos, dead people, unborn children, and even trees had voted. They had a sweeping victory."

"It was the same all over, except in those areas under our supervision. Our candidates had an overwhelming victory, but they were unseated by fraudulent methods. We went underground after that disgraceful trampling of our constitution. We decided that we can no longer put over our program for the peasants and workers through democratic processes; that an armed struggle in which every working man and woman participate is the only way to national liberation. This is our program at the moment, and we are sure to win because the common *tao** is behind us."

"You are planning a revolution?"

Hassim came back to the kitchen in time to hear the old man's question. Legaspi waited for him to answer it. Hassim studied the old man's face.

"It is the only way," Legaspi said. "The Katipunan had the same program against Spain. But there is a great difference between that revolution and the one we are setting in motion. For one thing, you fought against foreign tyranny and their native underlings; it was a fight for independence, which was successful until the Americans came to our country under the guise of liberators. Now the present revolution is different: we are fighting colonialism under the aegis of American imperialism and their native partners in plunder. That is the difference between the two revolutions: you fought against an oppressive government, but we are fighting against a system of exploitation, of the inhumanity of man to man. This system recognizes no national boundaries, racial classifications, and religious beliefs, for its main thesis is the economic slavery of the working class everywhere in the world. You are brother to the peasant in China, the coal miner in England, the factory worker in the United States, the farmer in Russia. There used to be many flags in different shapes, sizes, and colors, all over the world. But there is only one true flag, and that is the flag of the working class everywhere in the world. That is the flag of peace, progress, and human-

*Human being; hence, common people.

ity. All the other flags that you have seen or heard about are for domination, exploitation, destruction, and war. That is the flag of the ruling class; it has many shapes, sizes, and colors to differentiate their claims on the world, and the more gaudy the flag, the greater is the stake of the nation that the flag represents. They compel you to bow in abject subjugation to their flags because it is the only subtle way for them to purge you of all your individual freedom and sense of dignity. There is no bowing to the flag of the working class we represent, because it is a symbol of liberation from exploitation and the achievement of human dignity. We look at it proudly on our feet, with clenched fists tight and raised above our heads to warn potential aggressors that we are ready to strike in its defense. It is this constant vigilance that has kept us winning everywhere in the world. We don't put our hands on our breasts when we look at our flag, which is the practice imposed upon the people by the ruling class; the heart is faulty, it vitiates and abrogates the dictates of the mind. We don't crawl on our knees either, which is the common practice of some institutions like religion; supplication is useless and utterly foolish, fit only for slaves and hypocrites. We are not slaves. We are free men, and we want everybody to be free because freedom leads to a peaceful and creative world."

"You don't have religion?" the old man asked suddenly, looking from Hassim to Legaspi. When they remained silent, he felt an urgent desire to reach them, not knowing why he had to bring up this question. So he asked, "You don't believe in God?"

Their prolonged silence only aggravated the old man's desire for clarification. When their answer was not forthcoming, he said in a pained tone of voice, "We have to believe in something greater than any man. We have to believe in God."

Legaspi looked at Hassim for help. Hassim realized that the old man's questions were prompted by the death of his son, pushing aside the question of the revolution and the fight for man's freedom. He wanted to explain the political issue as it was tied up with the economic situation, but he knew now that he had to leave it for a while. The old man's most immediate concern was the death of his son, for even in death he had to be assured in some mysterious manner that evil would not come to him. Deeply religious, but not understanding religion, he somehow felt that there was a tie-up between the dead and the living.

So Hassim said to him, "The problem is not religion or the belief in God. That comes later. What comes first is man himself, his welfare and future. Is he secure? Is he free? Is he doing something toward a full life? Is he liberated from ignorance and superstitions? Is he healthy physically and mentally?" He stopped and waited for the old man to catch up with his logic in an interrogative manner. Then he continued, "When man is free from unemployment and his security is assured, when his freedom is complete to make full use of his capacities, when he is working toward the creative fulfillment of life, when he is enlightened enough to distinguish between reason and ignorance, when he has purged himself of all diseases mental and physical, then man, as himself, will have the time and equipment to attend to higher pursuits, to interest himself in something abstract beyond his domain, beyond nature and the visible world in which he is the sole creator, in something that concerns his spirituality as his own personality allows him, something, I should say, that lifts him up above the material interest of common humanity, because he knows that he is the most gifted of all animals. Give it whatever name you like, religion or God, but you have to achieve the first premises for man toward the fullest achievement of his divinity." Then he tried to be simple. He said, "You see, when you marry, the first thing that concerns you is a house so that you will have a place to start a family. In this house you will put in a few things conducive to harmony, including your harmonious self, and your wife also, and then your children when they start coming into the world. This example by one family is similar to the human family, in a universal scale of course, but the principles involved are the same."

"I don't know," the old man said. "I am just a peasant, and I don't understand these things. Yet you illustrate your point so plainly that I see no reason why it can't be done."

"It can be done, Father," Legaspi intervened. "But we need time and peace. Right now we are concerned only in the defeat of the enemy. That is our first objective; the rest will follow."

The old man nodded his head.

"Father," Legaspi said, "we will have to go soon. I don't want you to think unkindly of us. It is true that Francisco is dead, through us; but you know it yourself that he brought only shame and trouble to our family, to our town. Hassim had no other alternative, Father."

The old man got up from the bench. "Yes, I know. It is better so. Two sons dead, and you are the only one left; but you will go away again. You are always away from us, and will always be a stranger."

"Not a stranger, Father. Wherever we are and whatever we do, it is memories of our families that urge us to go on with our work. Not a stranger, Father. No. But a friend, a son, a comrade in arms."

"I give you my blessing, son. Whatever you do, remember us. And come again when you have the opportunity."

"I will, Father." But somehow Legaspi knew that he would not see his family again. He had to make a good lie, for the sake of the living, and for his own sake, so that he would go away without feeling sad. So he laughed and said, "We will come again soon. And do you know what, Father? We will bring that old man with us, so you can see for yourself how old he is. But he drinks all the time."

The old man smiled at his son. "You seem to have acquired the habit, too," he said.

Legaspi laughed loudly. It was the real Legaspi now: the Legaspi of the jungles and in the firing line. The old man joined him and turned to Hassim, whose brooding face had broken into a wide smile.

"Well," he said, "I had never dreamed of seeing you with my own eyes. I will tell my neighbor when you are gone, say, tomorrow afternoon. Will you be far away by that time?"

"Yes," Hassim said.

"And where?"

"I will not even confess that to the pope of Rome."

They all laughed.

"Let us join the women," the old man suggested.

"Yes, I would like to say good-bye to Mother," Legaspi said.

They went into the main part of the house where the two women were watching the dead body. Legaspi looked at his brother's face, and it seemed to him how young he looked. The body was covered with two thin blankets, which were soaked through with blood. And for a brief moment he thought that Francisco was still alive, for his face had not yet become bloodless and white. But he knew that Hassim always shot at the vital organ, the stomach, when he was on a level with the victim, and at the head when he was on a higher level. And as he looked at his dead brother all feelings of guilt in him were cleansed, for he knew that he would have been killed himself had not Hassim acted in his defense. He was glad now that Hassim was with him and not Dabu, who would have acted monstrously in the same situation. He walked over to the corner where Josefina was weeping.

"I am sorry, Josefina," he said.

The young woman looked up at him and said. "What am I going to do?"

"You can stay in this house and take the place of the dead," Legaspi consoled her. "My parents have no one now that my two brothers are dead. You see, I am going away today. So you are the only one left. Stay with them while I am gone, Josefina."

Josefina looked at Legaspi's parents, waiting for their approval.

"Stay with us," the old man said.

"Yes," seconded the old woman.

"Thank you," Josefina said.

"Be sure to take good care of the boy," Legaspi said. Then he turned to his mother and embraced her, saying, "We will go now, Mother."

The old woman began to cry.

"Shed no tears for me, Mother," he said. "We don't want tears. We want courage. Yesterday is gone, and in a few hours we will be gone; so look forward with courage, and be glad that tomorrow will come to give you another day of life. Now I want you to shake hands with my friend, because you may never see him again. When we are gone, Father will tell you something about him."

Hassim gave his hand to the old woman and said, "Think of me as your son. We are all your sons who are fighting for the liberation of our country."

The old woman studied Hassim's face. She said, "You look sad, son."

Hassim was touched, but he could not say anything.

"He has never had a childhood, Mother," Legaspi said. "He joined the movement when he was sixteen, but before that he had worked with the labor organizations in the provinces. He never had a home, and all his people are dead."

"All dead?"

"Yes. His father was the last to go. And as he says, he is your son now."

"Yes, you are both my sons. Go together. I will pray for you."

"Thank you," Hassim said.

Legaspi turned to his father and gave him his hand. "Good-bye, Father," he said.

"Be careful, son," the old man said.

"Don't worry, Father. He will take care of me," he said, nodding his head to Hassim. "We have a good group of men waiting for us. There is also a woman with us."

"A woman?"

"Yes."

The old man looked at Hassim, who nodded his head. Hassim gave his hand to the old man.

"When you are asked about him," he said, indicating the body, "it is suicide."

The old man took his hand and nodded his head.

"Good-bye," Hassim said.

"Good-bye," said the old man. "And give my greetings to Alipato."

"I will." Then Hassim turned to Josefina and said, "When the time comes, I will send word to you. I will ask you to join us, if you are resolved to liberate our country. There is a place in our movement for young women like you. We have several with us now."

"I will let you know," Josefina said.

"Good." Then he said to Legaspi, "Let us go."

They walked to the door where Legaspi picked up Francisco's gun. He gave it to his father.

"You will need it," he said. "Armando will talk to you when we are gone."

The old man took the gun and watched them go down the ladder.

He stood still at the threshold of his house listening to their disappearing measured footsteps. Then he put the gun under his belt and went into the main part of the house to look at his dead son.

They stopped at the edge of the cornfield. Armando surveyed the surrounding landscape to see if they had been seen, but the place was deserted. Peping stood beside his uncle, waiting for his command. They saw a few animals grazing across the river and stray goats on the grassy bank where the bermuda was thick and tender on sand near the water. Then they saw a woman with a clay jar on her head walking down the narrow lane that led to the makeshift shallow well at the bend of the river, where the bananas were in bloom and the bamboo trees were whispering under the slight wind from the west. The man and the boy nodded to each other and entered the cornfield, looking back for a second when they had been hidden by the cornstalks.

Armando led the way to the center of the field, while Peping followed him with agitation. The boy shared Armando's conspiratorial mission to the very core of his being. In his inexperienced mind he began to sift the truths from the lies, as he had heard them from the grown-ups. These were mostly about Legaspi; these were stories rumored about him since he went away. When his father was still alive, he was somehow blindly confident that he knew the truth about Legaspi; but when he died, through the betrayal of his uncle Francisco, he was all balled up and confused. Not that he did not understand Francisco when he talked about Legaspi and his father, but he found glaring inconsistencies in his approach to the lives of these two. He was unaware of the fact that Francisco was already dead; so as he walked behind Armando, he was pondering some vital questions that he would ask him when he returned home.

166  Armando stopped when they approached the center of the corn-

field. He looked back at the boy and regretted, when he saw his agitation, that he had brought him along. They were entering the rendezvous of men he had never seen and known, who might act impulsively before asking questions. And that, indeed, would be tragic for the boy.

"Are you afraid?" he asked.

"No," Peping said, trying to act like a grown-up.

"When we see them," he said, pointing toward the center of the field and bending down to his nephew, "don't say anything. I will do all the talking. Just watch and listen – and remember."

"Yes."

"Good."

Peping nodded.

"And one thing more," Armando explained. "Whatever happens, don't make any noise. Don't run. Understand, Peping?"

"I understand."

"They are our friends," Armando said finally.

Then they walked on, their eyes darting from left to right. They had gone ten feet from where they had stopped when Armando was suddenly surprised that the cornstalks around them were moving. He stopped and looked around. Then he saw them. He saw that they were surrounded. He moved back to hide the boy, and raised a hand.

"Dabu?" he asked in a low tone of voice.

Silence.

"Dabu," he called again, "I have a message for you from Hassim."

They came close to them in a circle, the ring tightening and tightening. First one came out from a cornstalk where he had been hiding, then another, another, until they were all visible to them, the menacing guns in their hands.

Armando did not move. But the boy, Peping, hung on to his uncle's shirt, his eyes wide with terror.

"I want to speak to Dabu," Armando said.

Dabu stirred, the gun still in his hand. "Yes?" he said. "What do you want to say to him?"

"I have a message from Hassim."

Dabu did not say anything.

"Don't you understand, man?" Armando said. "Hassim is with Legaspi. I am Legaspi's cousin. This boy – Peping – is my nephew."

Dabu put back his gun under the belt and nodded to his companions. He took Armando's hand, jostling the boy with the other. Then he laughed.

"We scared you, huh?" he said.

"Who wouldn't be scared?" Armando said.

Dabu led Armando to their knapsacks, while Old Bio took the boy's hand and followed them. The others followed close behind. When they reached the hiding place, Dabu told them to sit down. Armando sat on a knapsack and Peping sat on another beside him.

Now that they were seated in a circle, Armando saw Mameng, who was taking off her canvas cap. He had not suspected that there was a woman among them, for they were dressed almost alike. And Peping, when he saw Mameng and realized that she was a woman, looked at her with wonder. Mameng smiled at him, and he felt embarassed. He turned around to the others, wondering as he saw each face. He stopped at the old man's face, and knew for sure that he was indeed an old man. Perhaps as old as my great-grandfather, he thought. But when he saw Dante's gray hair, Peping was baffled. He noticed that Dante's face looked young enough, but the white hair confused his mind. Then he looked at Linda Bie, who was beginning to play with his flute. But even Peping knew that he was not like the others because there was something that was different from the others; there was something graceful and easy in his movement, and the boy wanted to hear his voice. He looked suddenly at Dabu, then at Armando and back to Dabu. And his heart swelled up with pride. The leader, he thought, waiting for Dabu to speak. And he was gratified.

"Where are they?" Dabu asked Armando.

"At the house of Legaspi's parents. The parents were there when I left, and Josefina with her baby."

"Who is she?"

"Well, she is – you know – sort of wife to Legaspi's brother." He looked at Mameng, embarrassed but trying not to be, and turned to see that Dabu was nodding his head. "The younger brother," Armando explained. "He was not at the house when I left. The other brother is dead."

"I see."

"And this boy?"

"Peping is my nephew. Legaspi told me to bring him along, I don't know why. Perhaps to show him Legaspi's companions."

"Suppose – ?"

"He is reliable," Armando explained. "You see, his father was betrayed by Francisco to the police."

Dabu's fiery eyes leaped to the boy, then back to Armando. "Well?"

"You will give me instructions, Legaspi said. I would like to start a unit here, and I would like to start on the right basis."

"I see."

Old Bio motioned to the boy. "Come here, sonny," he said. "Sit beside me, and I will tell you a story."

Peping got up reluctantly.

"It is all right," Mameng told him.

Peping went to the old man and sat beside him. Mameng turned to Dante. Linda Bie lay his head on one of the knapsacks and went to sleep. Old Bio opened the sack of whiskey and took a bottle. He drank. Then he offered it to the boy, who shook his head. Dabu started giving instructions to Armando.

"What is your name, son?" Old Bio asked the boy.

"Peping."

"That is a good name."

Peping did not say anything.

"So your father is dead?"

"Yes."

The old man wiped his brow with a palm. He was beginning to perspire. The sun was already high in the clear sky.

"You like to eat?"

"I ate already," Peping said.

Old Bio took another drink and said, "I need a little rest, son. Will you take my watch?"

Peping nodded.

"Good," Old Bio said. He reached for a knapsack and lay his head on it. "Be sure to wake me up when something happens, son."

"Yes, sir."

Old Bio closed his eyes and in a minute he was asleep. Peping looked at his face, then down to his sweak-soaked shirt. And he saw the gun under the belt. Now he knew where to reach for it when the time came. He sighed and looked in the direction of Dabu and Armando, who were talking passionately in a low tone of voice. He could not understand most of the words, but he was fascinated by Dabu. He listened attentively.

Mameng and Dante were sitting side by side, their backs on the others. They were so quiet that Peping wondered if they were asleep; but when he saw Dante suddenly light a cigarette with a flick of his fingers, he realized that they were not. They are guarding the place, Peping thought, and looked at the old man again.

The hours passed, and Dabu was still talking. Linda Bie got up and Dante took his place. After a while Old Bio got up too, and Mameng took his place. They are resting, Peping thought. They must have come from a long way. Then he looked at Dabu again. When is he going to rest? he asked himself. But he found no answer because the old man touched him.

"So you watched over me, eh?" Old Bio asked him.

Peping smiled.

"You will make a good courier like me."

"Is that what you are?"

"First class, son. Would you like to be a courier?"

"Yes," Peping said, and his eyes flashed with anxiety.

"Good. But you will have to wait awhile. We will come back for you when you are ready."

Peping was disappointed. He frowned.

"There is plenty of time," Old Bio consoled him. "You see – "

Then the shot from the town rang out clearly in the still air. Old Bio did not finish his sentence; he jumped to his feet and turned to his companions. They all jumped, looking at each other with wondering eyes. Dabu raised his hand; he was waiting to see if it was the signal. But when no other shot followed, he motioned to them to sit down.

"I wonder what it is all about," Old Bio said.

"Do you think they are in danger?" Armando asked Dabu, thinking of Hassim and Legaspi.

"I don't think so," he said. "We have a danger signal. And that is not it."

"I wonder."

"Do you have some firearms in town?"

"Francisco and his pals have firearms, supplied by the local police."

"How many are they, Francisco and his pals?"

"Nine or ten. No more. I am sure of that."

"You know them all?"

"Yes."

"Then there is no need to worry."

Old Bio said to Armando, "You need a weapon."

"Yes," he said. Then he asked Dabu, "Do you have an extra gun?"

Dabu shook his head.

"I have," Old Bio announced. He went to his knapsack and pulled out an automatic carbine. He said to Armando, "You have a big job here. I will give you a gun which was given to me when we started on this trip that will give you courage when you learn who gave it to me." He took the gun from under his belt and gave it to Armando.

Dabu smiled at the old man. Armando examined the gun, and looked at the old man.

"You can have it," Old Bio said. "I will use this one."

"I need it."

"Yes. That gun came from one of the bravest men in the underground. I hate to part with it, but I am giving it to you as a symbol of courage and friendship. It came from Commander Dimasalang."

Armando's jaw fell open.

"It is true," Dabu told him.

"Good God!" Armando whispered. Then he said, "I will not shame him. I will make good use of it. Thank you."

Old Bio reached in his pockets and gave him two fistfuls of shells. "The clip is full," he said. "But you will need extra shells – you have a big task."

Armando put the shells in his pocket and said, "Yes, I will need them."

"Do you want something to eat before you go?" Dabu asked him.
"Yes."

Dabu turned to Mameng. "Please give them canned sardines."

Old Bio snorted. "Sardines, always sardines," he said.

"What is wrong with them?" Armando asked, looking at the two cans that Mameng had given him.

Dabu laughed. "He does not like sardines," he explained.

Armando looked at the old man, then he understood the joke. He opened the cans and gave one to Peping. Mameng gave them a can of beans, and the two, Armando and Peping, sat on the ground and began to eat with their fingers. They were both very hungry.

Dabu studied Armando carefully. He looks lean, he thought. What a sacrifice he will have to make now, and I did not even ask him if he is married. Well, we have to make many sacrifices. He will make a good cadre – if I only have enough time with him? Then he looked at the boy and saw some similarities in his face with Legaspi's, and his heart ached so because now he knew that this innocent boy too is marked forever. When Peping suddenly looked up at him, he turned his face away. Dabu could not face the boy.

When they were through with their meal, Dabu told them to bury the cans. Peping was thinking of taking them home with him, where he could fill them with earth and plant mango seedlings. He knew where the seedlings were growing, near the house, but he would like them to be hanging in the windows, if he could take the cans home. But Dabu said they had to be buried, so Peping had to take orders. He had a reverential respect for Dabu, for authority as a whole, if it came from responsible persons, and evidently Dabu was one of them. He himself buried the cans while his uncle talked to the men and Mameng about the underground, about the men and women in it, and about the prospect of winning against the enemy. And he listened with fascination. The old man told him that they would come back for him when he was ready. When would that be? Tomorrow? Next year? When he would be old enough to carry a gun? Peping sighed. Maybe it would be too late. Maybe the struggle would be over. And he would like very much to go with his uncle Legaspi, only he knew him by the name of Fernacio. But there was his uncle Armando. Yes, he would work with him, and maybe when he was ready they would come back for him and his uncle. That was enough for the time being. He had something to do when they were gone. He wished they would give him a gun.

Linda Bie suddenly touched Dabu's shoulder and put his finger on his mouth, silencing them all. They stopped and listened. There was a slight rustle of leaves somewhere, then it seemed to be everywhere around them. Dabu motioned to his companions to lie flat on the ground, in the form of a circle, three feet apart. He grabbed Peping to his side.

"Wait until we see them all," he whispered to his companions. "Don't fire until I give the command."

Armando was trembling, for this was his first experience. He was lying on his belly between Mameng and Old Bio. He wanted to turn to Mameng to see how she took the situation, but he did not move his face. He looked straight ahead of him, waiting feverishly. Then he saw a man in his range of vision walking toward them with a gun in his hand. Then he saw the others, advancing slowly, surrounding them. Then he recognized the man, for he concentrated on the man walking directly toward him.

Then they saw all of them. Nine armed men, their guns ready.

Dabu lay flat on his belly and calculated their distance. Twenty-five feet away. He had to wait until they were fifteen feet away, to be sure to fell five of them in one volley. The enemies had not seen them yet. Perhaps they had expected them to be standing and talking, expected to surprise them.

Dabu counted the seconds, his eyes on the two men approaching him, but the gun was aimed only one one of them. It seemed a long time, and he could almost hear his heart beating. He was not afraid for himself but for the boy at his side. Not a single one moved, they seemed to stop breathing.

Then he whispered, "Fire!"

They fired as one man, and five of the enemies fell. They fired again, and two more fell. Two men turned back and fled. Dabu jumped to his feet, followed by Dante and Linda Bie. The two men split, and Dabu and Linda Bie split too, firing as they did, and one more fell. Behind them, Old Bio and Armando rushed to the fallen men, to be sure that they were dead. They were, for they had all been hit in the stomach. Mameng stayed on the spot with the boy, who was trembling and almost weeping.

Then from outside the field there was another shot. Linda Bie, who was still pursuing his man, stopped short when he saw that the man had fallen. He was bewildered for a moment, because he had not fired his gun. Then he saw Hassim running to the fallen man, and behind him, running in the direction of Dabu, was Legaspi. He ran into the cornfield and came to the spot where Dabu was turning over the face of his last man.

"You got them all?" Legaspi asked.

"I guess so."

"I saw nobody get away. Hassim got the last man, who was outside the field."

"Then we got them all."

"Anybody hurt?"

Dabu smiled. "Let's see if Armando can identify them all."

They went to the others. Hassim came running, and when he saw that nobody was hurt, he nodded toward Armando.

"Let's identify them," he said.

Armando nodded his head and followed Hassim. When they returned, Legaspi looked at Armando.

"I know them all," he said. "Francisco's pals, all right."

Hassim piled the enemy's guns and extra shells on the ground. Then he ordered Legaspi to put them in a sack.

"Look, Armando," Hassim said. "We are leaving right away. What do you think you are going to do now?"

Armando hesitated for a moment. Then he said, "I will take a chance. I will stay."

"Good. But you are all alone, you know."

"I am not alone, now." He looked at his nephew. "Peping will help me. Eh, nephew?"

Peping grinned. "Could I have a gun?" he asked.

Hassim picked a .32-caliber automatic from the sack and gave it to Peping.

"This is your gun, Peping," He said. "Armando will teach you how to use it. Be sure now: use it only for a good purpose."

"Yes. Thank you."

Hassim turned to Armando. He said, "One of our agents will contact you a month or so from now. Perhaps we will send Old Bio."

"Who is Old Bio?"

Hassim pointed to the old man. Armando looked at him, and for the first time he seemed to realize the importance of his task. Old Bio was looking solemnly at him.

"Could you not send a younger man, perhaps Legaspi?" Armando asked.

"It is too dangerous for Legaspi to come again. Are you worried about the old man?"

"Well, yes."

"Don't worry about him, Armando. Old Bio can outrun and outclimb anyone day and night. He is my personal guide. He made me pant like a schoolboy when we climbed down the mountains."

Old Bio laughed. "So you are worried because of my age, eh?"

"Well, I thought – "

"Don't worry about this old man, son," Old Bio said. Then he pointed to Linda Bie. "But worry about him. He is soft. Do you know why? He is the son of a capitalist, a big landlord in his province."

"Always the joker," Linda Bie said.

Armando looked at him. Yes, he thought. He has the marks of easy life. But he asked, "Are you, really?"

"I am telling you the truth, son," Old Bio said. "Of course he eats goat meat and fish like a peasant now."

Dabu and Legaspi laughed.

"How about him?" Armando asked, pointing to Dante. He was disturbed by Dante's silence. "He seems a little different."

Old Bio tapped Armando's forehead with a finger. "Here," he said. "Too much here. Thoughts. Ideas. But the mouth is closed most of the time. Do you know why?"

Armando shook his head.

"He has been a slave in the United States for fifteen years. That is why he has poison in his brain, which comes out in the form of words. He is the propagandist par excellence."

Armando looked at Dante's gray hair and reserved comment. He felt awkward in front of him, of them all, whose names he had heard from a long distance. And now they were all here, talking to him, instructing what to do, telling his part in the movement.

"You doubt my words, eh?" Old Bio said.

"No," Armando said.

Peping was also looking at Dante.

"And that one with the thick mop of hair and whose forehead is as low as an ape," Old Bio said, pointing to Dabu, "watch out for him. He will eat you alive."

They all laughed.

"Armando," Hassim said when their laughter had died, "do you think you will be able to organize a unit here in a month's time?"

"I can."

Hassim picked up the sack of guns and shells. He gave it to Armando.

"This is your first supply," he said. "We will send you some more later."

Armando took the sack. "This is enough for the time being, but I will need some more later," he said. Then he turned to the old man and said, "I guess I don't need your gift any more."

"Keep it," Old Bio said. "Remember Dimasalang when you use it."

"I will."

Legaspi shook Armando's hand. "I will see you again, cousin," he said.

"Go now," Hassim said. "We will move on when you are safe across the river."

"What about the bodies?"

"Let them rot in the field."

"Good-bye to all of you," Armando said. "Let's go, Peping."

"Be a good boy, Peping," Legaspi said. "Shake hands with Hassim," he said, pointing to him. "He is in command here."

Peping looked at Hassim. "I thought it was the other one," he said, pointing to Dabu. But he shook hands with Hassim like a brave little man. "Hassim," he said. "I will remember that name always."

"One more thing to remember, Peping," Hassim told him. "Follow Armando's instructions carefully. Will you do that?"

"Yes."

"Then go without delay."

Legaspi took them to the edge of the cornfield. When they had crossed the river, he returned to his companions. They strapped on their knapsacks and crept out of the cornfield. When they came to the bare land, Hassim looked at the sky.

It was already midday.

## CHAPTER FOURTEEN

. . . . . . . . . . . . . . . . . . . . . . . . . . . . . . . . . . . . . . .

They marched away from the town for an hour and came to a camachile grove. Here the cogon grass was tall, almost an average man's height. Clumps of talahib grass were in abundance, and their imperial white crowns were waving in the air. The sturdy reedlike grass was twice the length of the resilient cogon, which was bending under the noon heat. The camachile trees were bare, and already the stubby thorns were falling off the cracking barks; the fallen yellow leaves were thick on the ground, for in a few weeks, in the chilly climate of December, the little white buds would appear in clusters on the young branches; then, after two more weeks, the comblike green fruit would adorn the trees.

They stopped under the trees to hold council. Hassim told Legaspi and Linda Bie to keep guard at either side of the grove; on the north, where the town they had just left was visible through the parting grass, and on the south, where the village they were approaching was only a kilometer away. They were away from the houses, away from the town itself; but they had to be cautious, for they were not sure that the confusion in the cornfield was not heard. Hassim and Dabu squatted on the ground to discuss their plans, while Old Bio and Dante stood guard, their backs on each other, Old Bio facing east and the wide stretch of land rolling away into the mountains, Dante facing west and a narrow strip of swampy land that was cut by a river flowing westward to the sea. Mameng stood between Hassim and Dabu, waiting eagerly for the deliberation.

"We have to change our plan, Dabu," Hassim began. "I am not sure that the fighting in the cornfield was not heard. Even if the nine town police's stool pigeons are killed through their self-confidence and thuggery, I am sure they have other cohorts and small-time hirelings left. This town is a bad territory; I had to kill Legaspi's brother in his father's house. I regretted doing it, but there was no other course. He was going to round up his pals and the police to challenge us. If I had not done what I did, however much I regretted, we would have been exposed and delayed and perhaps lost some of our members. Legaspi's brother, Francisco, was responsible for the betrayal and murder of his older brother. And that is not all: he had mistreated a young woman who had begotten him a child out of wedlock. I don't want you to ease my conscience about the matter, because I know I did what I had to do. Of course Legaspi understands, and he made his father understand too; so we left the old man's house with his mind at peace, but his wife and the young woman will never forgive me. We can't win a whole house-hold, can we, Dabu?"

"Naturally not," he said. "Was that the shooting we heard from the town?"

"It was. A sad business, but necessary."

"I would have done the same thing."

"I am sure you would have. That is why we must change our plan; during the brief moment of confusion, Legaspi revealed my identity. I will not reprimand him for it because emotional conflicts were involved at the moment. His father wanted to challenge me with his crude bolo, so Legaspi had to stop the old man by revealing my identity."

"I understand. What shall we do now?"

Hassim nodded his head and picked up a twig from the ground. With the other hand he pulled up the dead grass on the ground between them and leveled the torn earth with his palm. Then with the twig he drew a map, marking off where they were and the next rendezvous, and connecting the two places with two curving lines, which revealed a space between them that looked like an egg. He marked another spot below the next rendezvous.

Dabu was following the lines and markings carefully. When

Hassim suddenly stopped and looked at him, Dabu nodded his head in silent agreement.

"We will split in two groups," Hassim said. "I will take command of one, and you the other. You have Legaspi, Dante and Linda Bie, and you follow this route. This is where we are, and from where we will start to the next rendezvous. Look." He pointed at the marked spot and slowly traced the line on the left to the next rendezvous and ponderously stopped at the marked spot. "Do you recognize this place, Dabu?"

Dabu grinned. "Surely," he said. "That is my hometown."

"Right. It is our next rendezvous." Then he pointed to the smaller spot below it and asked, "And this?"

"Of course! Why, I used to steal mangoes there when I was a small boy. It is a mango grove."

"Right. How far is it from the town?"

"About two kilometers."

"Good. Now we will take the other route, on the right. Mameng and the old man will come with me."

Dabu looked up and calculated the time. "We are about thirty kilometers from the mango grove," he said. "Do you think we can make it by ten this evening?"

"We can, if nothing happens on the way. But that is why we are splitting, in case something happens. Whoever arrives first should wait for the others until dawn. And at dawn, even if only one person is left, he should proceed to the city. You all know the details of our mission. Is that understood?"

"Definitely."

"Let us proceed immediately." Hassim got up and said to Old Bio, "We are ready, old one. Tell Legaspi and Linda Bie to come back."

Hassim watched the old man walk away and lit a cigarette. When the three came back, Hassim crushed his cigarette.

"We are leaving right away," he told them. "In two groups. Dante, Linda Bie, Legaspi – you go with Dabu. He will give you instructions on the way. Old Bio and Mameng will come with me."

Old Bio coughed behind his hand, looking at Legaspi like a lost dog. Hassim noticed him.

"Legaspi, give us a can apiece of provision." Hassim said. "And give the old man a bottle."

Old Bio could not wait for Legaspi to undo the sack of provisions. He put the bottle and can of meat in his knapsack, and gave the two other cans to Hassim and Mameng. They tightened the straps of their knapsacks. Then Hassim nodded his head to Dabu, and they parted silently. When they came out of the camachile grove and the tall talahib grass, they stopped and looked at each other across a space of fifty yards. They all raised their fists and went on their dangerous separate ways.

Old Bio and Mameng were walking five paces ahead of Hassim. Hassim watched them with a contemplating look, and he could not quite resist evaluating the lives of his companions. For it seemed to him now that he had traveled a long distance on the surface of the earth with them. And to what end and purpose? That there would be an end was sure enough, and he knew there would be an end; but he knew not when, and how far away. For their struggle was like chasing a rainbow, a rainbow so real and brilliant that it foreshadowed its distance and reality. They were propelled toward it by a common feeling of adventure, but he above all others, among all things; and it was almost gratifying for him to think that he was responsible for them, for the seeking and reaching of that rainbow, for the achievement of a strange adventure and the fulfillment of a burning dream. For he was qualified among all others to blaze a trail toward the end, where the purpose would be compounded with all their anxieties, fears, thoughts, tenderness, and joys; as though everything that they had lived for would come to this very purpose, would crystallize in it finally. And even now, following them thoughtfully with a measured stride, he was thinking of Dabu and his companions. There was something vital in an experience shared in common, he knew, that bound people together and that other experiences, met individually, could not and never do; for in such experience, the commonly shared, individual freedom and diversity were arrogated into a collective creative purpose, thus opening the way to a more wholesome activity for the common good. And though that adventure was dangerous, they would find themselves, in whole or in part, and that was its real meaning and significance, the regrouping of themselves at the end where they could look back and appraise what they had done. It did not matter how they would find their way back, for they had found the pieces of themselves at the end; and even when they realized the hazards of the return journey, the thought that they had made a world in reaching their destination would be more than they could hope for, in their journey back, where it all began, where the meaning was unclear until their triumphant return.

Was there no other meaning of life? Hassim could look back to the beginning, almost at the end of time, and seek out among the wreckage of other lives, all that he had known, if there was another, more tangible than what he had found among his companions in these last few hectic years. But he could not find any: for there at the beginning was a false peace, the peace of childhood that took nourishment from the unfailing roots of parenthood; not the peace of awareness, of knowing the world and the people in it, and their relations to each other as they were striving to weave a motif as a setup of their pattern of living. It was the false peace of childhood, deeply embedded in his memory and everybody's memory; yet he knew that from it started the yearning for real peace, the peace that came with maturity and awareness; and in it were first revealed the magic casements that revealed the dawn and murmur of real peace, becoming more murmurous and brighter as awareness grew, as it grew steadily until it became an imperishable reality. So that was the beginning of real peace after all, he thought. The family as a unit, then the community, then the whole country, then the system around which the country revolves with other countries, antiquating all national and geographical boundaries. It all comes to the incontrovertible fact, the beginning and end of man, the one race of man, which is humanity, always and forever. Yes, he thought again. The false peace translates itself into the real peace of awareness.

And war – why was there war? Was man instinctively warlike? He knew that man was not; he knew that many men knew that he was not; yet man had always shown himself as a warlike animal, for he showed no other concerted or gigantic project than war, to destroy his kind, to put to ashes what he had created. True, he had made attempts at creative activities, but these had always been superseded by his warlike activities, his destructive designs. True, he had built magnificent cathedrals where he consecrated his piety in luminous columns of marble and granite and stone, where he arrested in inspiring canvases and murals the greatness and bigness of creation, where his words haloed the awareness of his insignificance in the vastness of the universe, intoning or singing his highest praises for being allowed the everlastingness of that infinitude. True, he had invented thundering machines, Promethean of power, and strength and durability, with which he dug into the bowels of the earth for lifegiving matters and elements, such as iron and coal and steel, and even such luxuries as gold, silver, diamonds, and other brilliants, to satisfy his insatiable vanity to outrank the beauty of creation itself; or machines with which he spanned the longest rivers and crossed the widest oceans, to reach other places for more lifegiving matters and elements, and more astounding luxuries to assuage his ever-expanding vanities; or machines with which he scoured the skies ever higher and higher, in search of new islands and continents to conquer, for his need for lifegiving matters, elements, and luxuries had sorrowfully become insatiable. Because the skies were unconquerable and unrevealing – was it necessary that he had to come down to earth with his destructive machines, to destroy all that he had created and begin all over again, from his simple little needs to the unassuageable ones, following the same vicious circle from creative activity to wholesale destruction?

Was that why there were always wars? Hassim would not, could not, accept that war was the prime ambition of man – he had seen the purposeful and possible works of man everywhere, varying only in their usefulness to the world – so that finally, though he saw the wreckage of destruction everywhere, he refused to accept the end of man. Had man, then, become so complex that he had also become irreconcilable within himself? That the constructive and destructive forces within himself were forever challenging in their struggle for dominance over him? But that he refused to accept too. For within himself, as a man, there was no such struggle. He had accepted what to do with some procrastination at first, it was beyond denial, but as he studied the task given him objectively there grew within him a sense of responsibility, and he accepted it too, willingly and without reservations. It was the acceptance of the responsibility, then, the way he understood it – that brought about the forging of a concept that drove him to greater responsibilities of life, and revealed the true measure of himself, as he accepted one responsibility after another; and as he himself accepted the truth that man had no instincts for destruction, but for creating useful things conducive to the making of man's peaceable kingdom on earth.

Who, then, were responsible for wars? Hassim paused for a moment, looked at the surrounding fields around him, then at the sweltering sky, and back to the earth where Old Bio and Mameng, unaware of his meditations, had walked faster and were now far ahead of him. Hassim realized his absorption in the subject of war and peace, which had slackened his pace, so he evaded the question he had propounded to himself and walked faster.

They were now crossing an open field toward what seemed a cluster of grass huts a kilometer away. The land was so flat that there was not even a hollow or a rise behind which they could rest, or hide, if there was a need for it. Stalks of corn had fallen to the ground where animals had nibbled the remaining fronds of the dead leaves, and the creepers were eaten too, and the whole expanse of the field was a huge desolation, a wasteland; it looked as though a nomadic tribe had passed through with their animals and laid the land bare of growing things, leaving a footprint here and a dung there to indicate that they had camped briefly on this land. Even the trees were bare of fruit, though they were thick-leafed, and there was not a bird in them.

The desolation was complete. Hassim wondered what had happened. There was no sign of fighting: there was not even an animal around. And no man. There were only the grass huts in the approaching distance, where no sound disturbed the air, where no smoke came from the huts. What had happened? Hassim castigated himself. He should not have been too introspective; he should have been more watchful. Now it had all come to him so suddenly he had to think for lost time.

He walked faster. When he overtook Old Bio and Mameng, he fell in with them.

"Do you notice anything?" Hassim asked.

Old Bio looked sideways at him, then turned his face to survey the surrounding field.

"It seems very quiet," he said. "The land seems to have been uncultivated for quite some time."

"What do you think, Mameng?"

"The peasants must have evacuated the place," she said.

"This is part of Dabu's territory," Hassim said. "But I have not been informed of developments here, unless something happened only recently."

"Let us find out," Old Bio suggested.

"Has it any bearing on our work?" Mameng asked.

"Maybe not," Hassim said. "But it is always wise to know everything. It is a part of our task."

"We are approaching the village," Old Bio said. "I can investigate it alone."

Hassim and Mameng did not say anything. When they came to the edge of the village, they stopped behind a grassless high ditch and remained silent for a moment.

Then Mameng said, "I will go."

Hassim looked at her, then at the old man. Then he turned toward the village, deciding what to do. They were waiting for him to say something. But he was undecided, and he could not say anything. Old Bio knew what he was thinking.

"It is better for me to go," he said. He unstrapped his knapsack and gave it to Hassim. "I will not stay long."

"I will go with you," Mameng said.

"You stay," Hassim said finally.

Old Bio walked away without looking back. They watched him walking across the field in a steady gait, not slackening his stride, not even looking around. He walked as though he were walking home from a trip, as though he had a house in the village. He had taken off his canvas cap and stuck it under his belt, and when he came to the village road, he paused a moment and looked around him. Then he walked on and entered the village.

Hassim took the field glasses from his shirt pocket, screwed the lenses, adjusted the eyepieces, and focused them on the village road. He watched the old man walking under the trees until he disappeared behind the huts. Hassim kept focusing the field glasses, hoping to catch the old man. But Old Bio had disappeared.

Hassim looked at Mameng. He slung old Bio's knapsack on his left shoulder and lit a cigarette. He was resolving what to do, in case the silence of the village was a trap. For surely their presence in Legaspi's town must have already gone through the grapevine, and if there were people, the awaiting entrapment would be horrible for the old man. He had to wait. Meanwhile, he had to weigh the loss had Mameng gone instead of the old man; and he knew that, without reasoning too deeply, Mameng was doubly important to the mission. It was true that the going would be one man less had Old Bio not come with them. Still, it was the order from headquarters that the old man would accompany them.

Hassim hated to think of adverse results. He propped himself on the ditch and looked toward the village. Mameng watched him adjust the field glasses. Hassim screwed and unscrewed the eyepieces, trying to get a clear view of the village. He saw nothing. He stopped his vigil and lit another cigarette, while Mameng took the field glasses and focused them on the village. There was silence for a moment, then she made a sound.

"What is it?" Hassim asked.

"I see two men walking toward us," Mameng said.

"Let me see." Hassim took the field glasses from her and looked in the direction of the village, adjusting the eyepieces until he saw the two men clearly. "It is the old man," he explained. "I wonder who is coming along with him."

"I noticed that the other man is limping."

"He does. Yes . . . he is an old man." He gave the field glasses to her and said, "Watch them, Mameng. And stay here."

"Do you think it is a trap?"

"I don't know. Have your gun ready."

Mameng took her gun and put it on level with the ditch, aimed at the man with Old Bio. She held the field glasses with her left hand.

Hassim ran alongside the ditch ten yards away from Mameng and watched the two men coming toward them. He squeezed himself inside a hollow of the ditch that was wide enough to hold his body. He waited, and as Old Bio and his companion approached them, he began to doubt if the old man was in danger. Hassim saw now that the old man was a cripple. His right leg was crooked on the knee, so that he walked as though he were a hobbled horse. Still, he was not sure. He knew that peasants who had gone over to the enemy had many tricks to pull.

Old Bio's companion fell on his knees when they reached a dry ditch about fifty yards from where Hassim and Mameng were waiting. Old Bio stood beside him, waiting for him to get up. He did not offer to help him. And Hassim, watching them, almost laughed. For it was like Old Bio to show dispassion when he was contemptuous, or when he was angry, because he judged other human beings from his achievements and perspicacity to live, to meet obstacles.

They walked on when the cripple was on his feet again. Now Hassim saw that he was really a helpless old man; not as old as Old Bio, but old enough not be wandering alone. Perhaps that was why Old Bio's behavior seemed contemptuous, measuring the helplessness of a man younger than himself. Then they reached the ditch where they were waiting, and the cripple crawled over it to the other side, near Mameng. Old Bio climbed it with two vigorous strides and jumped on to the other side.

Hassim walked over to them and looked at the cripple.

"I found him in the village," old Bio said by way of explanation. "He is all alone. The place is deserted."

"Why did you bring him along?" Hassim asked.

"He said he is hungry. He claimed he did not eat for days."

The cripple, looking from Hassim to Old Bio, knew by his peasant instinct that Hassim was in authority. So he feigned respect and even subservience when Hassim turned to him, drawing away to a distance like a schoolboy who wants to ingratiate his teacher because he has done badly with his lessons. He pulled at his rags and scratched himself here and there, waiting for Hassim's words of authority. But when Hassim did not speak, he looked at Mameng and Old Bio again. Finally, Hassim pulled his ration of canned sardines from the knapsack and gave it to the hungry man.

Mameng took the can from the old man and opened it. He gave it with a silent protest, for he thought that she was taking it away from him. But when he saw that she was merely opening it, he nodded his head vigorously. Mameng gave it back to him, and he started to eat hungrily. He ate quickly, and when the fish was gone, he tilted the empty can to his mouth and sipped the sauce. Then he ran his hand inside the can and licked his fingers, one after the other, smacking his lips and tongue. He put a long fingernail between two loose teeth, where a piece of sardine had lodged, and sucked it. He smacked his lips once more and looked at them, waiting if they would give him another can. There were tears in his eyes.

"I am sorry, old man," Hassim said. "That is all we can afford to give you."

Mameng looked at Hassim, who knew right away what she wanted to say.

"You see, old man." Hassim explained, "we are going on a long journey, and we don't even have enough to carry with us for today. The can I gave you was my own provision, so I will eat nothing for the duration of the trip."

"Thank you," the old man said. "I didn't want to take away from you what you needed."

"It is all right," Hassim said, and smiled at him. "I can stand a few days without food. But you can't, I am sure."

"Thank you again, son. May God watch you on your journey."

"Yes, that is a good idea," Old Bio said.

The man looked at him sharply but refrained from answering.

"Tell me," Hassim said, "why is your village deserted?"

The old man looked at Hassim sharply with his lidless eyes and the fleshless jaws quivered, followed by a forecast of fear in his face. His withered hands shook slightly, and then turning his face away for a moment, he looked back at Hassim with piteous eyes.

"It is all right, old one," Hassim said amiably, "I just wondered why you are all alone. We are only passing through to a distant place where we have heard some jobs are available for those who are willing to work."

Somehow Old Bio, who sensed the man's reluctance to speak, pulled the bottle of whiskey from his knapsack and gave him a big swallow. Old Bio regretted his kind gesture, for the man helped himself gratuitously, giving back the bottle when he had drunk a third of what was left. Then Hassim offered him a cigarette, and

Mameng lit it for him. It was like bribery; it was extortion. But the man did not realize it in his desperation, and his oncoming feeling of gratitude for all that they had given him. The whiskey reddened his bloodless face so that it looked like he had a slight cold, and the yellowish color of his lidless eyes began to change color, like the beginning of gangrene.

"Three weeks ago a young man from the city came to live with us," he began. "He was not a student, I know that. He was a workingman, perhaps a factory worker. We old people did not pay too much attention to him because he seemed to be a quiet young man and easy to get along with. I said easy because after a week many of the young men of the village were always hanging around his place, especially at night, when there was nothing going on in the village. Of course there is no work at this time of the year in these parts, so we did not reprimand the young men for staying out almost all night. After ten days this man from the village disappeared with some of the young men, and we thought they had gone to town to look for work or maybe went carousing, as young men will do. We waited for three days, but they did not come back. On the fourth day of their disappearance, three important-looking men appeared in our village. They went from house to house asking for this young man from the city, commanding us to tell them where we had hidden him. We told the truth: that he had disappeared. However, we did not tell them that he had disappeared with some of our young men. But they did not believe us."

"Why were they looking for him?" Hassim asked.

"Why? They told us he was a communist. I didn't know what they meant because I didn't see anything different about him. I had heard of the word before, but I never saw a communist. So I wouldn't know if the young man from the city was a communist because, as I said, I never saw a communist. What does a communist look like?"

For a full second Hassim looked at the man with a blank face, then he turned his eyes to Old Bio and Mameng with the same blank stare, and for a moment there seemed to be a flash of recognition in his glittering eyes. When he looked at the man again, his voice changed from one of kindness to pity.

"I wouldn't know, old one," Hassim said. "We are only working people, and where we came from, a hidden valley, we devote our time to planting and raising animals. We did not hear much what was happening on the outside."

"What happened in your part of the country? Why did you leave it?"

Once again Hassim looked at Old Bio and Mameng; and when he turned back to the man, he knew the futility of imparting something of importance to him.

"Unfortunately there was a drought in our part of the country," Hassim lied. "But tell me: what was the name of the young man?"

"He called himself Lapu-Lapu. Is that a Filipino name?"

"I suppose it is, if he called himself that. Names are just names, given to us by our parents; when we were born we were to young to pick out from the calendar what names we would like to use. So one name or another does not make much difference. It is the person that counts, that means something to other people. But tell me: what did those three men do afterward, when they could not find Lapu-Lapu?"

"That is the most tragic part of it," the man said. "After they had terrorized some of the stronger men, they took the village chief to the small square and hanged him by the feet to a tree all day. After constant torturing, and at sunset, they beheaded him. I saw the head myself roll three times on the ground underneath the body, and the blood flowing from the trunk of the neck."

Old Bio shifted his weight to the other foot, making a loud noise with his throat; then, meeting the inquiring eyes of the man, he took a big swallow of the whiskey and handed it to Hassim. But Hassim waved it away to the man, who drank from it thirstily. When Old Bio had put the bottle back in his knapsack, Hassim looked at Mameng. But Mameng did not show any reaction, her unlovely face was as stolid as ever, although a glassiness began to appear in her eyes.

"Well," Hassim said to the man, "we are leaving now. Why don't you join your friends?"

"I don't know where they went. Besides, I am too weak to follow them."

"You can't live alone in the village."

"Will you take me with you, son?"

190

.........

*The Cry
and the
Dedication*

"I wish we could, old one. But we are going far away, and we don't have any provisions left. Besides, we are not sure if there are any jobs where we are going. I am really sorry. But some of your friends may come back for you after a while. Have you any relatives among them?"

The man shook his head sadly.

Hassim nodded to his companions. And he said to the man, "We'll have to leave you, old one. Take care of yourself."

The man looked at them helplessly. But when he saw that Hassim's decision was final, he climbed slowly over the ditch and walked forlornly toward the village. They watched him for a minute, then walked alongside the ditch away from the village.

They bypassed the village, following the ditch that led them to an open country. The sun was now nearing the horizon, and masses of clouds in varying shapes were sailing in the sky. Hassim glanced upward quickly and saw gondolas, chariots, dragons, fiery trees. There was even the face of a human being, and Hassim tried to place it among the persons he had known and knew. But in another second the face was broken by the high-altitude wind, and even on the earth the wind of December had risen, ruffling the trees in the village. And crickets began to sing in their crevices, the field birds scampered away from the diminishing sun, and little animals made rustling noise in the dead grass. For evening was falling, and the inarticulate living creatures in the field were all going back to their homes, where they would peep out into the big wide world of men. For night was a time of rest, and comfort, and mating.

They felt safe now that night was falling. Their first shadows appeared, lengthening quickly as they walked on into the night. And they walked side by side now, Mameng in the middle as always, so that in the darkness she would be protected against the alarms of the world.

Old Bio was the first to speak. "Do you think he was lying?" he asked Hassim, thinking of the cripple they had just left.

"No."

"I was just wondering if he suspected anything."

"I don't think so."

"Poor old man," Mameng commented.

"He is fortunate that he is alive," Old Bio said.

"Don't pity him, Mameng," Hassim said. "Pity the young who have yet to live in a confused world. And pity those who have not yet found out why there is so much confusion in the world. That man is through, he has lived his life, and he may have done something in his time. Of course there is a place for pity in human life, that is, great pity for those who are helpless and lost and forgotten and unable to participate in the making of life. Yes, there is a need of pity of that sort."

Old Bio laughed. "You are right, Hassim. He has lived his life. But not this old man!"

"You are right," Hassim said.

They all laughed. They walked on in silence. There was something on Old Bio's mind, so now and then he glanced swiftly at Hassim. Then he could not hold it any longer, so great was his desire to know the truth. He glanced at Hassim again.

"Do you know him?" he asked Hassim, thinking of Lapu-Lapu.

Hassim slightly nodded his head, and suddenly Old Bio looked down at Mameng who, when she turned to Hassim, did not see him nod. She saw only the glittering eyes, the masklike face, and the spreading darkness that was beginning to hide his youthfulness.

The night had come to the world.

CHAPTER FIFTEEN

. . . . . . . . . . . . . . . . . . . . . . . . . . . . . . . . . . . . . .

**F**ive kilometers away from Hassim and his companions, on the other route, Dabu and his companions were having the time of their lives. They were more fortunate. They found a river that was always dry after the harvest season until the month of May, when the rains began to fall. They followed the riverbed under thick canopies of intertwining mulberry trees and wild grapes, following

Indian style the narrow trails of animals and birds through grass and scrubs and ferns. It was cool in the shade, and they made good time creeping through the profusion of entanglements of tree and grass and vine. They came upon many big birds and huge lizards that tantalized their appetites, thinking of food, but they dared not waste precious bullets or attract attention.

So they walked on shaking with repressed laughter, telling jokes to each other that bordered on sexuality, but they felt free because Mameng was not with them. And they felt free from the prying eyes of the world, for they rarely saw human footprints on the sand. They stopped to rest awhile, an hour before sunset, and Legaspi began sorting his conquests on the way. For as they walked he reached out a hand here and there, grabbing bunches of grapes and rare fruits and edible grass. He had the natural instincts of a peasant, he could not pass by something edible without helping himself. To him it was all there for the taking, it was free, and he could help himself because there was no one to deny him.

So while he was sorting the edibles and putting them in the knapsack of provisions, of which he was sole custodian, his companions sat on the soft sand smoking cigarettes. When he was through with his chore, he sat among them and began toying with his gun.

"Is this not a part of your territory?" Linda Bie suddenly asked Dabu.

Dabu nodded his head and said, "We are not far from the rendezvous. This off-again, and on-again river passes by the town."

"How far are we?"

"About twenty kilometers. Are you worried we will not make the time?"

"Yes."

"We are two hours ahead of schedule. Enjoy yourself. I know where we are and I know where we are going. We are going home, Linda Bie."

"We are still far away from home."

"I am speaking of my home."

"Are you of this part?" Dante joined the conversation.

Dabu laughed. "Am I?" he said. "I used to prowl around this

territory as a little boy. With my cousin Silvio. I wonder what he is doing now – "

"He probably has beat you to it" Legaspi said.

"Eh?"

Legaspi raised five fingers. "Bambinos is what I mean," he explained.

They all laughed, except Dabu, who said, "Not Rosalia?"

"Who said about Rosalia?" Legaspi asked.

"Well, it is a personal story." And he turned his face away, trying to hide the shadow of doubt in his eyes.

They watched him in silence. When he did not want to talk any more, Linda Bie said to Legaspi, "How about a little drink?"

"That is a good idea," Legaspi said, opening the sack where he kept the bottles and giving one to Linda Bie. "Don't souse yourself, though. You might get lost in this jungle of a river."

Linda Bie looked at him with amusement. It was Legaspi's first time to moralize.

Linda Bie answered him with some reluctance. "Just a sip," he said. "The air is getting cold." He drank and passed the bottle to Dante, who took a big swallow and nudged Dabu's shoulder with the bottle. "It is good for you," Linda Bie said.

Dabu put the bottle to his mouth without comment and drank several mouthfuls. The heat of the alcohol seared his throat, and he began to breathe hard; coughing spasmodically, he gave the bottle back to Legaspi.

"I never choked before," Dabu apologized. "It is strange that I should cough now when I can usually drink a whole bottle of that stuff without blinking an eye."

"Drinking is partly psychological," Dante explained. "When you are disturbed by something, alcohol becomes nauseating, and you easily get drunk. The reason in your case, however, is the excitement you feel in coming close to home."

"I guess you are right," Dabu lied.

Dante understood his lie, for he knew that Dabu was thinking of Silvio and Rosalia, whoever she was in his life past. Linda Bie caught on too, but not the slow-witted Legaspi, who was watching Dabu curiously.

Linda Bie, however, did not want to continue their trend of conversation, which always reverted back to Dabu whatever they started.

"I read all your books when I was in college," he said to Dante. "The ones you had written when you were still in the United States. I enjoyed all of them, but I think, looking back to all that you have done, I like *Tales of My People* better. Is it not your favorite book?"

"It is indeed," Dante confirmed. "I have put in it the experiences of a little boy in Luzon who loved his countryside and the people and animals in it. But as a man and writer, I wove this boy's experiences with legends and folklore and lost tales. I found happiness and a feeling of closeness to the Philippines and the people when I wrote it. I can say with frankness that it was the beginning of my realization that I should come back to the land of my nativity. Its idea was so urgent that it did not take me long to decide. So I came back."

"And you came back to war and destruction," Legaspi finished it for him.

Linda Bie thought that Legaspi could not fathom their conversation. He looked at Legaspi with condescending eyes, then at Dabu, who was beginning to shake his mind from disturbing memories.

"Is it true about the old man who told you the stories that you finally put into the book?" Linda Bie asked Dante.

Dante was silent for a minute, not that he was reluctant to reveal the sources of his stories, but because he was suddenly reminded of a time long ago. Often in the United States, where he had written most of his books, he had lived in great loneliness. And even when he had written several books that had attracted favorable reviews, he was alone, and for a long time he had forgotten that he existed. So, with Linda Bie reminding him that he was once a precocious young man and a thinker of intellectual honesty, he suddenly felt lost and alone again. It was as though he were reliving that day when the first copy of his first book came from the publishers, and he took it to his hotel room where he looked at it for hours, fondling it this way and that as though it were a child of his own creation. It was his own creation of course, the only one he had, and there was no one to share it with him. He remembered that when he went out of his room that night, it was raining. He had the book inside his coat, hugged close to his body. He had thought of showing it to his buddies at the corner bar where he used to drink a glass or two of beer when he had the money. They were mostly illiterate day laborers, but he felt that they would share his joy. But there were only customers at the place, a friend of his and a whore who was passing the time because there was no business when the night was cold. Discreetly, he sat on the stool beside his friend. After a glass of beer he gathered enough courage to shove the book at him. His friend, who was called Paul, looked at the book with whiskey-shot eyes and grinned foolishly. It took Paul quite a while to decipher Dante's name on the cover, and when he realized that he had written it, he grinned foolishly. They had started talking in Ilocano then, which was Paul's language, regarding the book. It was not much of a book, Dante had assured his friend, for surely it was not to Paul, who was illiterate, since the book was a volume of poetry. And when the whore had heard that they were talking about poetry – angered that Paul was not ministering to her drinks – she grabbed the book off the table with anger.

"Poetry, huh?" she cried, tearing the pages with savage anger. "Puit – puit – that is what! Poetry my ass!" And with that vilification of a golden ideal, the dreams of youth, the yearnings of a lost soul in a strange land, she flung the book outside in the rain. Then she screamed at Paul, "Buy me a drink, and sleep with me tonight! You too, Shakespeare – if you have balls!"

Ay, ay, Dante thought. Should he tell them that incident? In this twilight of beauty and tranquility – for it was now twilight – should he blacken the purity of their thoughts about women? But as he was pondering, he heard Linda Bie's voice from a distance, urgent, reaching him with warmth and tenderness.

"It is true about the old man?" he was saying. "He seems to be out of this earth, a figment of imagination, a beautiful creation by one who has a great longing for his country and people."

"It is true," Dante said at last, blowing a cloud of smoke and watching it trailing in the air and disappearing about the branches over their heads. And dreamily he continued, "It is true there is a high mountain that is green all the year round bordering the north side of my province. It is true there is a wide fertile valley under the shadow of this mountain on which the peasants have been scratching a living since the dawn of history. These peasants, primitive in their ways and simple in their understanding of life, still use the crude farming tools their forefathers used centuries before, in the beginning of a settlement that became one of the densely populated sections of the islands. The passing of time and the intensification of settlers in this valley helped preserve a common folklore that was related from mouth to mouth and from one generation to another, so that now it is no longer possible to distinguish which tale is indigenous to the tribe living there and which is borrowed from other tribes. But the telling of these tales is so enchanting, so charming, that no one questions the truth of their origins and the validity of their existence.

"It is also true there is a town called Pawan in this valley where a beautiful river runs unobstructed and waters the plains generously in its slow journey to the open sea. Here the farmers plant rice when the rains come from the mountains in the north, and corn when the sun shines in the east, and again sugarcane when the soothing winds come from the south and sometimes from the west, so that the fields are verdant with vegetation beyond the singing of it every day of the solid year.

"It is true that when the moon was bright in the sky an old man whose age no one could remember – because he was born long, long ago, in the era of the great distress in the land – came down from his mysterious dwelling and went to town where children followed him noisily in the streets and threw stones at him when he would not stop to tell his tales of long ago.

"It is also true he sometimes sat under an ancient mango tree in the plaza and related a story over a cup of red wine or a handful of boiled rice, and the children would scatter attentively in the grass around him, and the men and women would stand silently farther away to hear every word that fell softly from his aged mouth, for there was no telling when he had a bright new tale about the people who had wandered and lived and died in this valley years ago.

"It happens it is also true that I heard this old man tell his tales many a time when I was a little boy. At first he did not notice me in the crowd of children who listened to him, but as time went by he began to see me, until at last he concentrated his stories on me.

" 'I have noticed your attentiveness,' he said to me one day. 'Do you believe these tales?'

" 'I believe them, Apo Lacay,' I said.

" 'But why?' he asked. 'These are merely the tales of an old man who has lived beyond his time. There are others – educated men – who can tell you fascinating stories about what is happening in the world today.'

" 'There is great wisdom in your words,' I said respectfully. 'Besides, I'll go away someday. I would like to remember what kind of people lived here a long time ago.'

" 'You will go to a land far away?' There was a sudden gleam in his eyes, but it vanished suddenly and a deep melancholy spread over his wrinkled face. And he said sadly, 'But you will never return – never come back – to this valley.'

"I could not answer him then, or the day after, or long afterward – not even when I went to that land far away, remembering him.

" 'Everybody dies,' he said that day. 'No man comes home again. No man comes back to bathe in the river of home, to watch the golden grain ripen in the fields, to know the grandeur of the meadowlark on the wing. No man comes back to feel the green loam of the land with his bare feet, to touch the rich soil with his loving hands, to feel the earth move under him as he walks under the familiar skies of home.'

" 'I will come back, Apo Lacay,' I said.

"He looked at me silently and long, and there were tears in his eyes.

" 'Son,' he said at last, touching my head with his fading hands, 'I will go home now.'

"Nervously he reached for his twisted vine cane and walked slowly away. He did not come into town again. Many years passed and we thought he was dead. Then that fateful year, I decided to look up the old man. I went to the mountain and looked for him, shouting in the wind and climbing the tallest trees to see some signs of human presence in the huge caves on the mountainside. At last I found him sitting quietly by a stream.

" 'Good afternoon, Apo Lacay,' I greeted him.

"He stirred, but his face was toward the sun. I looked at his eyes – it came to me that he was blind.

" 'I came to say good-bye,' I said, sitting on the fallen leaves beside him.

" 'It is you, then,' he said, reaching for his cane. 'I thought you had left long ago.'

" 'Now is the time, Apo Lacay,' I said. 'But tell me this first: is it not dangerous to live all by yourself in this wild mountain?'

" 'What is there to fear? The beasts, birds, trees, storms, and tempests – would you be afraid of them? There is nothing to fear in the night, in the dark heart of night. But in the daytime, among men, there is the greatest fear of all.'

" 'Why is that, Apo Lacay?'

" 'In the savage heart of man there dwells the greatest fear of all creation.'

" 'But man has a marvelous mind. He can think, analyze, break apart and put things together.'

"That is the seed of all living fears. The mind. The beasts in the jungle with their ferocious fangs are less dangerous than one man with a cultivated mind in a civilized city. It is the heart that contains the world of truth and beauty. The heart is everything – "

" 'Is that why you tell the kind of stories you told us? To make us laugh because of all these fears?'

" 'Laughter is the beginning of wisdom, because it starts warmly in the heart and goes up to your nourishing mind and spreads throughout your growing body. But real laughter springs from tragedy. The more hilarious the laughter, the more tragic is the tragedy from where it springs, and life is the greatest tragedy of all. That is why laughter is double-edged, cutting both ways, eliciting tears of sorrow and happiness at the same time. It is a weapon for those who know how to use it.'

" 'There is a great truth in what you said. That is why I came to see you. I will leave our country soon, and I would like to remember all your tales of long ago.'

" 'But why? In that land where you are going – will the people give you something to eat while you retell them? Will you not be afraid the children may stone you in the streets of their cities?'

" 'I don't know, Apo Lacay,' I said. 'But this I know: if my retelling your stories will give me a little wisdom of the heart, then I shall have come home again.'

" 'You mean it will be your book as well as mine? Your words as well as my words there in that faraway land, my tales going around to the people of high culture? My tales will not be forgotten at last?'

" 'Yes, Apo Lacay. It will be exactly that. Your book as well as mine.'

"He was silent for a long time. I made a fire by the stream because the day was becoming cold. Then it seemed to me that, watching him lost in thought, he had become a little boy again living all the tales he had told us about a vanished race, listening to the lost cries and agonies of men and women and children in the midst of abject poverty and ruthless tyranny. For that was the time of his child-hood, in the era of great distress and calamity in the land, when the fury of an invading race impaled their hearts on the tragic cross of slavery and ignorance. And that was why they had all become that way: sick in mind and soul, almost devoid of humanity, living like beasts in the jungles of their captivity. And this man who had survived them all, surviving a full century of change, but living now in the first murmurs of twilight and the dawn of reason and enlightenment, was the sole survivor from the cruelty and dehu-manization of man by man, but whose tales were taken for laughter and the foolish words of a lonely man who had lived far beyond his time.

"When I looked at him again, he was already dead. His passing was so natural and quiet that I did not feel any sadness. I dug a grave by the stream and buried him. And the birds sang gloriously around, and the night had come. Then I walked down the mountain to the valley of home. Then sometime afterward I boarded a big boat that took me to a land far away.

"And in that land, writing many years later, I didn't exactly remember which were the words of the old man of the mountain and which were mine. But they were his tales as well as mine, so I hoped I had written a book that really belongs to every one in that valley beautiful beyond the singing of it."

After Dante finished his recollections, nobody said a word for a long time. They all felt the depth of Dante's attachment to his valley, which was the scene of all his books. And even Legaspi, who had not read a single word written by Dante, felt it. For it epitomized man's love for his land, family, and home, and they all felt it when Dante was talking. Their silence was broken by the sound of music drifting to them in the deep twilight. They looked in the direction of the music.

"What is it?" Linda Bie asked.

They all listened seriously. Dabu's face broke with happy recognition, but Legaspi, whose ears knew only the sound of death, frowned foolishly. Even Linda Bie and Dante recognized the music now, and they felt at ease; not that they had expected something calamitous, but because it was so long ago that they had heard such music.

"There is a wedding nearby," Dabu announced. "Somebody is getting married. Were you ever married, Dante?"

"No," Dante said disinterestedly.

"Not even in the United States?"

Dante shook his head.

"You missed something," Dabu said.

"You have never been married yourself," Dante told him.

Everybody laughed.

"You should see these peasants when they get married," Dabu continued. "Thirteen, fourteen, fifteen years old. They want that something unbroken."

Dante was getting bored.

"Why," Dabu went on, "I had a neighbor who married when he was eleven years old. I wonder if he was old enough to procreate. Do you know, Linda Bie?"

"I wouldn't know," Linda Bie said.

"But I know!" Legaspi said.

"The hell you know," Dante told him. "I bet you've never even seen a woman's breast."

"Don't tell me," Legaspi protested.

"What does it look like?" Linda Bie challenged him.

"Well, it is round. It is soft. There is something pinkish on the top."

"Did you ever touch it?"

"No."

"Did you ever put it in your mouth?" Dante asked him.

Legaspi looked at him with confusion. "Are you supposed to put it in your mouth?"

They laughed at Legaspi. Their laughter was cut short by the sudden sound of music. Simultaneously they turned in the direction of the music and listened for a moment.

Then Linda Bie said, "What is it?"

"Don't you recognize it?" Dabu asked him.

Linda Bie shook his head.

"Of course you don't," Dabu said. "You were a city man, and that kind of music is strange to you. You are listening to a village wedding music."

Linda Bie seemed relieved.

"Didn't you say we are two hours ahead of schedule?" Legaspi said.

Dabu nodded.

"Why don't we join the wedding and dance with the girls for ten minutes?" Legaspi suggested.

"That is a good idea," Linda Bie said.

Dabu was silent. The he said, "We have to be careful, though."

"Do they know you around here, Dabu?" Dante asked.

"No."

"Ten minutes is all right if we are careful," Dante said.

"Let's go by twos then," Dabu agreed. "I will give you the signal when we make the exit. Go ahead with Legaspi, Linda Bie. Dante will come with me."

"Is it far?" Dante asked.

"Half a kilometer away is my guess," Dabu said. "We will leave our knapsacks here, but not our guns."

They began hiding their knapsacks in the bushes, covering them with grass and leaves. And they felt young and excited again, for this was their first time to see what they had all known years ago.

They knew they were risking their lives and mission, but their blood was young and alive and pounding in their veins. Legaspi was the most excited of all, because this was his first attendance at a wedding; and as he worked to hide his knapsack, he wondered if he would be clumsy with the girls. Somehow the gun under his shirt had given him courage. But what kind of courage? He was confused.

"Are you ready?" Dabu asked Linda Bie and Legaspi.

"I am ready," Linda Bie said.

"Go this way," Dabu told them, pointing to a path crossing the river and up the embankment. "Just keep following the music. It is not far. We will be right behind you."

Linda Bie and Legaspi started to go. Dabu and Dante watched them cross the river and climb up the embankment. When they had disappeared behind the trees, Dabu looked westward to the setting sun.

"It will be dark in a few minutes," he said. "I hope they know what to do."

"I think they do," Dante assured him.

"Let's go, Dante," Dabu said finally.

They followed a path across the river and climbed up the embankment. When they reached the trees, night had fallen. They walked slowly in the shadows, following the music, which was now becoming louder. They stopped when they reached the edge of the yard where the wedding was going on. They saw Linda Bie and Legaspi walk into the crowd and disappear. Then they nodded to each other and entered the yard.

A man looked at them surreptitiously when they mingled with the crowd. They walked straight to the dancing pavilion and stood in a corner, appraising the place in one sweeping glance. Then they saw Linda Bie and Legaspi in another corner doing the same thing. But the young men and women in the pavilion seemed unaware of their presence. They watched the dance in progress and nodded their heads silently. When the musicians stopped for a few minutes to select another number, Dabu saw a girl he wanted to dance with. It was the bride, all dressed in white, sitting beside an old woman, who was probably her mother. But when the music started again, Linda Bie was ahead of him. He touched Dante and made a beeline to another prospect, who was not as beautiful as the bride. He was not disappointed; the girl leaped to his arms before he could say something to her. And then they were dancing, close, almost cheek to cheek; and it was when they had gone around the pavilion that Dabu looked around to see his companions. They were all dancing. Legaspi had chosen a fifteen-year-old girl, while Dante picked a woman of about his age or older, for her hair was all white with age. But she was not bad looking; she had more of it than the young girls. And Dabu almost laughed. They looked at each other across the dance floor, and by silent agreement they started dancing toward each other, toward the center of the pavilion; and when they were crowded in the center, touching elbows, they all felt good. Dabu and Linda Bie exchanged partners in silence, and Dante and Legaspi did the same thing. Dabu almost howled when he saw Dante dancing with the young girl, he seemed out of place; the girl was almost half his size. Then the music stopped, and they escorted their partners to their seats. They stood awhile beside their partners, looking across space. When the music started again, Dabu grabbed the bride; when he turned around he saw Linda Bie's disappointed face. Linda Bie stopped when Dabu took the bride; when he turned around all the girls and women were taken, except a young peasant girl who was barefoot. Linda Bie danced toward her and bowed, but the girl seemed reluctant or terrified. When Linda Bie bowed for the second time, she slowly got up and gave her hands. Then they were dancing.

They were watching each other at every turn. Dabu was about to say something to the bride when he noticed something unusual. The groom and several men had come into the pavilion and were watching him. They had not noticed that he saw them because of the crowd around him. He murmured his apology to the bride and took her back to the seat, where he murmured his apology once more and walked to the door. As soon as he was outside, he walked leisurely through the crowd and went to the dark side of the yard. He stood against the fence and watched the door of the pavilion, waiting for his companions. The groom and two husky men appeared at the door searching for Dabu in the crowd, but returned to the pavilion when they could not locate him. Then he saw Dante coming out and walking straight to the darkness where Dabu was waiting. Then he saw Linda Bie and Legaspi coming out the other door, followed by the groom and the two husky men. When they stopped Linda Bie and Legaspi, Dabu's heart leaped; and he leaped automatically, crawling along the darkness of the fence, closer to his companions. And as he crawled, he noticed that Dante had done the same thing, taking the other fence, crawling closer to his companions. Dante quickly looked across the yard through the crowd to see if Dabu was there, for it was their usual tactic when they were in a crowd to surround it. Dante saw him.

Linda Bie was doing the talking. The groom seemed to be belligerent. The three men had not noticed it, but Legaspi had stepped aside three paces, so that the men were between him and Linda Bie. It was a perfect angle if the four of them suddenly started shooting. They had not noticed that Legaspi had looked quickly on both sides of the fence and saw Dante and Dabu watching the whole performance. What Dabu hated most was the killing, if there had to be some action. He had enjoyed himself in the dancing pavilion, and he hated to smear the memory with blood. The same thought was in the minds of his companions, the same sickening regret if there had to be some killing. That was why Linda Bie was trying to explain the situation pacifically, while Legaspi remained silent, watching, waiting.

The groom suddenly struck Linda Bie with his fist. Linda Bie staggered backward, and as he did so, the two husky men fell on him. Legaspi held himself, and so with Dante and Dabu. But when one of the husky men pulled a knife to strike Linda Bie, Legaspi pulled his gun, and at the same time Dabu and Dante leaped upon the crowd. Three shots rang out all at once, and the groom and the two men fell on the ground. It was all done so quickly that before the people realized what had happened, the four of them were already running in the darkness toward the river where they had hidden their knapsacks. They jumped down the embankment of the river and dashed to their rendezvous, where they grabbed their knapsacks in silence and started running away from the village, down the river and through the wild entanglements. When they had gone a kilometer, they stopped running and looked at each other. But they could not say anything. So they walked on silently, knowing they were safe.

"Breathe no word about this incident," Dabu told his companions.

They nodded their heads in silence.

## CHAPTER SIXTEEN

**H**assim and his companions reached the edge of the town a few minutes before ten o'clock. They stopped in the open field to locate their rendezvous, for it was a new territory to them. Hassim knew the location of the rendezvous on the map, but the newness of the place and the time of night made him unsure what side of the town they were approaching. When the moon came up, and after a quick mental calculation, he realized that they were on the right side of the town.

The silent sky was lucid with sharp and pointed stars, and already the night was cooling off with a slight breeze that was creeping leisurely across the fields. Crickets were chirping gaily in their hidden little crevices, frogs were croaking somewhere in the night; and Hassim wondered if there was a pond nearby, where frogs were bound to habitate before the rainy seasons came. The grass seemed wiry and dying in the moonlight, although it was already past the middle of December, when the midnight dews fell on the waiting earth to give sustenance to growing and living things.

Hassim crouched low to the ground, his chin touching the grass, to see the shadowline of the mango grove, which was their rendezvous. He saw it in the distance, about two kilometers away. He knew it was the mango grove because of the gnarled shadows of the stout branches. He got up and pointed a finger in the direction of their destination for the information of his companions.

Old Bio nodded and looked at Mameng, who took Hassim's information in silence. And in silence they walked on toward their destination, becoming aware of the fact that they were hungry and tired. They had not touched food all day for fear that Legaspi, who was the custodian of the food sack, would be delayed with his companions. They had not rested on the way except when they talked to the old cripple in the village near their last rendezvous. They had walked ten hours straight without rest and food and water, because Hassim had forgotten to take one of the water bags from either Linda Bie or Dabu. But they were nearing their destination, and in another fifteen minutes they would know if the others had arrived before them.

When they approached the mango grove, Hassim realized that there were more trees than indicated on the map. There were more than twenty trees in the grove, from Hassim's calculation at a glance, covering an area of about two hectares. It was a safe temporary hideout, even if there would be some unavoidable action. With the inevitable edging his mind, Hassim studied the position of the grove and its relation to the town and the open fields. And his heart faltered: if it happened, they would have to fight it out among the trees. They would have to do it to the last man, and when they seemed doomed that last man would have to make a desperate getaway and go on alone with the mission.

And then? Hassim thought as he walked.

But it was then that they entered the shadows of the trees. They stood beside a huge tree trunk in silence. They listened to any unfamiliar noise under the trees. Then Hassim took the flashlight from his knapsack and made the signal: two short flashes, and darkness. A quick flash of light came between the trees, meaning –

*Who?*

Hassim answered it: two short flashes, and darkness.

And the answer came: two short flashes, and darkness.

Hassim nodded to Old Bio and Mameng. It was the second time that Old Bio had seen the signal, but Hassim had never explained it to him.

They walked under the trees toward the source of the other light. The dry leaves made a crunching noise under their feet, and no matter how stealthily they walked, there seemed to be hundreds of people under the trees. They walked abreast, about three feet apart, looking to the left and right. But as they approached the spot where the other light had flashed momentarily, the silence seemed to increase in depth.

Mameng sighed, walking between Hassim and Old Bio, her gun in her hand like the guns of her companions. How many times had she been trapped in a heartbreaking anticipation such as this, she could not remember now. She could not even remember when it began; she knew only that it had started years ago, a long, long way back. And where would it end now?

Old Bio was more complaisant to his fate. Had he not known more than a half century ago the meaning of silence? Had he not encountered nights such as this many times long before his companions were born? And so it seemed to him, walking quietly to the left of Mameng, that to live a hundred years or a day, from this moment on, did not mean much anymore. What really meant something to him was no longer the length of his life on this earth, for he had lived a long time already, but how heroically and magnificently he would live that time. He knew that if the end had to come, it had to come; and it would come to him heroically and even magnificently. But if it would not come now, it would come sometime; and he would meet it heroically and magnificently. The time and place did not mean much, not anymore. But how to meet it was the meaning of his existence now. He cocked his gun in readiness and walked on, smiling with bliss because he had found the meaning of living.

Hassim had also found the meaning of living, but it was entirely different from old Bio's viewpoint. He was the epitome of life defying death. Life, to him, should be lived to the very end of its existence, for each individual, and for a tribe or a nation, each giving equally to each, thus ensuring a longevity commensurate with the innate timber and capacity of every person. So Hassim did not want death for himself or for anyone, because it meant to him the final backdrop of a tremendous play where every person could participate unselfishly, gloriously. Death was nil, a noneness, a nothingness. It did not exist, although its reality and immediacy were everywhere around him. The only comprehensible truth was life fully lived, without compromises or vacillations, and he would like it to be known and available to everyone. He could not smile like Old Bio because he could not accept death the way the old man did, which was a pessimistic acceptance of the end of one's life. But Hassim could only hack away at death and its manifold prefigurations with a determined fierceness, believing strongly in life for himself and for everyone, for all living things on the earth. So he walked on courageously, hugging that imperishable belief close to his soul.

In the night the noise came quietly, from under the trees, so near them. But it was loud enough for them to know a presence in the night. Of what? Hassim could hear the old man sighing, knowing that he was accepting what was inevitable, be it the provocation of his pessimism or a retreat from it. He wanted to know what Mameng felt, but the flutter of any eyelid would beleaguer his concentration on the source of the other light. There could have been other nights, he knew, when he would have sat under a tree and talked to Mameng about plants and animals and birds and other things that belonged to a world of peace. Now it seemed strange to him, as his cautious feet crept slowly on the dry leaves, that that time was pushed away indefinitely, perhaps forever. And he groaned inwardly as he realized that that was probably the sad truth of all their living.

Then the light came on again.

*Who?*

Hassim answered it. The other light streaked the darkness. He jerked his head quickly to his companions.

"Something is wrong," he whispered.

"Is that not our signal?" Old Bio asked.

"It is, old one. But something is wrong."

Old Bio did not answer for a moment, then he said, "Shall we spread around them?"

"It's no use. They are watching us."

"Do you think that is Dabu?" Mameng said.

"Yes," Hassim said. "Stay here, and don't move until I give you the signal. I will approach them alone."

Hassim stepped forward, while Old Bio and Mameng walked behind a tree. They watched Hassim crouching low about five feet away from them, then he disappeared in the thick darkness. And Hassim, walking straight to where the other light had flashed, knew that the moment was charged with many types of loyalties. There was the loyalty to himself, if he surrendered all that he held honorable and noble; and in doing that, he would live a lonely and meaningless life. There was the loyalty to his companions, and if he did not surrender that, all that he held honorable and noble would remain behind in the bright sky of his life, because he would have to surrender himself, he would have to die. And there was the loyalty to the cause, which transcended even the loyalty to himself and his companions, transcending everything that he had known, even the world. Which loyalty would he sacrifice now?

"Halt!" The command rang out in the night.

Hassim stopped, but the gun was still in his hand. Then he saw them in the darkness approaching him, two menacing shadows detaching themselves from the body of the night. He saw them coming toward him, and at that moment he seemed to feel as if a wide abyss had opened before him, and that there was no alternative but to plunge into it. Yet the hand with the gun was steady, for somewhere in his consciousness was the primal instinct to preserve himself, through irrationally, unreasonably. He waited in agony.

"Hassim?" It was Dabu's voice.

Hassim winced. "Yes."

They came to him, Dabu and Linda Bie. What was the meaning of the danger signal? Hassim wanted to know, but he controlled himself.

"Are you safe?" Dabu asked.

"Quite safe."

"The other two?"

"Safe," Hassim said. "What is wrong?"

"I will show you."

"Wait. I will make a signal for the two to come." And he did, flashing the light in the direction of Old Bio and Mameng. Then he turned back to Dabu and Linda Bie. He said, "Have you been here long?"

"An hour."

Hassim kept silent. When Old Bio and Mameng were with them, Dabu led the way. Linda Bie followed behind them. They had walked a few yards when Hassim noticed the outlines of our men in the darkness. He immediately recognized Dante and Legaspi, but the other two men were unknown to him. When at last they reached them, Dabu clicked his flashlight and focused it on the faces of the two unknown men, one after the other; first the old man, then the young man, and back to the old man.

Hassim studied their faces: the old man was about fifty-five, the young man was perhaps thirty. They were both grave and tired and lean.

"They are outlaws," Dabu explained. "We have disarmed them, but the decision is yours."

Hassim slowly wiped his brow. Then he said, "Return their firearms."

Dante and Legaspi had the guns, but they hesitated to surrender them. There was an awkward silence, deep as an abandoned well.

"Return their firearms," Hassim repeated.

Dante and Legaspi returned them without comment, but in the dark Hassim felt the tension. He himself had his gun still in his hand, and he was watching the men retrieve their guns. But somehow he knew that the father and son would not be belligerent, for it would be foolish if they showed any resistance.

"Where did you find them?" Hassim asked.

"Here," Dabu said. "Lucky we did not start shooting, we had taken them unaware. They were sleeping like babies."

"We were tired," the old man offered to explain. "Besides, we will not harm our own kind."

"My father and I, we are the only ones left in our family," the son said.

"They took my daughter away," said the father. "They killed my wife and one son."

"Who are they?"

"The constabulary."

Old Bio grunted, and they all turned toward him.

"Where did you come from?" Hassim continued the interrogation.

"A town thirty kilometers from here," said the father. "To the west, near the sea."

"You have never come here before?"

"No."

"Why did you come here?"

"It is the nearest exit. We had to fight our way across the open field this side of our town."

"They will probably follow you here."

"It was already dark when the fighting started. We lost them in the night."

"What have you done?"

"Look here," the son intervened. "Who are you that you ask so many questions?"

"It is all right, son," said the father. "Let them ask us questions. We will tell the truth because we will stand or fall by the truth."

"If you say so, Father."

"Yes," said the father. Then he said to Hassim, "We killed a man during the occupation."

"Why?"

"This man was working with the Japanese, pointing out those families who had relatives hiding in the hills. He was a very dangerous man, so we had to kill him. I personally did the killing. Now this dead man's brother is the mayor of our town, because he has the support of the present national government. The president himself came from Manila and appointed him to office. The first move he did was a reprisal against my family, for the death of his brother. He brought the local police and a platoon of constabulary men to my house. That was this morning. We killed seven of them, but they got two of us. They took my daughter away."

There was a sob in the man's voice. Old Bio murmured something, and they turned to him again.

"They took my granddaughter too," he said. "Only she is dead now."

"That is their code of honor," Hassim said to the father. "They are not human beings anymore."

"If only they were not our own countrymen," said the son with regret.

"There are no longer national and geographical boundaries," Hassim explained. "There is no longer 'my country' or 'My countrymen,' because these barriers have been scaled. There is only 'my fellow workers' now, and it is being used everywhere in the world by those who understand that we have a common enemy."

"I don't understand," said the father. "But we will go back."

"We will go back," the son repeated.

Hassim could not see their faces, but he knew even in the darkness that there was a fierceness in their eyes. He knew they would go back and take revenge against the mayor. He had seen many of these people who took the law into their own hands, blinded by grief. They lacked a wide scope of comprehension: they translated the struggle against the common enemy from family losses. And he knew that he could not dissuade them from acting irrationally, independently, blindly. Even if he could point out that there was a better way, a large fight in which they could participate toward a bigger freedom for all, he knew that they would bring with them into the underground their individualistic, even anarchistic, attitude toward the enemy.

But he said, "There is a way of achieving a better end."

"There is no other way," said the father.

"Have you heard of the underground?"

"Yes. But it is too far away. Besides, we don't know who they are."

"Seek it out," Hassim said. "The underground has many members everywhere, perhaps they are even in your hometown. If you go back, I suggest that you look for them. Make an alliance with them, and obey orders."

"Is the underground widespread then?"

"It is."

"Then we will go back. And we will look for underground members, after we are done with the mayor."

"Kill him?"

"Yes."

"What is there to be gained?"

"He must pay for his crimes."

"And be criminals yourselves?"

"They forced us into criminality."

"You kill this man, and another, and another. You can't kill thousands of people to avenge your family. You don't have enough time for it, not counting the energy and luck."

"What is there left for us to do?" the son said.

"Perhaps you have never seen your family butchered like pigs?" the father asked.

Hassim wanted to strike the man, but he said calmly, "That is precisely why I am advising you to join the underground, because it has a long-range program toward the liberation of our people from the local and national lackeys of the landlords and the rich, who in turn are lackeys of foreigners who want to exploit our people into slavery. I have seen many people die, including my whole family. There are two of you left, but I am the only one. And the case is true with practically everybody here."

There was silence for a moment. Then the father said, "I am sorry to hear that. We are not the only ones then?"

"You are not. Everywhere in our country are people like you, people whose families were murdered or scattered in the hills. We are suffering together."

"We have heard of it," said the son.

"Are you of the underground then?" asked the father.

"Yes."

"We would like to know more about it."

"You will," Hassim said. "I am on an errand right now, but the others will stay here and explain the work of the underground to you and your son."

Dabu moved to Hassim's side. Hassim felt Linda Bie's hand.

"This is your task," he said.

"I will take care of it," Linda Bie said.

"You stand by," Hassim said to the others.

They nodded in silence.

"Keep them here until we come back," Hassim ordered. Then he said to Dabu, "Let us go."

They unstrapped their knapsacks and gave them to the old man.

"You know the signal, old one?" Hassim asked Old Bio.

"Yes."

"Watch for it."

"I will."

"We will not stay long."

They watched them walking side by side under the trees. When they were still in the grove, Hassim looked up once and saw the bright moon shining between the gnarled branches of the trees. He saw a cluster of pointed stars around the moon, and the whole sky seemed to be swinging into space. He felt light; even buoyant, as he walked beside Dabu. It seemed strange that on a night like this there seemed to be a song of joy in his heart.

But Dabu was grave, for he was approaching his home. He had not seen his family for five years, since the beginning of the war when he joined the regular army. It seemed too long ago now, because he was only eighteen when he went away. He felt his hand in the darkness, and an agonizing sob broke out of his heart. For he was touching the hand that had killed many men, the hand that was smeared with the blood of dying men.

What happened to that clean little boy? he thought. Why did they drive me into killing? Once when I was growing up I wanted to own a little farm and then perhaps get married. But what happened to it all? And Rosalia – where is she now? Goddamn them who have forced me to kill! I can never go back now, back to cleanliness without thinking of the past, without being haunted by the ghosts of the past. No more. Where is the end?

When they came out of the mango grove, they stopped and looked toward the town. Most of the houses were still burning with light, but some were already in darkness. They saw the gray roof of the town house glimmering in the moonlight, and a light was showing through one of the upper windows. The church across the street was dark, except the belfry where a lantern was shining.

Then they walked on.

"The same old town," Dabu said. "No change except a few deaths, marriages, births, and perhaps an adultery here and there."

"Quite a town," Hassim said.

## CHAPTER SEVENTEEN

. . . . . . . . . . . . . . . . . . . . . . . . . . . . . . . . . . . .

They walked in silence across the wide-open fields and the drying river. When they entered the town, Dabu began to talk. The sensation of coming home aroused in him a volubility that was unnatural; memories moved in concentric circles in his mind, shifting and reshifting, crowding in and out from the mist of the past until he was able to find a common thread in his life to string them together and examine each item with a new perspective.

Hassim listened eagerly, for every homecoming of his companions was also his to share, if only to feel the pulse of everyone when they returned to their most cherished places in the world. He had come home with them a hundred times in the course of five years, and each homecoming had given him a solid understanding of what home and family stood for, especially when you had been away for a long time. The home assumed a significance beyond its natural proportion, and cherished inch by inch in remembrance, it arose in the mind like a beacon stabbing the darkness of night with a brilliance such as you never saw before, illuminating your prodigal path homeward. And family meant more than home, for it consisted of familiar faces and voices, all moving in a world that was your childhood. Yet home and family were always coexistent, inseparable and interdependent, each giving character and meaning to the other.

Yes, that was the indestructible truth.

"I hope they are all well," Hassim commented.

"I hope so too," Dabu said.

"How many are you?"

"Three. I am the only child."

"At least there are less mouths to feed."

"That is surely one way of looking at it. But my father wanted several sons to help him on the farm. He was greatly disappointed when the midwife told him the sad truth when I was born. He kept trying with his manhood and rosaries for years, but he finally gave up and took the midwife's words as gospel truth. So he began to concentrate on me, hoping to put the strength of his unborn sons in me. He was a stubborn man. But I was not much help to him because the war came sooner than he had expected and nipped me off the family stem."

Hassim knew he had succeeded in surceasing Dabu's grave mood. "He will be proud of you now," he said.

"Not my old man."

"Is he that tough?"

"Tough? He is made of iron."

"I wouldn't want him for a father. I want the easy kind, like my own father."

"The iron hand helps sometimes, especially when you are naughty like this boy. As I told you before, I used to steal mangoes from that grove behind us. Wouldn't you need an iron hand like my father's for that kind of mischief?"

Yes, Hassim had succeeded in his purpose pretty easily. "You are right," he said.

"Did you ever steal anything?"

"Who did not?"

"I heard some men say there are honest politicians."

"And honest rich men?"

"Why, yes."

"They will claim your ass if they know there is any value on it."

Dabu laughed suddenly, uproariously. It was his first time to hear Hassim talk like that, and he was genuinely tickled to death. He himself had used such language beyond Hassim's ears, but to hear it from him made him guiltily happy.

Then they were both laughing.

They were approaching the plaza now. They stopped and looked in the direction of the *presidencia*, on the other side of the plaza. They could see two policemen in the hall sitting on a bench, but were not sure whether they were drinking or playing cards. Outside the night was too quiet, even the church across the street, where there had always been someone going in and out the open door. There was no one in sight, although some of the houses around the plaza were still blazing with light.

They walked on into the plaza, their canvas shoes sliding softly on the dewy grass.

"What, no wedding?" Hassim asked.

"Not even a wake," Dabu said.

"Or birthing."

"I will bet you the whole sky there is some fornication some-where."

"I will bet you the whole earth it is in the mayor's house."

"I will bet you the whole ocean it is in the police chief's house."

"I will bet you the whole wind it is in the judge's house."

"I will bet you the whole dark night it is in many houses."

They laughed again.

"I will bet you the skin of my teeth the mayor's wife is an adulteress."

"I will bet you the lint in my belly the chief is a cuckold."

"I will bet you my eyeballs the judge has several mistresses."

"I will bet you my ass balls there are several adulteries and cuckholdries in this town."

They laughed hysterically.

They reached the marble monument in the plaza and stopped to look at it.

"Who is it?" Hassim asked.

"Rizal," Dabu said, suddenly remembering that he used to climb the monument as a little boy. "I did not know he is everywhere until I joined the army. In plazas, paper money, stamps, beers, and whiskeys."

"He is probably turning in his grave now."

"Lucky he did not have any grave. What happened to his body?"

"The Spaniards probably fed it to the dogs."

"That is a hell of a way to kiss the world good-bye."

"He probably thought the world is full of gentlemen."

"Is it true he was a heretic?"

"I read it in one of his books that insurgency has the condonement of God."

"And so he was godded."

"Well, there is always a Rizal monument to build when the politicians run out of tricks during elections."

"Amen."

What was the meaning of their sudden bantering? Was it a premonition of some tragedy?

Hassim pondered about it silently as they walked away from the Rizal marble monument. He felt that underneath Dabu's merriment was an artificiality, quite unlike the genuineness of his laughter in other places. Like that night when he first contacted his companions with Old Bio on the hills, when he and Legaspi tried to put something over on the old man. And many other times that stretched back to the breakup of the regular army, and Dabu joined the underground then with his easy laughter. Hassim realized, however, that laughter belonged to the young and healthy; and Dabu was only eighteen then, and too healthy to be carrying a loaded gun among unarmed people.

But tonight?

Hassim cast a sidelong glance at Dabu. His face was still creased with the fading shadows and lines of laughter. He felt pleased somehow, knowing that Dabu enjoyed his joke. Well, would it hurt if he went on with this mood?

"Did I ever tell you that I grew up in Tondo, the slum district of Manila?" Hassim said.

"You do not say much about your past," Dabu commented.

"I was born in the Bicol provinces."

"I thought you were Tagalog because you speak the language perfectly."

"I didn't know you are Ilocano either, because you speak good Pangasinan."

"Well, Dante is not Pampangenio. He speaks Pampango fluently."

"Do you know where he came from?"

"You will soon know. But that is our advantage: we speak most of the important languages in the islands. Look at Linda Bie: you wouldn't know he is a Visayan."

"I know he seldom uses the Visayan language, but I know he is a Visayan."

"Very few speak Visayan, that is why. Linda Bie is very fluent in Spanish."

"I know. The sons of the middle class have Spanish education."

"Spanish is what they speak at home, and some Filipino languages to their servants."

"You were going to tell me about Tondo." Dabu said.

"Yes. Well, we had a little house on Calle Fernandez. I was fifteen when I became aware of the great change in me. At night I used to stand by the window smoking cigarettes. I stood there for hours thinking why we left the province where there were fields and rivers and hills. In Tondo there were no such things; there was squalor, misery, vice, and unemployment. But those were beautiful nights, beautiful in an aching way. It was the beginning of February and the nights were really beautiful. I could see the glorious

reflection of the bay in the silver sheen of the sky. I could see the bright lights glimmering tantalizingly, where the rich people lived. Those were so beautiful they seemed unreal, out of a storybook. It was like a huge dream, with so many bottomless canyons floating in space and disappearing at the foot of a scintillating rainbow, at the end of one's fondest dream. And there was a strange lovely voice calling, that seemed far away, behind a tumbling roller on the sea. And I was desperately fighting to find where it came from, and what for, and why it stayed on at the edge of night. And there were tiny bells, far off, faint, coming closer to me.

"Yes, I used to stand by the window looking out into the street. There was a soothing breeze from the bay that came into my room like the tenuous fingers of a girl found only in a dream. In the farming towns skirting Manila, the lowland rice lay golden in the bright moonlight. I could smell the enchanting fragrance of the ripening grain on the back of the wind from the mountains that crept across the rolling fields into the city. Not far from the house was a wedding in progress. I could tell it from the music and the laughter of the men and the shrill cries of the children.

"I used to stand by the window watching the people pass by. It was like broad daylight. I saw girls look up when they reached the periphery of light streaming from my room like a steel blade into the street below. I saw a particularly good-looking girl in a yellow dress, and boldly made the sign. She was undecided for a moment, looking swiftly down the street and back to my window, then walked on with that telltale sway of the fanny that street whores have in common.

"But there is really nothing romantic in a city, especially if you live in the slum district. Especially in Manila. Manila is a very old city, perhaps as old as any old city in the world. It was called Maynila by our pagan ancestors, but the Spanish conquistadores changed it to the present spelling. In Manila there are still curious relics from the past. In the crowded markets you can still hear remnants of languages left by venturesome travelers who had fought their way across the uncharted seas in lost times. But now these are only for the copious specialists and uninitiated tourists who discover with sadness that people everywhere also blow their noses and break wind like anybody else.

"There is nothing mysterious in it, either. Perhaps there is a little intrigue that itches in the curious mind like a sickening unfulfilled sexual desire. You understand, I read Jose Rizal and understand how lonely he must have been walking unfamiliar European streets, or seeing the striking miners in France and Belgium, or the unemployed mill workers in Manchester and London. But he was a naturally lonely man, and the mad rush of a commercial world was too terrifying to him. This is one kind of loneliness. There is another: when you are in the midst of people and you feel detached and far away from them all. Dante had this kind of loneliness in America, and although he has never spoken about it, the loneliness has followed him even to our own land. I grew up in the slums of Manila, but you can never be lonely in Tondo. The section where I grew up was always bursting with activity, and there is no room for loneliness, not the physical kind anyway. But there is a wide room for spiritual loneliness, the kind that eats you away. For example, there is wide room for robbing people of their hard-earned money when night falls without being stricken by the pangs of conscience. And there is also room for murder. When I remember the conscienceless robbing and murdering, I feel a terrifying loneliness within me and a mental impotence sets in my mind. But it is not a sentimental loneliness. It is not the desire to return home, to see family and friends once again. It is the kind of loneliness that drives a man to seek out among his fellow men a deep and lasting fellowship. Perhaps this was what Rizal wanted to find in his worldwide travels, but he lived in a mad and swirling world. If this was so, then it is to the loss of our heritage that he did not seek out a broader fellowship outside his class, seek out above all an understanding of the problems and aspirations of the workers wherever he went. He could not see the challenge of a chauvinistic society except from a scientific viewpoint.

"So I used to look out the window watching the good-looking girls pass by. Later, however, it would have been another story. I would not have stood there foolishly making futile signs. I would have done something very practical. Was it really long ago? Seven years, perhaps? I was already fifteen – so suddenly? What happened to the preceding years? Oh, I was paralyzed with remorse. I was young once in a roaring city and played in the crowded streets with boys and girls of my own age. When the girls walked by with their come-and-get-it swagger; we boys blushed with extreme innocence. But in the dark alley, when one of us gathered enough courage, we grabbed the girls and roughly mussed them up. Nothing serious, of course. Just kissing wetly and fumbling about them, trembling at the slightest touch of their sprouting adolescent breasts. And then we would run furiously down the street, hiding in the protective privacy of our rooms. But later, in the first flush of youth, there were no longer stupid fumblings and frustrated desires. The approach had become methodical. It was studied. There was only the fear of pregnancy, the poignant fear of involvement, and most fearful of all – marriage. But there were always the quack doctors, the sly ones who worked in great secrecy, and the miscarriages and abortions and bloody deaths were plentiful. But the girls loved. They loved to be loved. And some of them loved children too. Those were the unfortunate ones. Or were they? Then suddenly – was it before or during the war? – it did not matter anymore. No overtures were necessary. Practically nothing anyway. We laid them. It did not matter anymore. It was all the same then. They were all the same then. A dirty world had made us all that way."

Hassim sighed deeply and looked at Dabu, who was walking with his head down.

"But in that small house in Tondo, I used to stand by the window watching the good-looking girls pass by, Hassim continued. "There were the usual noises of men in the neighborhood loving, and the women cackling in their rusty beds. Standing there I thought of the day when the war came. There was a strong wind that rolled down the mountains and swept across the plains. It rushed madly across the face of the land and broke through other mountains and finally disappeared in the swirling sea.

"Then the rumor came that the war had ended. But nobody knew for sure that it had really ended. There was still some fighting up north, on the scarred hills and in the deserted villages. There were guerrillas who had no direct contact with the army of liberation. And in the south, where towns stretched out thickly along devastated beaches, the planes were still dropping bombs. The bombing seemed to increase by the hour. You could see the leaping red flames licking the black sky. You could hear the thatched huts crumbling and the terror of the people fleeing in the fiery darkness.

"The sky was clear, and a gentle wind came from the sea. Hungry birds scattered from fallen trees and swarmed hungrily at the rims of flooded fields, picking up worms and seeds floating on the water. Starving ants fought savagely on masses of leaves floating down streams and rivers.

"And so, finally, the rumor became a reality. The war had indeed ended, and the season of heavy rains came and passed. The sun burst forth gloriously and stood clearly on the earth. The machines of destruction had stopped, and for a while there was silence in the hills, and some of the guerrillas went back to their towns and villages. You could hear the pitiful noise of the living and see the sorrowful tears of the lonely crying over their dead.

"The terms of surrender were signed and released to the world. Peace had come at last to the beleaguered islands, and soldiers began marching wearily on muddy roads and ruined fields. In Manila you could see the politicians carrying bulging briefcases and darting furtively into dark buildings, and the people stood in lengthening lines waiting for immediate medical care and food and shelter.

"And dead comrades were rotting in forgotten hills and unknown fields. Others were drinking heavily in cynicism: the same corrupt politicians were in power again. These comrades were confused: they did not know what they had fought for. And many were sick. And more returned home disillusioned and became complete strangers in their own country. Some went into banditry: these were the dangerous ones. And there were the bitter ones, the angry ones, the lost ones. And some trekked back to battlefields where they had fought looking for the fragments of their lives and broken pieces of their ambitions."

Hassim stopped again and looked at Dabu.

"Where is the peace?" he asked. "The real freedom? The equality among men? The democratic ideal?

"That was the kind of loneliness that filled me when I was standing by the window of our house in Tondo. I had gone home to see my family, after the fighting. But a panic seized me. I felt its steely fingers clutching me inside, pulling me away. I felt myself falling, and my impotence was so great that a tearless sob of desperation choked me. A surging wave of darkness reached out for me, leaping like a flash of lightning to enfold me forever. And in one frantic movement my hand went to my throat: the effort seemed so powerful that my whole body shook, releasing the loneliness slowly until I was all spent and still.

"When I looked out the window again the bright moonlight was in the trees. The earth-born magnificence of the surrounding landscape opened up a new field of hope for me. It filled me with an intense desire to go out and seek someone who could understand me. I wanted to go back in memory to the innocent years and start a new life with promises. Yes, it was the time of fecundating earth and oranges in bloom. I could smell the blossoms drifting in the air, and it made me feel good.

"I went out of the house and walked down the alley. It was truly a beautiful night, fragrant with flowering plants and cool with the falling dew.

"I walked all night to the hills, where I found the answer to my loneliness among new comrades. I have been there since, Dabu."

It was then that they reached the gate. They looked at the house where a faint light was showing through the small kitchen window.

"I am glad you told me that story before we go into the house," Dabu said. "I have learned a lot during these last few minutes. I have learned more from it than the fighting we have had together against the enemy. Now I know what to say."

"I am glad you did." It was really what Hassim wanted to do, for his premonition of tragedy was so strong that he had to tell it to Dabu to fortify him. "I am glad you did," he repeated.

"Let us go in now," Dabu said.

. . . . . . . . . . . . . . . . . . . . . . . . . . . . . . . . . . . . . . . . .

**D**abu climbed up the polished wooden ladder. Hassim followed close behind him. They paused at the narrow landing to locate the source of the light, which was so faint that writhing blades of the moonlight, penetrating through the decaying grass walls and roof, almost absorbed it in their lucidity. The light came from behind a huge hand-woven cotton blanket of crude design hanging on a rope in the center of the house. There seemed to be nobody home; the only sound was weird, elicited by the tiny feet of mice scampering in the gray darkness of the kitchen, where unwashed clay pots and earthen bowls were strewn profusely on the bamboo floor.

Dabu and Hassim looked at each other in silence. Then Dabu pointed to the hanging blanket, and together they approached it quietly. Dabu lifted the edge of the blanket with his left hand so that Hassim, who was standing on his right, could see what was behind it.

And behind it was an old woman kneeling on a reed mat, her back toward them. She was kneeling before three *molave** statuaries, her cracked lips moving soundlessly. Her legs were neatly folded side by side, but the arches of her bare dark feet were black with dried mud. Her long hair was gray and disheveled. The rags on her bony body were so torn that she was very near to nudity. There was a nauseating odor in the house.

Dabu's heart leaped wildly, and there was a streak of anguish across his face. For even in that awkward position, he knew that it was his mother. He would know her anywhere, even in the darkness of night. The smooth black hair that he well remembered had turned gray and untidy in his absence. The once fastidious woman had become a scarecrow, a beggar of life, a shadow of all that Dabu had emulated in the past.

Call on the angels too, Dabu. Once you believed in their righ-

*A hardwood tree found in the Philippines.

teousness, and now you must believe in them again. For again you are a little boy, innocent to all the world. Call them: because of their righteousness, which you believed in once, they will give you a pair of wings to rise above the terror and ugliness and hate of this world. There in their infinity they will give you a heart so big it could contain all the beauty and truth that are left in man. Call the angels, Dabu . . .

And call the spirits, Dabu. For wherever they are, they will hear your call. For the cross of life that you will have to carry until death is their burden, if you call to them now, if you plead guilty to all that you have done to give yourself freedom. Call them now: there are hundreds of them, and they are everywhere in the land. Call the spirits, Dabu . . .

And call the Morning Star too, Dabu. If ever there is one light in the whole universe that is forever faithful to the lost, it is the Morning Star. The Morning Star will give you a light to see your way through the darkness of the world, and with it you can separate the evil men from the good men. There in the eastern sky the Morning Star awaits, first during the day and last at night, and if you want to call, call now, Dabu. You must have that ever-faithful light in your heart to guide you in the darkness. Call the Morning Star, Dabu . . .

But above all call Christ, Dabu. For the cross he had borne for mankind is your cross now to bear through the thorny roads and parched lands of the world. What tortures he had suffered will be yours now. For your heritage is pain, and loneliness, and deprivation, and you will carry on your bare shoulders that cross of suffering. Christ above all others will not deny you. Call Christ, Dabu . . .

"Mother!" Dabu whispered. In his aching heart he knew the truth now. He looked at Hassim and asked, "What shall I do?"

Hassim choked with emotion before he could answer. Then he said, "Didn't you say your father was still alive when you left?"

"Yes. But I doubt if he is still alive, what with that wreckage in the kitchen."

"Something awful must have happened," Hassim said quietly. "Do you have any relatives?"

"I have an uncle in the village."

"Let's take your mother there and ask your uncle what happened. How far is it?"

"About five kilometers."

"Then let us not lose time."

Dabu turned to his mother; nodding to Hassim, he lifted one arm. Hassim took another arm, and together they guided the witless woman through the house and down the ladder. She walked obediently between them, almost like a little girl. They stopped at the gate, and Dabu gently closed his mother's mouth. Then they walked on in silence.

All the houses now were in darkness. But the moon was full and bright, so the fields they crossed were clear. They passed through several farms before they came to the river, where they carried the woman across. And after an hour of walking in silence, they came to the edge of the village. A dog barked at them twice, then retreated in silence under a house. They walked on undisturbed to Dabu's uncle's house. It was the longest journey that Dabu had ever made in his life.

The house was actually a hut, made of cogon grass. And it was in darkness. They entered the gate and paused in the yard for a moment. Then they walked on to the ladder, which Dabu knocked heavily with his knuckles. There was no movement in the house. Dabu knocked again, louder this time. There was a slight noise in the house, the pattering of bare feet going to the door, where it stopped suddenly.

"Uncle Peto!" Dabu called.

The door opened a little, the closed.

"Open up, Uncle Peto! It is Fernacio, your nephew! And Mother!"

The door opened again, and a dark face looked down upon them.

"Who is it?"

"Your nephew – and Mother!"

The man hesitated to answer. Hassim flashed the light on the man's face swiftly, then on Dabu's and his mother's. Then back on the man's face. And in that instant, Hassim saw the wizened old face breaking into terror.

"Let us up, Uncle Peto!"

"Not so loud," whispered the old man. "Come up quietly."

Dabu helped his mother up the bamboo ladder, and Hassim followed them. The man crept across the darkness of the hut and scratched a stick of match against a post. A spurt of blue flame leaped out of the darkness and bloomed in the cup of his dark hand. Then a rugged white wick hanging at the edge of a conch shell was lit, and the interior of the crowded hut was revealed, revealing a woman crouching on a mat in one corner.

The old man turned around and looked at them. The terror-stricken face froze. The drooping mouth opened, but no words came out.

"It is Fernacio, Uncle Peto," Dabu said.

The old man nodded his head, but the terror was still on his face.

"Yes, I know," he said. And then, pointing to Hassim, he asked, "And this man?"

"A friend."

The woman rose from her corner and walked to Dabu, studying him and Hassim. Then she took Dabu's mother by the arm and led her to the mat, where they both sat down facing the three men.

"Where have you come from?" the old man asked.

"Never mind that now, Uncle Peto. What happened to my mother?"

The old man looked at Dabu, then turned his face away.

"It does not matter how horrible it was, Uncle Peto. I have to know the truth. You must tell it to me straight."

Still avoiding their eyes, the old man began the sad story in a low voice. "It started six months ago, Fernacio," he said. "When the government organized what it called a Neighborhood Association. The name is harmless enough, and the local officials explained to us that it is some sort of a club where we could gather socially and discuss common problems on a friendly basis. I was reluctant to join, but friends and neighbors began avoiding me on the streets. I thought that if that was all, I did not mind it. But then, the more aggressive members began to pressure me. They ruined my crops. That was all right with me too, but when they killed my work animals – " He turned to Dabu and choked. "What could I do?" he cried in anguish. "How could I plant rice or corn without my animals? How could we live? There is no other way to make a living except to work the land? Do you blame me for joining the organization?"

Dabu waited. He wanted to know the details. But the old man was coming to it, so he asked, "What about Father?"

"I am coming to it. I joined the organization, as I was telling you. But your father was not a member. Some of the members kept asking him to join, but he refused. Then they told me to talk to your father. I talked to him, I begged him. I pleaded with your mother also, but to no avail. They ruined his crops too, and killed his animals. Still he was adamant. They could not do anything to make him join. They even beat him up two times when he came home late at night from the field. But he would not change his mind. Your father was a stubborn man!"

Dabu glanced swiftly at Hassim.

"Then it happened," continued the old man. "It got around that you had joined the underground. This meant to the members that your father was in league with you. They asked him where you were hiding, and he told them the truth that he did not know. They would not believe him. From then on he was a marked man, he was marked for death. And so it happened not long afterward. It was horrible."

The old man broke into tears. Dabu watched him. His mother was also weeping, but the sound that came from her throat sounded inhuman. It was like the groan of a wounded animal, a dumb animal who could not tell what hurt her or in what part of the body. Dabu turned to her, and when she stopped, he looked at his uncle again.

"Tell me the rest, Uncle Peto."

"Your father disappeared, and not a trace of him since. We found your mother lying in the field, her tongue cut out and her head crushed. The blood had hardened in her mouth, and it was quite a task to pry it out. We kept her in our house because we knew that she was not safe in your house, but she disappeared one night when we were sleeping. She was still a little sane then, but when we found her wandering in the streets of the town, she had already completely lost her mind. We wanted to take her back, but she kept pointing in the direction of your house. We took her there, and carried food for her there every evening. That is what happened in brief, Fernacio."

Now the old man seemed to melt in agony. And his strength seemed to have left him completely. He walked to a plank chair and sat down heavily.

"You have not found any trace of my father?" Dabu asked.

The old man shook his head and said, "We kept hoping he would come back. Now we know he is gone forever. There are dogs running loose in town that have been feeding on human flesh."

Dabu walked to one of the windows and opened it. He looked out into the moonlit night, trying to suppress the welling tears in his heart. He stood there a long time, thinking and then not thinking. For what could he think about when his father was torn to pieces by hungry dogs? And his mother was mutilated into insanity? What could he think about in a night such as this? When even nice memories were blackened by the ungodly sight of his mother. What were thoughts to him now when he was surrounded by the horrors of other men's thoughts? Where in this whole world could he sit down again and find peace when there was horror everywhere? Not here, not anywhere.

Dabu closed the window and turned to the others. He said calmly, "Our country has become a lair of madmen."

The old man nodded and added, "The Neighborhood Association is an organization of spies, of neighbors and friends spying on each other, betraying each other, even killing each other. That is what it is truly, and none other. Yes, Fernacio. Our country has become a lair of madmen."

They looked at one another briefly, each thought they were afraid of each other. And although they did not pay much attention to Hassim at first, he was now the center of their attention.

Then the old man asked Dabu, "What are you going to do now?"

"We are going soon, Uncle Peto."

"But why?"

"We have to go, because we have something to do."

"And your mother?"

"That is why I need your cooperation and confidence," he

explained, looking at Hassim. "I would like you to keep her here for me. I will try to reach you with a message or some help to answer her necessities from time to time. I know I am asking you a great deal, but you are the only one I can trust. I want you to understand my position, Uncle Peto."

The old man sighed. "Yes, in times like this we need one another." he said. "I am an old man now anyway. I don't have much time left on this earth. I am thinking only of your aunt, not your mother because she can't be hurt anymore. Your aunt and I – "

"I understand your predicament, Uncle Peto," Dabu intervened. "You have to make some sacrifices, for what is the use of living in cowardice?"

"No use at all, son. Death is much better now."

"We all die, but don't accept death that way. To live is a matter of many years or a few hours, but how heroically you live is our concern. And even dying has many degrees, many forms, many qualities. This much I have learned since I have been away. Your seriousness of meeting life should be equal to, if not greater than, the seriousness of meeting death. That is a thought that I would like to impart to you before we go."

The old man remained silent. Then he asked, "You were not seen coming into town?"

"I don't think so. It was very quiet, and we did not see anyone."

"You were taking a great chance coming back."

"It is a part of our job, although to me it has a personal aspect."

The old man nodded. "I am not going to ask you what you are doing," he said. "But whatever it is, I hope we will meet again."

"I hope so too, Uncle Peto."

They walked across the floor and shook hands vigorously. Dabu's aunt crept on the floor and knelt to him, grabbing his hands to kiss them. Dabu wrung them again from her in anger.

"Don't do that, Aunt Marciana," he said. "I am not a priest or a mayor, not even a landlord or a moneylender, nor a tax collector or a clerk."

The woman drew back, bewildered.

"And don't kneel to me, Aunt Marciana," Dabu told her. "You have knelt all your life, so your servitude to whatever it is that you were serving is over. You have knelt so long that your knees are hard as stones. I used to see you crawling from the church door to the altar, and that was quite a lot of kneeling on rough stone and sharp bricks. I don't remember what you got for kneeling on your bruised knees, but you must have had something because it made you happy despite the bleeding knees. You used to kneel in the mud too, planting rice under the heavy rain. But I know what you got, because it was a harvest, be it bad or good. But I don't understand why you knelt in your yard when the mayor came to get your chickens or goats for nothing. And I don't understand why you knelt to the moneylender, priest, clerk, and landlord. As I remember now, you have knelt to many things. You have spent most of your life on your knees, Aunt Marciana. And above all, don't kneel to me. Your kneeling days are over, Aunt Marciana."

The old man watched Dabu bend to his kneeling aunt and lift her up with both hands.

"Don't you feel better standing on your feet, Aunt Marciana?" Dabu asked. "Look at the world from your height, and don't bow or stoop to anyone. We are all human beings, not idols or priests or rich men or politicians. To stand on your feet is your personal friend. That is why you have legs, Aunt Marciana. Don't crawl on your knees when you are in danger. Stand on your feet and fight or run, depending on your chances of living or escaping. Remember all this when I am gone."

Then Dabu took the woman to his mother. He kissed his mother's forehead for a moment, then walked back to his uncle. He gave the old man a gun and some shells.

"You will need these, Uncle Peto," he said.

The old man accepted the gun and shells without comment. Then he asked Dabu, pointing at Hassim, "He – ?"

"It is better for you not to know him," Dabu said. "You don't know his name, and you have never seen him. It should be that way until the time comes."

The old man studied Hassim in the faint oil lamp. He seemed to sense something about Hassim, but he held back what he was thinking. Hassim was looking straight at the old man, and his eyes that were used to darkness, that seemed to gain fierceness in the darkness, were staring at the old man. In those eyes the old man saw the shadow of death, and the rage of one who had seen many men die in agony. Slowly he turned back to Dabu.

"You are right, Fernacio," he said. "I have never seen him."

"It should be that way," Dabu said. He nodded to Hassim. "We will go now."

"Take care of yourselves," the old man said in parting.

They walked to the door, followed by the old man. They did not look back, and the old man closed the door after them. They crossed the yard swiftly and kicked the gate open. They stopped when they reached the road and looked back to the grass hut, in time to see the light go out.

"I don't know if I will ever be happy again," Dabu said.

"You will," Hassim said, talking for the first time. "And greater happiness you will have, now that you understand the necessity for it. Happiness, like all human goals, is beaten out of our hearts and minds. At least, in this kind of world, that is so. Would that there were another kind of world, where happiness is as common and cheap as the air we breathe. We know the possibility of that world – we see it in the collective future of our work – so let us not begrudge ourselves of some sacrifices, however large or small, however unpleasant or terrible, toward the making of it. That is the meaning of our work; that is the attitude we must take. Otherwise everything will be chaos within and without ourselves and anarchy in our work and in the broad world."

"I have to cry."

"I know."

"She is my own mother."

"The more that you should cry. Cry for your brave father also."

Dabu suddenly burst into tears. All that he had repressed in the house found expression in his tears.

Hassim tenderly held Dabu's shoulder and said, "Cry away all the years, Dabu. Yes, the long years. You have seen many of them. The years of growing up with a great urgency, and loving without shame, and living without fear. Yes, the lost long years. You have walked to the very end of them, and back, back to the beginning of them. Here in this haunted town the years began with the tender notes of your youth. They came passing you by, and then without knowing, they came back and took you away – away to the wilderness and the far world's crossroads where you knelt crying peace to all the living. There were years on the back of the quiet wind from the south, saying, 'Now, now, don't you cry.' There were winds from the north, tenuous and soft like the fingers of a dream. And there were years from the west suffused with rain and wind, calling far into the night. But the years from the east, warm with the sun and cool with the Morning Star, those were the golden years saying, 'Now go out into the world and live.' So all the years came and went, leaving you only a pocketful of memories. Where are the years, Dabu? Let us go back to the very beginning of them, to the very heart of them – there in the barren fields of our land and the fighting jungles of our new home!"

## CHAPTER NINETEEN

. . . . . . . . . . . . . . . . . . . . . . . . . . . . . . . . . . . . . .

**H**assim and Dabu walked in long strides toward town, but in silence.

The night was clear and quiet. A proud chariot of clouds was brushing the moon with its fleecy wheels, rushing southward where the sky rose majestically on its imperial blue dome. In the east the Morning Star's brilliant light was shared by lesser stars. At the dip of the western sky a huge mass of formless cumulus clouds was undecided which way to go; the wind from the sea had not yet conspired to drive it away. And in the faraway island of the northern sky a falling comet flashed in amazing speed from one cone of silence to another, streaking the silent face of the night with a fiery sharp light, then it vanished. Then there was a deep-throated rumble in the southern horizon, announcing that rain was approaching.

They quickened their steps when the rolling thunderclap broke behind them.

"Rain will come at dawn," Hassim said.

Dabu nodded. "It is good for us," he said.

They were now approaching Dabu's house. They stopped when they reached the gate and looked at the house.

"Wait here," Dabu told Hassim.

"All right."

Hassim watched Dabu go into the house, then turned around to see the lay of the land. When he turned back to the house, he saw a spreading tongue of flame licking the window. He was about to run across the yard and into the house when he saw Dabu jump from a window into the yard. Then Dabu was running toward Hassim.

"What happened?" Hassim asked.

"I set the house on fire."

"Why?"

"It is of no use now."

"Your mother may want to go back."

"She will never go back."

"It is a foolish thing to do, because even if your mother does not want to go back, some dispossessed peasants could use it."

"I want to burn the past, that past part of me, and forget everything attached to it."

A wall fell to the ground.

"Let us go," Dabu said, "before anybody finds us here."

Dabu started to run. Hassim ran too, coming abreast with him. They ran straight to the plaza where they paused to look at the Rizal monument. But without pausing long this time, Dabu swerved to the right and continued running to the *presidencia*. Hassim paused for a while, not comprehending Dabu's course of action.

"Come back!" Hassim called.

But Dabu kept on running straight to the *presidencia*.

"The crazy fool!" Hassim cursed, and started running after Dabu. He turned his face back as he ran, and saw the house aflame. He heard the noise of pounding feet running toward the burning house. He heard dogs barking and animals stampeding. But he ran on, following Dabu, trying to catch up with him. He knew now what Dabu was up to, but his strides seemed to slacken. Dabu seemed to be going farther and farther away from him. When Hassim realized that he could not catch up with Dabu, he cursed again, "The crazy damn fool!"

Dabu did not run straight to the *presidencia's* open door. He turned aside, to the protection of the left brick wall, where he crouched under the window looking inside the building. The gun was in his hand.

Hassim ran to his side. "What is the idea?" he asked.

Dabu did not answer him. In spite of his question, Hassim knew. He looked inside through the iron bars of the window and saw the two policemen playing chess on a crude piece of board. Hassim stepped back and looked up at the second floor of the two-story building, to see if there were any other policemen around. He knew that a town of this size always had more than two men on guard, perhaps four, on a night like this. A light was in one window, perhaps the mayor's office, where nightwatch policemen took turns to rest or sleep while the others were on duty. He knew now that there were at least four, and the other two were perhaps sleeping in the mayor's office. He jumped back to the side of the wall to warn Dabu, but Dabu was already rounding the corner of the building next to the entrance.

There was no time left for hesitation. There was no time left for anything, not even to think of escape; surely the whole town would be awake in a few minutes. But escape, that most precious word to all belligerents in the world, would come and find a way when the time came, if it ever came to the two of them.

So Hassim plunged into the darkness, following Dabu to the *presidencia's* door. And the two chess-playing policemen were taken by surprise, when Dabu fired at them. Dabu fired first at the older man, who clutched desperately at his chest as he fell from the wooden bench where they were playing. There was a look of surprise in his eyes as he fell, and even sadness, for tears trickled down the corners of his face when he rolled on the cement floor to die. The other was a young man, about twenty-two, who was quick enough to unsheath his gun from its holster when Dabu fired the first shot. But it was too late: the gun was halfway from the holster when Dabu fired again, firing twice, hitting the policeman in the stomach and then in the chest. The young man, however, was stubborn to die. Even as he fell that gun was still in this hand, aimed at Dabu. But even that display of courage and alerted discipline was cut short, for Dabu fired again, three times in rapid succession. And the young man fell to the floor without consummating his courage, his personal valor, his departmental discipline. He fell without knowing what hit him, without even showing in the slightest contraction or expression of the eyes his reaction to it all. He fell, then he died; and his blood poured on the cold cement floor, commingling with the blood of the older policeman.

And all this happened in less than half a minute. At the end of it, Hassim was already on the landing of the stairs facing the lighted room. When the man came out of the room with sleepy eyes, the gun loosely hanging in his hand, Hassim fired and jumped to the side of the door. And in that instant, he saw the other policeman getting up from his cot bed and fumbling for his gun, which was lying on a bare table at the foot of the cot. Hassim fired twice at him, and again at the man who had opened the door. Then he ran downstairs, then to the door and out, where he saw Dabu's shadow cutting across the lawn toward the main highway. Hassim ran after him, and as he ran he noticed that there was no more flame in the sky. The house had crumbled to the ground, for he saw only a thin veil of smoke, violet in the bright moonlight.

Hassim ran after Dabu. There was no time to think. There was no time to lose. In a few minutes the town would be awake. He did not know where Dabu was going, but he knew that he had to follow him. He knew that he had to be with him, to help him, whatever was in Dabu's mind. So he ran faster. When he saw Dabu cut across the plaza, running in the direction of the houses, he followed him without thinking. And he ran without looking around or back, knowing that time was the element.

But even as Hassim ran after Dabu, he thought of Old Bio. What if the old man would mistake the shooting for the signal? What if they would all rush to town? Hassim ran faster than he had ever run before. He could hardly feel the earth now, for he was flying through space. His thoughts were far ahead of him, in the grove, in the city, in their bivouacs among the hidden hills.

Then Hassim saw Dabu kicking the tall gate of a middle-class house. Then Hassim knew, and knowing it, he fumbled for the other gun in his shirt. When he reached the fallen gate, Dabu was already dashing up the polished teakwood stairs. He rushed across the wide yard to the door, which Dabu had left wide open after him. Then he was at the foot of the stairs, and he heard the loud report of a gun upstairs. And in that instant, Dabu came rushing down.

Hassim looked up at him and the smoking gun in his hand, and as he looked, Dabu turned to a side of the living room and fired. Swiftly Hassim turned aside, just in time to see a servant emerging from a side door. He fired. The servant was hit in the belly. He jumped to the side of the door, to see if there were others inside the house. Dabu had also jumped to the side of the living room, waiting to see if there were others. But none came. So together they rushed out of the house and the gate, flinging themselves into the night, against all the world.

They kept away from the plaza and the *presidencia*, away from all the lighted places. They ran through the dark alleys, under the silent houses. They ran under the whispering trees, across some fields and pasturelands. Then they came to the junction where they had departed from their rendezvous to the town. Here was a cane field, and Dabu plunged into it.

Hassim followed. He found Dabu beating the earth with his fists.

"My mother," Dabu was whispering. "My father. My father and mother."

Hassim leaned over him and said, "That is enough now. Let us go."

"O God!"

"Let us go, Dabu," Hassim urged him, lifting him to his feet. "The old man and the others might be running to town, then we will have a hell of a job on our hands. Let us go – "

They started to run, crossing the cane field. When they emerged from the other side, their faces and arms were bleeding. They had been cut in several places by the sharp blades of the cane leaves. But unobstructed now, they ran with all their might. How many places, in the far-flung stretches of the earth, did they run together like this? In what village did they defy armed constabulary men, running like wild animals under houses and trees?

It had always seemed to Hassim that they had been running away from something all their lives. For even as he reached Dabu, who had slackened his stride, Hassim knew that he would be running like this to the very end of his days. When they were together at last, running side by side with all the power of their legs, Dabu had forgotten his madness of a moment before. He was even chuckling, his head a bit forward, his elbows even at his sides.

Hassim was relieved. "Who was he?" he asked.

"The mayor," Dabu said.

"I thought so."

"He should have died a long time ago."

"He is dead now."

"I gave it to him between the eyes. I woke him up first and then fired. You should have seen his face."

"I can imagine. I have seen many faces like his."

"You can't imagine this one. I shoved the gun in his face and fired. He never knew what hit him."

"Did you know him?"

"As a little boy, yes. But I remembered him all right. Of course he had grown fatter. If we had time I would have asked how he beat the world. He was a worldbeater. And a good one."

"Well, he has no more world to beat."

"I hope not, although I remember that he used to say there is another world."

"Did you see his wife?"

"I had no time. She was probably asleep in the adjoining room."

"Did you know any of the servants?"

"No."

"The policemen?"

"One of them. The young man at the door of the *presidencia.*"

"Too bad."

"Yes. I would have liked to talk to him. We used to play together. In fact, he saved my life once. When there was a flood in the town. We were swimming across the river when suddenly there were cramps in my stomach. I fainted, and he towed me against the strong currents. He saved my life. Now he is dead."

Hassim felt sad too. They could have talked to the dead young man. They could have given him something to remember them by. He could have been convinced, he could have learned the truth of their cause. Now he was dead. What could Hassim say to Dabu, to the night, and above all to himself? He did not know. But he knew that he had to keep on running, and be on the lookout for Old Bio and the others.

"He is better dead," Dabu said.

"I guess so."

"I didn't want to shoot him, but when he reached for his gun, I had to do it."

"I saw it. There was no other way."

"I hate to hit him. But he is better dead. Poor Perfecto."

"Yes, he is better dead."

"Do you think Old Bio and the others will come running to our rescue?"

"We have to look out for them."

"I see shadows ahead."

Hassim looked. It was the Old Man and the others. They were running toward them. But their figures were becoming fainter, for the moon was darkening. The cumulus clouds in the west had been blown skyward, and now they had covered the moon's bright face. As they ran, they looked skyward.

"It will rain," Hassim said.

"Yes."

And it began to rain when they met the others. Warm dark rain, pelting them heavily. Big-seeded rain from the west, running eastward to the rice country. Warm rain for the planting, to inundate the waiting fallow land. In this valley of the big rain, where the rice grew so tall that man is a dwarf beside it, the rain came and stayed for weeks at a time. This was the first big rain, and it would stay until the lands are all plowed, if there were any men left to do the work.

They all looked at the rain in silence. They let their bodies soak in the rain, for it had been hot all day long. It softened the outer walls of their bodies, loosening their stiff joints and tight minds. They stood there silently under the rain, soaking themselves to the bone.

Then Old Bio asked, "What happened?"

"Some accident," Hassim answered.

"Everything all right?"

Dabu laughed. "All right is right," he said.

Hassim noticed that the old man and his son were still with them. He touched Linda Bie. "Did you give it to them straight?" he asked.

Linda Bie nodded.

"Now look here," Hassim said to the old man and his son, "we have no time to lose. Four policemen, the mayor and his two servants are dead. There may be trouble, though I doubt it. Nobody saw us. But it is better to make precautions."

"I understand," the old man said.

"Have you decided where to go?"

"We are going back," the son answered.

"If this is so, let us part right away."

"Yes," said the old man.

"All right then. We will hear from you?"

"You will."

"Do you have enough shells?"

"Well – "

"Give them some," Hassim told Legaspi.

Legaspi gave them a handful of shells each, after asking them the caliber of their guns. Father and son put the shells in their pockets in silence.

"Now let us part," Hassim said.

"God be with you," the old man said.

"Same with you," Old Bio told them.

"Run as fast as you can for the next five kilometers," Hassim advised them. "We will do the same. If there is some trouble on your side, we will not be able to help you. And it is the same thing on our side: we don't expect you to help us. We both have missions of our own."

"That is understood then," said the father.

"Good-bye and good luck," Mameng said.

They all saluted and parted, running in two groups as they parted. The rain was pouring in torrents now. It was so thick that they could hardly see each other. In this kind of rain they would not be seen easily, unless the enemy were a foot distant from them.

They ran two abreast, with Dabu and Old Bio ahead. The last was Hassim, who saw Old Bio slacken his stride until Legaspi was at his side. Legaspi pulled the bottle of whiskey from his food sack as he ran. Old Bio put one hand on Legaspi's shoulder while he tilted the bottle with the other, running as he was drinking; then when he was finished, he let go of Legaspi's shoulder and ran faster until he came abreast with Dabu. Hassim saw him give the bottle to Dabu, and suddenly he felt thirsty too. He ran up to Legaspi and asked for a bottle.

"What happened over there?" Legaspi asked.

"Dabu lost his mind for a moment." Hassim said.

"I have never seen him lose his mind."

"You would if you had seen what they did to his mother." Then Hassim, between drinks, told Legaspi the whole sad story. "That was what caused it all. I don't blame him."

"I don't either."

"Still, we would have met some difficulties. That was why I had to help him."

"I would have done the same thing."

"I know."

"How far is the next rendezvous?"

"Thirty kilometers."

"Is that Mameng's town?"

"Yes."

"I thought so."

"The poor girl."

"I hope nothing serious has happened to her family."

"I hope so too."

"Have you ever been in this part of the country?"

"No."

"Well, you will see it now."

"And sooner than you think, with this breakneck speed we are having."

Hassim returned the bottle to Legaspi and told him to give some drinks to the others: Linda Bie and Dante. Then he was at the end of the line again, watching from side to side as he ran.

But the heavy rain had afforded them a screen against the enemy, a shield, a weapon. If it would keep up all night long, they would be at the next rendezvous at dawn. And that would be another day in Hassim's life of daring adventure, and another day of knowing what was happening in the land. Even as he ran, he thought of the city where he grew up, and of Consuelo, who had shown him magical days and unforgotten nights.

What happened to her? he asked himself, looking straight ahead for fear of losing track of the others.

There was a flash of lightning in the dark sky. Then the roar of thunder. Still they did not stop running. And they had run ten kilometers before they eased their strides, for the rain had become light and gentle.

Hassim sipped the water that dripped from his head to his face. It tasted salty: his perspiration was mixed with it. Or perhaps it was his tears.

At dawn they stopped running. They were approaching the next rendezvous. Mameng's town, which announced itself in the thinning rain with high towers of coconut trees and buri palms. And the rain had ceased falling.

They rested in a wide field of okra. The okra was the length of a man: so tall that they could stand without being seen. They sat in a circle and unburdened themselves of their knapsacks and wrung their clothes dry. Old Bio looked very drunk. Dante was trembling from the rain. Linda Bie was as pale as a ghost. But Legaspi and Dabu were in the best spirits, laughing and telling jokes as they smoked their cigarettes.

Hassim looked at Mameng, but remained silent. There was a mist in her eyes. She knew that she had come to her town; she had known it a long way back that she would come to her town. And now she was here. And now she looked sad, sadder than she had ever been. For truly it was the saddest moment of her life. She looked at Hassim hopefully.

"There will be light in another hour," Hassim announced.

"Yes," Mameng said.

"Do you know that you and I have to go into town?"

She nodded. Then she said, "I would like Dante to come with us."

They all looked at her, then to Dante, then to Hassim.

"I want it that way," Mameng said.

They looked at Hassim.

"All right, Mameng," Hassim said.

The others smiled and lit their cigarettes.

"Give me the bottle, Legaspi," Old Bio said.

They all laughed.

## CHAPTER TWENTY

. . . . . . . . . . . . . . . . . . . . . . . . . . . . . . . . . . . . . . .

In the dawning they looked at each other in silence. They were dripping wet from the heavy rain, but could not build a fire to dry their soaked clothes and bodies. It would attract attention, it would be too dangerous. But the mist was gradually drifting away from the fields, giving way to the first peeping rays of the coming sun. The grass gleamed whitely. The trees around them were whispering, for the large drops of rain on the leaves fell to the ground in a sweet rhythm. And the okra vines shook as they moved about in their hiding place.

Old Bio had wrung his shirt dry and was now slapping it vigorously against his thighs, to make it dry faster and quicken the circulation of blood in his shaking body. He jumped from one foot to the other as he did his chore, grunting like a pig and murmuring inaudibly.

But nobody was paying any attention to him. Everybody was busy with his own private business.

Legaspi was poking into his food sack, wondering if anything was spoiled. The tender leaves and vines that he had snatched off the trees as they walked through the entanglements of the dry river near Dabu's town had benefited by the rain. The ferns had uncurled their furry stems, while the leaves had become greener and more delicious looking. When he was satisfied that nothing was spoiled, he opened the sack where he kept the bottles. He smiled with satisfaction because they were all tightly corked; and with his glowing smile, he opened a bottle of whiskey and put it to his mouth. He closed his eyes as he drank the hot liquid, searing his throat and stomach with its hotness. Then he put back the bottle in the sack and lit a cigarette.

Mameng's shirt had stuck close to her brown skin. You could see the small mounds of her breasts neatly molded by the wet shirt: the hard yellowish tips were almost visible, challenging you until you were dizzy with your unspoken thoughts. But she was not aware of the provocation she aroused. She was used to the company of men, and in fact she felt at times like a man. It was only when she was alone that she was aware of her sex, stroking her gleaming thighs and cupping her breasts firmly in her hands. That was before she had become a woman with Dante, back there on the hillside of their first rendezvous. After that consummation of all that she had dreamed of, after loving Dante, the need to caress her body had shifted itself to another sphere: that of admiration of her body, of giving it suppleness so that it would be more yielding and glowing when Dante touched her with his gentle hands, and made much of her, rubbing and kneading the sensitive contours of her awakened body. So now she sat there before her companions, but her thoughts were far away. She was thinking of home.

And they did not want to disenchant her thoughts. They let her alone in her world of memories.

Linda Bie was coughing spasmodically. He was kneeling on the ground and bending double, his palms tightly pressed against his mouth. He did not want to make any unnecessary sound, lest their presence would be detected. He looked at his palms now and frowned when he saw the big blobs of gray phlegm. Then he wiped his hands with the wet grass and asked for a drink from Legaspi.

They did not watch him either. They did not want him to know the sad truth about his health. It was a silent lie that they had all conspired not to tell.

But Linda Bie knew. It would be a matter of weeks now, he thought as he put the bottle to his mouth. It did not matter much for him to know the truth. He had lived and fought with his companions, and he had found a truth bigger than himself. His only hope now was to impart a portion of it to someone receptive enough to assimilate its wonder and glory. That was all he wanted. Perhaps when he reached home he would be able to find fertile ground in which he could plant the seed of this truth. And that was why he was way ahead mentally, thinking of his father and brothers.

Dante was not thinking. He was not even interested in his soaked clothes. He was smoking one cigarette after another in silence.

Dabu was getting drunk. He was drinking from a bottle and eating sardines. His thick mop of black hair had fallen to the left side of his head, which he kept brushing back into place without success. He finally gave up and concentrated on his drinking. He was sitting cross-legged, the gun in his lap, the canvas cap in his shirt pocket. When he finished the sardines, he dug a hole between his legs and buried the can. Then he started to laugh.

Hassim was busy writing his report. He was still dripping wet; raindrops fell on his notebook. But he kept on, for he was using a lead pencil. When he was through, he put the notebook and pencil in his knapsack.

Now Old Bio had put on his dry shirt. He felt better. The blood in his withering body began to circulate. He felt his heart beating regularly.

"This cold weather always gets me," he announced.

"It is because of your age," Dabu told him.

"My age? What has my age got to do with it?"

"Everything. Your bones creak. Your eyes blur. Your head aches. Is not that so, old one?"

"Stop there now. And listen."

"I am listening."

"I feel younger than I have ever been. Of course not as young as when I was seven years old. Didn't you know that I was a hero when I was seven years old?"

"I didn't know."

"Well, I was a hero. Where were you at seven?"

"Not in the cradle by any means."

Everybody laughed. They were watching Old Bio and Dabu. Old Bio turned his face and looked toward the rising sun, then back to Dabu.

"The sun is rising," he said. "I mention it because it started the rising. I mean my becoming a hero. Listen: it happened like this."

They sat smoking their cigarettes. And the old man told his tale of long ago.

[*The manuscript breaks off here.*]

## CHAPTER TWENTY-ONE

. . . . . . . . . . . . . . . . . . . . . . . . . . . . . . . . . . . . . .

**A**fter Hassim had finished his report, and a light and quick breakfast, he rose to his feet and looked up at the brightening sky. The clouds were drifting away to the far horizons, driven by a western wind from the ocean. And Hassim knew all at once that it would be a sunny day, perhaps until five in the afternoon, when the rain would continue to flood the land. He parted the tall okra vines in front of him with both hands, making a narrow view through which he could inspect the surrounding fields. He looked as far as his eyes could see, but there was no one around who might discover their hiding place. He put the vines back in place and turned to his companions.

"Are you ready?" he asked Dante and Mameng.

"I am ready," Mameng said.

Hassim looked at Dante, who nodded in assent.

"Leave your knapsacks and caps," Hassim told them. "But keep your guns, and enough shells."

Dante dropped his cap on the knapsack beside him. Mameng gave her cap to Old Bio and smoothed down her uncombed black hair with the palms of both hands.

"We are ready," Dante and Mameng said simultaneously.

Hassim stepped forward and said to the others, "Be on the lookout for us."

"We will," Dabu said.

Hassim, Dante, and Mameng crept through the okra field single file. When they came out of the vines, their shoulders and waists were soaked by the raindrops that showered them from the okra leaves. But the sun was beginning to be hot, and in another half hour they would be dry again.

They crossed the fallow land that stretched between the okra field and a fishpond whose water was also used for irrigation. They followed the narrow, tall ditch surrounding the pond, teetering almost into imbalance as they skirted their way around the water. When they reached the corner of the ditch that adjoined a wide strip of flooded field, they jumped off the ditch and followed a narrow path that led them to clumps of flowering talahib grass. Here they beat their way through with dangla brush, scaring away quails and blackfooted herons from their roosts. When they came out of the talahibs, they heard at once the gathering roar of the river. But they walked on in silence, and when they came to the high cliff of the river where a pathway was cut downward to the water's edge, they stopped to calculate the depth and swiftness of the water.

Hassim was unfamiliar with the river, especially at this time of the year. The map he carried with him indicated almost everything accurately but did not mention the river's characteristics.

"Are you familiar with this river?" he asked Mameng.

"Yes."

"Is it deep?"

"A man's length. We can easily swim across it."

"Let us do it then. Be sure to keep your guns and shells dry."

They sat on the grass and took off their shoes. Hassim and Dante took off their shirts also, and wrapped their shoes, guns, and shells with them. Mameng was for a moment hesitant, but she turned her back on them and took off her shirt; likewise she wrapped her shoes, guns, and shells with it.

Hassim and Dante stood on their feet and looked across the river. Then they turned around to Mameng to see if she was ready. She was. She had bitten the knot of her bundle, almost covering her bare breasts. But at a swift glance, Hassim saw the firm bases of the brown molds that were not wholly covered by the bundle. Her stomach was narrow and deep like a man's. Mameng looked at Hassim and lowered her eyes.

"Let us go," Hassim said. "You go ahead, Dante. Mameng will follow. I will be at the end."

Dante descended the pathway to the water's edge. Mameng followed him, the bundle still hanging from her mouth. Hassim looked quickly back to where they had come from, then followed them to the river. Dante waded into the water and began to swim, the bundle lifted by the left hand just above his head. Mameng followed him, taking the bundle from her mouth the moment the water reached her waist. Hassim watched them for a second, then walked into the water and began to swim.

The water was deeper than Mameng had imagined. It was about seven feet deep, but the current was not strong. Perhaps on their way back to the rendezvous the crossing would be more difficult. The water was dark brown because of the mountain clay that had been dissolved in it as the tributaries merged somewhere beyond the farming lands. Small logs and thick branches of trees were floating, and birds were sitting on them. But it smelled sweet and clean.

As Hassim swam after them, looking straight ahead, he felt the muscles of his body tighten around him. He was a city man and was not used to swimming. But he could see that Dante seemed to be gliding smoothly – and it seemed to him that the water was loving Dante – they seemed to be flowing together and laughing as they moved their sinewy arms. And Mameng seemed to be a sister of the river, for she turned around once to see if Hassim was safe. She even stopped swimming and raised her stroking hand to Hassim, then smiled and continued toward the other side of the river.

Dante and Mameng were already wringing their shirts dry when Hassim came out of the water. Hassim put on his shirt without drying it, for the sun was already hot enough to do the job for them. He put the shells in his trouser pockets and hid the gun under his belt. When they were all ready, they walked to the clump of bamboos atop the high embankment. The embankment was sandy and broke easily when they put their weight on it, but there were stout shrubs growing profusely. They held on tightly to these and climbed up the way mountain climbers do. They dusted their trousers and shirts when they reached level ground.

It seemed mysterious under the bamboo trees. The somber light that had penetrated through thick clumps seemed to be writhing in agony. The diaphanous green leaves were whispering softly. And the air was soft and cool and fragrant. There was the smell of moss and mushroom.

Dante looked under the trees and saw shoots two feet above the ground. And he thought of Legaspi, because he knew that he would not pass by without cutting some of it for the food sack. He smiled as he thought of Legaspi, thinking of his creditable peasant ways.

Hassim led the way. They walked under the bamboo and came out to a fenced guava orchard. The guavas were leafing; there were rotten fruits under them. Most of the fallen fruits had been pecked at by birds. There were also a few coffee bushes, but these seemed uncultivated. There was a tall mulberry tree in a corner of the orchard, but it was flowerless and dying. The whole orchard seemed to be neglected. And once again Dante thought of Legaspi. Dante knew that had the orchard been Legaspi's property, he would have worked it into a garden of beauty and abundance.

They climbed over the old wicket fence and came out to a deep lane. Hassim knew, at first glance, that it had been a path through which the water ran, during rainy seasons, seeking for level ground. Man had found it passable and more accessible than the tangled undergrowth on both sides, so he had begun using it.

They were walking abreast now, down the narrow lane.

"You lead the way, Mameng," Hassim said.

"It is not far from here," she said.

"Go ahead then. I will stay behind."

"I will walk with her," Dante suggested.

Hassim nodded.

They walked down the lane about half a kilometer when they saw a man riding on a carabao approaching them. Mameng and Dante turned quickly to the left, crawling under the fence and crouching breathlessly behind a big ipil tree. Hassim followed them. When the man came to the spot where they had crawled through, he stopped his animal and peered somewhat disinterestedly behind the ipil tree. Perhaps he saw them; perhaps not. He grunted and kicked his animal. And the carabao moved on leisurely. Then he was out of sight and hearing.

"Let us take a shortcut," Mameng said.

Hassim and Dante nodded.

They cut across the field, crossed several fields and fences, and came to a cemetery. They stopped awhile, sitting on the inscribed gravestones. The sky was completely clear now and the sun was getting hot. Vapors were rising from the gravestones and wooden crosses that marked the resting places of some unknown dead. The graveyard was neglected: the grass and shrubs had grown wildly all over the place, almost making it a veritable jungle. Creepers and vines covered the four walls. Even the gate was thick with morning glories.

Mameng had suddenly become solemn. They watched her get up from the gravestone where she was sitting and walk to a corner of the graveyard. She stopped beside a grave with only a wooden cross that marked where the dead had been buried. Then she reached out to the guava tree nearby and broke off a branch. She laid the branch against the cross and stood there for a minute, looking downward.

Hassim and Dante looked at each other.

Mameng, pray for the dead. Or was prayer taken away from you, too? Did they take away your songs for the dead, like Hassim? You who had once burned a candle every evening and knelt to it when the curfew called? You who had offered a prayer when you awoke in the morning, before you went about your daily work? Have they taken away your only language with the dead? Did they destroy your last thread of communication with the forever dead?

Pray anyway, Mameng. Pray if you still remember some of the consoling words. For the dead are dead forever. And whoever is buried under your feet will somehow feel your presence, hear your words, taste the salt of your tears of sorrow. And hallowed be thy name.

When she came back to them, it was Dante who greeted her.

"A family member?" he asked.

"My brother," she said. "He died when he was quite young. Nobody could diagnose his sickness."

"Because there were no doctors?"

"Yes. Only a witch doctor who burned roots and leaves and applied the ashes on his stomach and legs. He bled to death through the mouth and nose."

"Probably hemorrhage of the brain," Hassim said.

"Probably."

"Any other members of your family except yourself?"

"Three. Father, mother, and an older sister."

"You have not heard from them since?"

Mameng shook her head. They were quiet for a while, evading each other's eyes.

Then Hassim said, "Let us proceed."

Mameng led the way to the gate. Outside the graveyard was a field of cactus and maguey. A pig was eating cactus fruit, but it remained undisturbed when they passed by. It went on eating as though nobody was present.

After the cactus and maguey field, they came to a grove of acacia trees. This was formerly the plaza, but that had been removed to the other end of town. Now it was thick with bushes and weeds and grass. The monument in the center was desecrated by vandals with their indecent inscriptions, while around it were telltale marks left by clandestine lovers. There was even dried human excretion, and the monument itself had been repeatedly trod by dogs.

The desolation was complete. The plaza was like a town that had flourished with grandeur and had died at the height of its glory. It died, and nothing remained now but the skeleton of a past.

They passed by the scandalized monument without pausing. When they came to the wilderness of the plaza, Mameng stopped. She looked up and down the road bordering it, but saw no one. It was still too early for town people to be stirring.

"Only three blocks now," she said.

"Let us hurry," Hassim said.

"Lead us through a safe way," Dante said. "I feel that some people are looking at us through their closed windows. I feel it in my bones."

"Follow me then," Mameng said.

They followed her down an alley. At the end of the first block, the church bell started tolling.

"What is it?" Hassim whispered.

"It must be Sunday," Mameng told him.

Dante nodded.

"No wonder the whole town is deserted," Hassim commented. "But let us hurry. The devotees will soon be out, and we don't want to be the center of attention."

They turned to the left on the second block, then to the right at the end of it. Then they were in Mameng's block. She led them around it, sidetracking the few houses. When they came to her own yard, she told them to stop by the shallow drawing well. And she did what she used to do: she looked at herself in the still, clear water of the well. And she frowned, almost with tears. How old she had grown! She desperately held down the hot tears welling in her breast.

"Does it matter now, Mameng?" Hassim asked, for he knew what she was thinking.

"No," she said. "Now let us go into the house."

Hassim and Dante followed her up the ladder. They did not knock, they did not make any noise to make their presence known by whoever was in the house. So when Mameng's mother saw them standing at the doorway, she stood still at the very spot where she was walking to the small kitchen. She put her hand to her mouth in surprise, then screamed aloud.

"Alicia!"

Mameng ran to her mother and grabbed her. "Mother, Mother."

They embraced in silence, while Mameng's mother wept copiously. Neither Hassim nor Dante knew that Mameng's name was Alicia, for like all others in the underground, they had changed their former names. They had all covered up their pasts as part of the underground strategy, in case they were captured and tortured. They would then force confessions from them, naming their towns and families. Then reprisals.

Mameng's mother looked at her with that shine of disapproval in the eyes of Filipinas when they see one of their sex dressed as a man.

"You must have had a terrible life," she commented.

"It is a hard life, but it is also a good life," Mameng said.

"Then it is no better than ours."

"It is better than this."

"How could it be?"

"It is a long story."

Hassim and Dante were watching them, not stirring. Mameng knew it, and she knew also that she had to make some explanation easy enough for her to understand. She had to begin somewhere, in the common thread of their lives, for her mother to understand what she had been doing all these years.

"Of course you know where I have been all this time, Mother," Mameng said.

Her mother nodded, and in that instance a shadow crossed her face. Mameng had started from the wrong end, and she was a little confused. She knew it was difficult to begin a long story, after all these years. She tried another angle.

"And how is Father?" she asked.

Her mother frowned, then looked at Hassim and Dante. Then she said, "Your father is gone – two years ago he left and never came back."

"Where did he go?"

"To the north. I have heard he is working in the gold mines in the mountains. But if he is, we have not heard from him."

"But why did he leave?"

"He just left, that is all."

"I will try to find him when I am in that part of the country again."

"You have been there?"

"Yes."

"And you are going back?"

"Yes, Mother. I have to go back. We have to go back."

"You should stay and settle down like other girls. You should get – "

Mameng knew what was coming. She reached for Dante's hand and said, "I would like you to meet my husband, Mother."

Mameng's mother looked at Dante, who was offering his hand, sighed, and gave her hand. Then she turned to Mameng. "He is one of them?" she asked.

Mameng did not answer.

"And the other one?" her mother asked.

"A friend of ours."

Her mother looked at Hassim for a long time in silence, then to

Dante, then to Mameng. Then she cried, "Ay, Alicia! What have you done with your life? You who have been a dutiful daughter? Now you are wasting your life in the jungles and mountains. What have you found that you tenaciously cling to that kind of life?"

"I have found a great deal, Mother," Mameng said quietly. Then she asked, "Where is Petra?"

"She is at church."

"How is she? What is she doing now?"

"She is a teacher now, at grade school. Lucky she has a job, otherwise we would have starved to death."

"How long has she been teaching?"

"Almost two years now."

"I am glad for both of you."

"She should be here now, Alicia."

"Good. I would like to see her before we go."

Her mother looked at Dante again. "Your face is young, but your hair is gray," she said sadly and in a tone of voice that implied that she had already accepted him as a son-in-law. "You must have had a difficult life, son."

"I guess that is what it is, Mother," Dante said.

Mameng's mother nodded. "What part of the country are you from?" she asked.

"Well, I'll say from everywhere. You see, Mother, I spent many years in America. That's why I come from everywhere. Yes, that's the word: everywhere."

"So much the better. Will you take good care of my daughter?"

"I will, Mother. We'll all take good care of her."

She nodded. Then she looked at Hassim and asked, "And you, son – ?"

But it was then that Petra appeared at the doorway. She had a black shawl over her head and a rosary in one hand and a book of prayers in the other. She was a little fatter than Mameng and of fairer complexion, which revealed the fact that she had not been overexposed in the sun. A schoolteacher, a woman of the house, a domestic woman. Now Petra stood in the doorway trying to identify the three of them, and when she finally recognized Mameng, she rushed to her. Her skirt fluttered about and whispered and sang a song of piety as she ran to Mameng.

"Sister!"

"Petra!"

They embraced, and parted. Then they looked at each other.

"You look so serious," Mameng said.

"Why not? There are so many things going on and they make me dizzy most of the time."

"Now what could it be that bothers you?"

Petra turned to the two men. "Well – "

"First of all, Petra," Mameng said, "I would like you to meet my husband." She introduced Dante. "And our friend." She introduced Hassim.

Petra studied the two men, and turned to Mameng. "You are all from over there?"

Mameng nodded.

"Your husband looks distinguished," Petra whispered. "And that other man, there is something about him that I can't give a name."

Mameng did not say anything. And she thought, *Just like a woman. Always measuring men, always thinking of a possible marriage. If she only knew the truth that I am not really married.*

But she said to Petra, "Tell me about these things that make you dizzy."

"In the first place everybody in town thought you were dead. We thought so too, but after the retreat of the army some of the men who were called bandits were executed in town. One of them was able to pass a word along to us that you were alive and in good company. We did not know what he meant, but there were two other messages. Then we understood who you were with and what you were doing. I can't understand what you are doing, but I am glad you are alive."

Mameng nodded.

"Nobody in town knows what you are, and it is for the best. Are you going to stay?"

Mameng shook her head.

"Why not?" Petra asked.

"Where my husband goes, I go," Mameng lied.

Petra looked at Dante, then to her mother. "That is a courageous statement," she said.

"It is better that way."

"I understand. I would do the same thing."

"Now what about those other things that bother you?"

"Well, one of them is the new problem at school. An official from the national government arrived a few days ago with a bunch of papers that we, the teachers, must sign. Nobody seems to understand what it is all about, but they call it a Loyalty Oath. The official explained that we should sign it to show our loyalty to the government. It is ridiculous because we are already loyal!"

Mameng glanced at Hassim. Petra noticed it. But Hassim did not speak.

"Of course it is one of those things," Mameng pacified her sister. "An appointed official in the national government had nothing to do, so this loyal business was created for him."

"But it is silly. The paper states that if we are communists or members of the underground, or have relatives in any of these organizations – "

"Let it not bother you, Petra. You are not a member of any of these organizations and you have no relatives in them."

"But you – "

"Let us talk about the other things that bother you."

Petra looked at them for a moment, then she said, "The school principal told us the other day that a detachment of soldiers was on its way here."

"Which way are the soldiers coming from?"

"From the south. From the capital. But they must be in town now."

"Are you sure?"

Petra did not have to answer. The heavy rumbling of trucks and jeeps was heard from the direction of the plaza. Then the voices of men.

"Yes, they are in town now," Petra said.

Mameng looked at Hassim.

"It is time that we go," Hassim said.

Mameng turned to her sister and mother. "We have to go now," she said.

"Must you take her away?" Petra asked Dante. He did not answer. Then Petra knew that she had to ask Hassim, "Can't you let her stay? I beg you!" But Hassim did not move, did not say anything. And Petra began to cry, "Alicia, Alicia."

"If you must go," her mother said, "have my blessings."

"Thank you, Mother." Mameng embraced her mother and Petra. Then she said, "Good-bye."

The three of them walked quickly to the door and climbed down the ladder. The two women in the house rushed to one of the windows and saw Mameng scrambling up the fence. When she jumped to the other side, her gun fell. And that was the last time they saw her, her dark hand reaching for the gun on their side of the yard.

## CHAPTER TWENTY-TWO

. . . . . . . . . . . . . . . . . . . . . . . . . . . . . . . . . . .

**T**he contingent of soldiers was making an unnecessary noise. But Mameng, Dante, and Hassim did not lose any time. They circled the town, avoiding the houses. They saw people rushing to the plaza from all directions. They saw army trucks along the road and jeeps racing to the *presidencia*. They saw the late churchgoers mingling with the surging crowd under the acacia trees. And they knew that they had to hurry without making themselves conspicuous.

When they reached the river, the water had already increased its volume. They took off their shoes and shirts without speaking and looking around, for they knew what they were doing. Mameng did not even bother to hide herself now; modesty had given way to the intense desire to escape. Her breasts shook as she plunged into the water ahead of her companions, the bundle raised above her head. Hassim and Dante followed her, swimming in swift strokes side by side. The current was strong now, but the urgency to reach their rendezvous was paramount in their minds. And they crossed the river in less time than when they went into the town.

Once they reached the other side, they put on their shoes and shirts and rushed to the field of talahib grass. They did not circle the fishpond; they waded through the shallow, brackish water. Then they were in the open field, making a shortcut to their rendezvous.

Hassim looked up at the sky, to see if rain would come sooner than he had expected. And sure enough, the sun was beginning to darken and already the west was painted with thick, dark clouds, engulfing the whole horizon. Already, somewhere in the west, rain was falling. And when they reached the okra field a slight drizzle began to fall, hiding them from their enemies.

Dabu met them halfway. He wanted to know what was going on in the town, but he remained silent until they were with the others. And the others were eager too. They looked at each other in silence.

Then Dabu asked, "What is going on over there?"

"Soldiers just arrived from the capital," Hassim said.

"That is bad."

"We are safe. We will stay in hiding until the heavy rain comes."

"How many men?" Old Bio asked.

"Perhaps a whole company."

"Then it is not merely a maneuver. They are after something."

"No doubt."

"Did you get enough information?" Legaspi asked.

"Quite enough. From Mameng's sister. Petra by name.."

Dabu looked squarely at Mameng and said, "Why didn't you bring me with you?"

"Four is a crowd," she said.

"Not when I am the fourth member."

"Two is enough of a crowd when you are around."

"Not when Petra and I are around."

"Your filthy mind again."

"My mind is in the right place."

"You will soon place it right enough," Linda Bie said. "When we reach the city. But don't overwork it."

Everybody laughed.

"By the way," Dante informed them, "didn't you know that Mameng's real name is Alicia?"

"It is a pretty name," Dabu said. "If it is in the right place."

They laughed again.

"The big rain is coming," Hassim told them.

They all looked at the sky. The rain was approaching them from the west. It came like a mammoth school of hungry locusts, darkening the sky. It came with that noise of locusts hungrily devouring a whole field of corn. It came with its heavy downpour, completely hiding them from their enemies.

And they felt relieved. Rain was their companion, their weapon , their shield. Always there was rain to hide them, to soak their tired, hot bodies. And always it was a warm rain, for there was no cold rain in their country.

"We will leave soon," Hassim said. "Be ready."

"Always moving," Old Bio complained. "I don't even have time to close my eyes."

"What are you crying about?" Dabu told him jokingly. "You can always sleep while walking."

"That is the honest truth."

"And you live on truths," Dante told the old man.

"Truth or no truth," Old Bio said, "I need a drink."

"No more," Legaspi said. He had a grave concern for the supply of liquor, which might not last until the end of the trip. But when he noticed the old man frowning, and after turning to Hassim's condescending face, he said, "There is a little left, of course."

Old Bio took the bottle from Legaspi's extended hand and said to him, "Your mouth still smells of your mother's milk, young man. When you get to be my age you will know that it is a privilege to drink." He swallowed a big drink and looked at Legaspi scowlingly. "What do you say now?"

"Nothing."

"That is better. Learn to respect other people's virtues or faults. Eh, eh?"

"Eh, eh?" Legaspi repeated.

They all laughed.

"Let us go," Hassim told them.

It was dark enough. They walked quietly through the okra field. Hassim looked at his wristwatch. It was nine o'clock. Enough time to reach the next rendezvous, he thought. If only the rain will not stop.

Their formation was as usual: two abreast, Dabu and Old Bio ahead, Hassim at the last, the others in between.

Hassim had time to think now. Dragging his feet through the mud, his mind became active again. It was when he was walking long distances that his mind worked clearly, sharply, and sometimes sadly. It was only when he was walking that he had enough time to think, and he was at peace with himself. The other times of his life were for action, for planning, for reporting, for defending himself or killing someone. And when he slept, he was troubled. But he was not troubled when it was a dreamless sleep. Those times were rare when his sleep was untroubled, like his waking life. So it seemed to him that he had never known rest, not anywhere or anytime, in the whole world.

What would his next report be about? He thought of Petra's problems and dizziness. And he smiled patronizingly, thinking of Petra's intellectual inadequacy to understand what was going on around her. And he remembered Mameng's silence when Petra asked her startling questions, startling because she was innocent of their implications, which would have probed deeper into their activities in the underground had Mameng chosen to answer, but she remained silent. At that moment, Hassim saw the inferential differences between the two sisters: Mameng wise and grave, though not as soft and beddable as her sister: Petra bewildered and flamboyant, a little on the sexy side, and how beddable! Hassim smiled at his private thoughts.

Then he became preoccupied by writing an imaginary report thus:

*This dislocation of family relations and the general disorganiza-tion of this locality is due to the introduction of an incipient method of testing the loyalty of teachers in the public schools. This in itself is a violation of the national constitution which guarantees the individual a definite privilege to join any organi-*

*zation of his own choosing, or thinking thoughts and the social forces attendant to these same thoughts. Actually this method leads to fear, that most dangerous human instinct, that ravisher of private initiative and creative activity.*

*I recommend the following items for the committee to discuss pursuant to the preparation of counter-methods to expose the danger of the loyalty oath among schoolteachers.*

And Hassim began cataloguing the items in his mind. The rain had become stronger, the sky darker, the fields more muddy. He could hardly see the trees through the thick rain; it seemed like ghosts passing; ghostly as he approached them, and passed by.

Ahead of him, Dabu was telling a story to the old man. But they were safe now. Hassim calculated that they had gone seven kilometers from the town. And the rain was growing bigger, as they walked southward. All right, he thought, let Dabu tell his story.

And Dabu was saying to Old Bio, "So you thought you were the only hero? Eh, eh?"

Hassim heard Old Bio laugh sarcastically.

"Listen, old one," Dabu was saying. "I was a hero, too. A greater hero than you have ever been, or will ever be. You were a hero with a horse, riding like nobody's business through the rough terrain of your world. What is that to my kind of heroism?"

"All right, all right!" Old Bio answered. "I am listening. These are not a dead man's ears hanging on my head. You were a hero? Ho, ho, ho!"

"I was a hero, all right," Dabu said. "But not on this earth, old one. I was a hero in the sky."

"What, what?"

"Yes. I was a hero in the tall sky, where I found a glittering city, a city made of mist and hanging in the air. And you could have seen an august assemblage of men from all over the world, adorning that imperishable city with their wisdom."

Old Bio laughed again, but at the same time he felt that this Dabu would outdo his tale of heroism. Somehow he felt it coming.

The others were also listening, but Legaspi most of all, because he thought that when they had time to rest again he would tell them something far beyond their expectation of him. Dante was interested only in the veritability of their tales; but he knew that peasants peppered them with fantasy, religion, folklore, and common history. Peasants are great storytellers, he thought. If they could only write –

"Listen," Dabu was saying to the old man. "It happened when I was seven years old, too. Not a day like this. The sun was in the sky. The birds were in the air. The grass was laughing. The earth was singing a song. All the world was singing. There was joy all over the world. Now you see, old one, joy is a man's passage to a greater joy. Listen – "

Old Bio listened. They were all listening.

And Dabu began his story about a city in the sky.

[*The manuscript breaks off here.*]

## CHAPTER TWENTY-THREE

. . . . . . . . . . . . . . . . . . . . . . . . . . . . . . . . . . .

**H**assim wondered if the rain would ever stop. He glanced swiftly skyward, then looked at his watch. It was three o'clock. He walked on, dragging his feet through the mud. And it rained heavily all day, flooding some of the fields knee deep. When nightfall descended, the rain began to diminish until it finally ceased at ten. Gradually, the sky cleared, and a few stars appeared in the heavens. Then the wet moon showed its drying face.

Hassim was relieved. He was relieved twice, for they were in safe territory now. He was relieved of the rain, though shaking from the cold. He peered ahead of him into the night, trying to locate the site of the town, and their rendezvous. The mist was still impenetrable, far ahead, but slowly lifting now above the plain. He felt tired and hungry. And he sneezed so loud that Linda Bie, who was ahead of him, looked back not without reproach. Hassim waved his concern away with a weak stroke of a hand. He sneezed again.

They walked on without slackening their strides and at midnight reached their rendezvous. They stood side by side under the open sky, in the sheltering night, looking at the town with its few lights blinking in the darkness. They could count the lights, one here and one there, in a town with an area of five square kilometers. Then they waded across a flooded field to look for a hideout.

They found refuge in a cane field. The canes were young, fit only for animal fodder. The leaves were long and sharp and fuzzy, cutting them as they sought the center of the field. They sat in the hollow of two rows, under the growing canes. And they began smoking cigarettes.

"Does the place look familiar to you, Dante?" Hassim asked.

"It does indeed. And I won't be surprised if this cane field doesn't belong to my brother."

Hassim nodded his head almost invisibly. He knew Dante had a brother, according to his dossier kept by the underground. But he did not know he was alive. He was beginning to know Dante's past.

"You mean to say you have a brother in this town?" Old Bio asked.

"Yes. This is my hometown."

"He must be some brother."

"Quite a brother."

"A landlord?"

Dante noticed the sudden interest in his companions' faces. But he had nothing to hide, nothing at all to be kept secret, because he was one among them. He was with them and would always be. Yes, he would give them an idea what kind of brother he had.

"A landlord and a priest," he answered Old Bio.

"What luck!" Dabu exclaimed. He meant it negatively, for he had an aversion to priests. He had seen his mother bruising her bare knees on the cobblestones of churches. And remembering his mother, he repeated, "What luck!"

Old Bio looked at him strangely. Then he said to Dante, "A landlord is bad enough. But a landlord and a priest – "

"That is what you have when you come from an educated family whose members know how to get along with the powers that be. Some of them anyway, because there is always one in every such family who revolts against the others, against compromises, against authority. I am one of those who revolt, as you already know."

"You don't have to tell me, Dante," Linda Bie interrupted. "I came from that kind of family. And what a family to come from. But I am also one of those who revolt. I have revolted."

"A landlord and a priest," Old Bio was still murmuring. He shook his head, sighing deeply. "It is unbelievable."

"Any other members of your family, Dante?" Hassim asked.

Dante shook his head. He smiled tolerantly at Old Bio and said, "Only the landlord and priest."

"It is quite enough."

"I should say so," Legaspi said.

"I would like to see your brother," Old Bio suggested. "I have never seen a landlord and a priest in one person. I have heard of them but have never seen one. I have lived a long time in the world and now, at the very end, I would like to see one. I don't know why – "

"You will see him," Hassim told the old man.

Old Bio nodded and chafed his hands.

"You will not like him," Dante warned.

"Why?"

"He doesn't like me. He doesn't like our kind of people."

"What kind is he?"

"I have told you already: a landlord and a priest in one person."

"Ah."

"Slow to catch on this time, old man?" Dabu mocked.

Old Bio looked strangely at him again. He wanted to say something, but withheld it. He was waiting for his time.

"It is true, then, what is in your dossier concerning your brother?" Hassim asked Dante.

Dante pondered Hassim's question. He wanted to assay how much he knew. Is there anything to hide? he asked himself. Is my past liberalism a guilt to this man who is a product of fighting and discipline? Should I be ashamed of my liberal past to this man who thinks that liberalism is the most criminal of all bourgeois decadence? I don't know.

Old Bio was looking from one to the other. He seemed to sense that there was some kind of a duel, but he could not place the cause of it. He was waiting like a hunter waiting for the game to make a dash out of hiding into the open. Then he became impatient. He stabbed the air with his fist.

"Well?" he said.

Dante smiled. "It is all true," he explained. "When I returned from the United States to the Philippines, I started a liberal weekly paper in town. I wanted to reach the common people, to let them know what was going on around them. I didn't have much money, so it was only a small paper. Only the landlords have big papers, and the politicians too. But I won quite a following among the people. And my brother came into the story. He put me out of business by calling me a heretic. He attacked my views from his pulpit, making it so abhorrent and foul that even those who were behind me stopped their support, friendship, and even ordinary courtesy. Fear? Yes, definitely. Fear of their homes and lives. My brother beat me to it, all right. Then he drove me out of town with the help of the local police and angry citizens. Is that what you wanted to know, Old Bio?"

"It is enough," said the old man. "I understand. And the more that I would like to see him."

Hassim held his breath. Dante's question was directed to him, he knew. But it was enough to him that Dante did not hide what he already knew. It was enough that the old man said he understood.

"I understand too," he said.

"Quite so," Dante said, smiling. "But my brother probably doesn't want to see me. However, it is about time that we meet again."

"I understand how you feel."

"Not vengeance or recrimination. I just want him to understand where I stand now, and where I stood before."

"That is best."

Old Bio nodded his head vigorously. Then he said, "That was some rain."

"It is good for the land," Hassim told him.

"It is not good for me. My old bones are rattling. Do you hear them rattling, Legaspi?"

Legaspi laughed and said, "Here is a tonic for your rattling old bones, old one."

Dante knew the inquisition was over. He lit a cigarette. He passed one to Hassim, then to Linda Bie and Dabu.

Old Bio took the bottle of whiskey from Legaspi and drank a mouthful. Then he said, "You are beginning to understand life, son."

"It is your rattling old bones that I understand, old one."

Old Bio nodded his head happily and asked Dabu, "How about you, fool?"

Dabu knew Old Bio was in his angry mood again. He glanced at Hassim, then at Linda Bie. Then he said, "I understand a few things."

"Tell me, then: is your city in the sky raining now?"

So that is what is bothering him, Dabu reflected. He knows I have something over him. But he said, "It never rains in my city."

"If it does not rain up there," Old Bio demanded, "how do they raise crops?"

"With the goodness of their hearts."

"I wish we could do that on earth."

"The time will come."

"Yes, the time will come," Old Bio murmured in defeat. "And death, too."

"Meanwhile, there is some whiskey," Legaspi chided him.

Dabu laughed. Linda Bie wanted to laugh too, but he was afraid it would make him cough. Old Bio looked at Legaspi. He was defeated by Dabu again.

"Give me the bottle, son," he said.

"Don't take too much," Hassim advised him. "We are going into town soon. I believe it will rain again, and the town will be too dark."

Old Bio swallowed another mouthful and gave the bottle back to Legaspi.

"I am ready anytime," he said.

Mameng was busy wringing her shirt dry. Dabu noticed her preoccupation.

"What is the use of doing that, Mameng?" he asked jokingly. "If Hassim is a weather prophet, you will be wet again."

Mameng suddenly turned around to answer Dabu, but she remembered her condition. In the second that she had turned around, Dabu saw the dark blots of her breasts reflected in the faint sky light. And he grinned, thinking of the suppleness of the rounded bases.

"It is my own shirt," she said softly.

"I am only reminding you," Dabu said.

"Mind your own business."

"I need your cooperation."

Legaspi slapped his thighs. "That is a good one, Dabu," he said.

"What is a good one?" Old Bio interrupted.

"Nothing," Legaspi said. He did not want the old man to participate in their joke. He would not approve of it anyway. So Legaspi repeated, "Nothing, nothing."

Old Bio looked at him doubtfully. Dante walked over to Mameng and murmured something to her. She nodded her head and put on her shirt. Then together they walked down the row, slapping away the sharp cane from their faces.

Hassim sat down and lit a cigarette. He looked up at the sky through the bending long leaves.

"It will surely rain," he said.

The others, except Old Bio, looked up too, then sat down around Hassim. Old Bio stood looking in the direction where Dante and Mameng went.

"Sit awhile, old one," Hassim told him. "We will go into town when we are rested."

Old Bio sat down reluctantly. Legaspi put a bottle of whiskey in front of them. Then he suddenly laughed.

"What is funny?" Old Bio asked him.

"I remembered something. Well, a story. I thought of it on our way here, when Dabu was telling you about his city in the sky."

"You, too," Old Bio said with disgust.

"What do you mean?"

"I never thought you had imagination."

"Even dogs have one, old one."

"You are right," he said sarcastically.

"What, what?"

Dabu intervened, "Tell your story."

Legaspi grabbed the neck of the bottle and drank. He lit a cigarette, smiled widely and began, "You see, it happened when I was seven years old too. It was a bright morning also, like Dabu's day – "

[*The manuscript breaks off here.*]

## CHAPTER TWENTY-FOUR

· · · · · · · · · · · · · · · · · · · · · · · · · · · · · · · · ·

**T**hey came out of the cane field and walked abreast. Dante was between the old man and Hassim. Dante felt walled in, for the two tall men towered high above him. As high as the sky, it seemed to him. But he felt protected, being guarded on either side by valiant men, by two glorious comrades of the underground.

Hassim struck a match and looked at his watch. It was one o'clock. He glanced skyward and saw that the moon had vanished, and the few stars were vanishing. The night was becoming darker, the wind colder. He looked sideways at his companions and walked on in silence.

Then it began to rain.

Old Bio sighed, for he saw a long, cold night coming toward them. Nobody knew but he, being an old man and alone within himself, the agonies that he suffered in his tired old bones from the cold rain, and the loneliness of night. And he sighed, for even during the day the loneliness crept up like probing steel fingers within him, tearing at his heart. Once he had grown into an old man, he would never be young again, never be warm again; and the world would never know that he was once a young man who had laughed and cried, and had raised a family and had worked industriously to keep that family; telling hilarious tales as he walked across the far world's crossroads; growing old at last to this aching loneliness and the coming long, cold night, and the world would never know his agonies. He struck a match, and as he lit his cigarette, the tiny blue flame faceted his face, revealing deep tracks of the years.

"Do you think your brother is awake this time of night?" Hassim asked Dante.

"He's mostly awake," Dante said. "But if he's sleeping, it doesn't take much to awaken him. He has a big cache of gold in that big rectory of his, and bundles of banknotes and gold-edged securities. A man like him doesn't sleep much, and can't sleep much. His deep concern for the big cache is too disturbing. So conscience stricken is he that he has terrible nightmares night and day, even when he is delivering his lectures."

"I wouldn't be in his place."

"Worried about the big cache, eh?" Old Bio asked.

"Worried to death is more appropriate for him, old one. When he's at his pulpit, he sends an acolyte to guard the room where he has hidden the cache. And when he's through with his Gospel talk and prayers, he goes hurriedly back to the mysterious room and strips the acolyte naked to the bones for fear that he may have found the hidden cache and secreted some of the gold and banknotes on his person."

"He does that all the time?" Hassim asked.

"Always."

"They always get that way when money is concerned."

"Money is an evil power, if it is that much honored," Old Bio commented. "Exposing a boy to his nakedness, especially a priest, especially a servant of the Lord."

"Yes, my brother does many impious things."

"I hope we will get some information from him," Hassim said.

"He's a tough man. Hard is the word that best describes him."

"They always get that way."

"Leave him to me. I'll talk to him. I know where his sore spots are located. Above all, it's in that hidden cache."

"He is as bad as the Spanish priests in my time," Old Bio said. "I mean the money part of it, and the disregard for human dignity to acquire it. The only difference is, in my time, the *guardia civil* routed the people from their homes and places of work with their fixed bayonets and drove them to the church. Even the sick ones, who were flogged to death or very near to death when they complained. But even that is not as bad as the practice of priests nowadays who spread malicious gossip themselves about certain citizens and attack them at the pulpit when the gossips have done enough damage. The bitter part of it is, they are our own kind."

"That's exactly what my brother had done to me, old one."

"The more dangerous they are if they are your blood relations," Hassim said.

"He is not fit to give spiritual advice to the people," Old Bio said.

"You'll soon see who's dangerous, according to his own light."

"I have seen many vile men in our country."

"Many of them are men of the church, old one," Hassim said.

"You don't have to tell me that sad truth, young man. I have lived long enough on this earth to know it. When you are born you give money to the priest. When you get married you give him money. When somebody in your family is sick you give him money. When somebody dies you give him money. On top of that, between your birth and death, you give him money every Sunday. Sometimes twice when he wants to add something to his rectory or has taken a fancy on some good land. It seems that you are always giving from the very hour of your birth to the last second that you are buried in the ground. You never get anything in return. Never that I know of. I would have become a priest myself if I had known it is an easy life, eating the best food and drinking the best wine and wearing perfumed clothes. I would not have been a peasant, a small tenant farmer at that, working like a carabao in the heat of the sun and in the cold rain, if I had known that there is comfort and leisure and pleasure in priesthood, if I had known you don't only get the best necessities of life but also the most desirable of women and the money and handshake of the rich landlords and the influential politicians. Instead I chose to be a peasant, wearing rags and eating grass and leaves of trees. Yes, I will barter my soul to the devil himself to be born again, for an easy life in the priesthood."

"It is too late now," Hassim said.

"That is just it, son. Everything is too late for me. It was too late for me to be born, when there was still plenty of good land to be acquired for nothing if you were willing to work it. When I was born, it was all grabbed by glib-tongued brigands in the capital and anonymous men in faraway countries. When I realized what is wrong in our country, it was already too late because this gang of brigands had spread throughout our land, penetrating and controlling every facet of our life: politics, religion, education, and many other important things. It is too late because they have surrounded us, they have put chains on our necks and ankles, chains on our minds, hearts, and souls. What can a man do? He is not even free to speak his mind anymore. Or to worship as he knows how. Or to live as he is prepared to do. No wonder many of us have given up, cavorting with and lackeying for those brigands who would want to despoil our country's wealth and beauty at their pleasure. But I am not giving up easily. I have some defiance left in me yet. I will make a dent on their wall of defense yet, even if I have to use my own head to butt it with, even if I have to use my fingernails to bore my way through it."

"You are in a heroic mood tonight," Hassim said.

"That's the spirit, old one," Dante told him.

"Why not? Hassim has taught me a great lesson. He said that even the very air we breathe is foul if there is one foul man left in the world. I am not a philosopher, a thinker, a learned man. But I can see that the foul men are thriving, increasing every day, every hour everywhere in the world. But I can also see that we haters of foul men are increasing as rapidly as they, if not more rapidly; so somewhere, across some barricade of reckoning, we are bound to collide against each other, if not to fight it out to the very end: to see who is fit to live in the world, the foul men or the good men."

"The good men always win," Hassim said.

"It has to be," Dante corroborated.

"Yes, it has to be," Old Bio said. "It says so in the Good Book, even though I have not seen it yet. But it has to be. I feel it in my old bones that it has to be. Otherwise there is no sense in all this striving toward the good, this sacrificing for the good of all."

Hassim felt that the old man was in a nebulous mood of thought. And Dante, walking between them, wanted to be a part of them more than ever before. But he was thinking now of his brother, whom he had not seen for five years. Not that there was anything special that he wanted to resuscitate or anything personal in their relationship that he wanted to clarify. He knew where he stood. His brother knew where he stood. Dante wanted, then, to exact from his brother the width of his demesne, in both spiritual and geographical planes. For in that knowledge, as he himself knew, he could pit his own against his brother's, even the amplitude of his demesne against his brother's, to see which was more durable and enduring, his, Dante's, or his brother's, who had started their breach with a pittance of hypocrisy five years before.

The black rain fell upon them. And on them the cold harbored, soaked their tired bodies through, coupled the night's danger and loneliness. And the gray land spread out around them with its stirring water, crying and crying, like children orphaned and lost, lost, lost: and they were not unknown to the world. Reaching the edge of town now, a light or two blinked at them: the darkness engulfing them dropped away, revealing them to watching hidden eyes.

"Hassim." It was as though the shattering sky crashed upon him, as did the lancelike rain, as did the danger at his side. Hassim turned.

"Did you speak to me, Dante?" Hassim asked.

"Yes."

Hassim's eyes, shining in the darkness and rain, could not see Dante's face. How little he knew about this man who had lived in a land he had never seen; and he felt lost.

"I've a strange feeling, coming back to my hometown, to my own brother," Dante said. "It seems as though I've walked the length of the world, reached the end of time. At thirty-five, I feel as though everything has come to an end, to a dead stop, and there is nowhere else to go: either retreat or advance. It's very strange."

"You are tired."

Even the old man, remote in his loneliness, consumed by his private agonies, heard the anguish in Dante's voice, felt his sudden terror.

"Yes, you are tired," Old Bio seconded Hassim.

"It must be the rain, and the night, and the whole world that we can neither comprehend nor seize with our hands."

"We will be there soon," Hassim consoled him.

"We should rest when we get back to the hideout," Old Bio suggested.

If we will ever rest, Hassim thought. If there is ever rest anywhere, sleeping or awake. How soft and gentle and kind is that word. Rest.

They entered the town. No dogs challenged them, exposed their presence. No windows opened, revealing their identities. No flitting shadows even to spy on them, to follow their movements. Here and there the houses were bright with light, but no one came out to greet them. The silence was grave, deep, dark, and ominous. It was as though it had been stamped officially on the cold night, as though it was its official seal.

Hassim knew at once that he should have brought Dabu with him, even Legaspi, instead of the old man. He knew now what a load, a responsibility, he had on his hands. It seemed to him that someone was warning him from the other side of the night. There from the core of darkness far away, he heard the warning voice. Was this the night of all nights?

Hassim walked on with his companions, seeking the dark side of the street. They passed the marketplace, the plaza, the *presidencia*, the schoolhouse. Then they were in the cobbled yard of the church. They stopped behind flowering banana trees.

The church door was closed, and they saw no light coming through the windows. They watched in silence, contemplating.

"Maybe he is asleep after all," Hassim said.

"I guess so," Dante answered. "The rectory is at the back, and that's where he sleeps."

"He has servants around?"

"Several, and they are scattered all over the place. The acolytes also live here."

"Where?"

"The rooms adjoining their master."

"Let us be on the lookout, if they are all over the place."

"They have any weapons?" Old Bio asked.

"That I don't know," Dante said.

"All right," Hassim said. "Lead the way."

Dante nodded his head slightly and motioned them to follow

him. He plunged into the darkness, through the banana trees, into a trellised alcove, with a high scaffolding of cement walls on either side, opening into a circular patio, then into a long hallway where the rooms of the servants, attendants, and acolytes were located, and at last to the stairs that led to the priest's living quarters. They stopped at the foot of the stairs, looking up and listening for sound. When they were sure that their presence had not been detected, they made ready to go up the stairs.

"Be ready with the flashlight," Dante whispered. "Don't show your guns."

Old Bio was disappointed. He grimaced in the darkness. He followed Dante slowly, his grip of the cold iron bannister was strong. Hassim followed close behind him. They placed their feet on the cement steps one after the other, slowly and softly, so that it took them almost ten full minutes to reach the landing that opened up into three winding hallways, and, spreading out, into darkened corridors.

Dante crept through the hallway on his left. Old Bio and Hassim followed. They stopped at a huge door of teakwood, paneled handsomely, even artistically. There was a fat and tall candle by the door; straight and decorative in green porcelain, it beamed somewhat fatuously, even garishly, there in the mystery and silence of the priest's abode. And even in that strange light, Hassim saw the religious designs and medieval carvings on the teakwood panel. He half-smiled.

Dante knocked quietly. There was no answer. He knocked again. A chair scraped the bare floor. Then slippered feet approached the door.

"Who is it?" a voice called from inside.

Dante nodded to Hassim.

"A messenger from the mayor."

"What, this time of night and in such bestial weather?"

"It's very important, Father."

"Very well."

The door opened slowly. Hassim flashed the light full upon the pajamaed priest. Dante wedged a foot between the door's edge and the wall. Old Bio pushed the door with his broad shoulders. And in an instant they were all inside, the door closed safely behind them, while the priest was still recovering from their sudden intrusion into his privacy. He was completely unprepared, and there was terror in his face. The light from Hassim's hand was still on his face, and he began to shake. Dante waved a hand at Hassim, who immediately clicked off the flashlight. There was a candlelight beaming from an inner room, and it wreathed their faces, half revealing their identities. When the priest recognized Dante, his face changed into anger.

"I should have known!" he shouted.

"Relax, Father Bustamante," Dante said. "We just came to pay you a visit. It's raining outside, and we'd like to share the warmth of your hearth before we go out into the night again."

So that is Dante's real name, Old Bio thought. Soon I will know his first name. Father Bustamante! Ha, I will laugh at his face if he does not show me that fire to warm my old bones.

Father Bustamante looked from Old Bio to Hassim, then back to Dante, and the corners of his mouth twisted bitterly. "You have no right coming here," he said.

"You have not changed, Father Bustamante," Dante said. "Where is your humanity? We are waifs of storm and stress; don't you have human kindness left in you?"

Now Hassim knew that this was the other Dante, speaking quietly and intelligently, yet behind it was a controlled anger, about to break, if it had not yet broken. He watched and listened. How tragic and utterly dismaying to see two intelligent brothers dividing the world, parting as they had parted, and meeting the way they had met: the imposed conclave of two opposites, the hates and fears of man walling them up, making them total strangers.

"That warm hearth of yours, Father Bustamante," Dante said.

"Don't call me Father Bustamante."

"Should I call you Pontius Pilate?"

Old Bio almost roared with laughter. He was enjoying it all. He turned slightly to Hassim, who was smiling almost invisibly. Old Bio winked at him.

"What do you want with me, Conrado?"

"Not so loud, Father Bustamante."

So that is his name, Old Bio thought. Conrado Bustamante. Now where did I hear that before? I must have heard it somewhere? I am sure of it. Was not there a famous man in this part during the reign of Spain? I must think. Think. Yes! Why did Dante's face escape me? Of course, it is his new name. It does not seem possible that they are brothers, the only grandsons of a man who had fought like I did against Spain, only in a bigger way, far, far bigger way. And right away Old Bio wanted to impart to Hassim what he had just discovered, to tell him that he knew Dante's antecedent and that he felt closer to Dante now that he knew it.

"I don't want you in here."

"We're men of peace, Father Bustamente."

"I told you to go!"

"You mean 'command,' Father Bustamante?"

The priest rushed to the door where they had come in to call for the servants. Hassim grabbed his arm and twisted it around to his back. He looked at Hassim with hate in his eyes.

"Your brother told you that we are men of peace," Hassim said. "Believe him, and don't make any trouble for yourself. Take us into a room where we can talk quietly."

"Let go of my arm!"

Hassim released him. Father Bustamante strode across the room. They followed him almost at his heels. They entered a bigger room with a burning fire in a corner. There was a rug on the floor, an ornate table with four similar chairs around it, and on the table was a tall wine container and several clean glasses. These attracted the attention of the old man, although he walked immediately to the fire and put his back to it, shaking his legs as he eyed the wine with great attentiveness.

Father Bustamante stood at one side of the table, studying them one by one. Dante sat at one side of the table, opposite his brother. Hassim leaned against a wall between them, so perfect was their distance, the three of them, that the priest was exactly on the right angle of each of them.

"You don't only force your way into my place, but you don't even have respect for the finer things in life," Father Bustamante said, watching Dante soaking the polished table with his wet clothes.

"I suppose you have never intruded into the lives of others, Father Bustamante?" Dante said. "I suppose you never told them to do this and to do that? I suppose you have never intruded into their minds and hearts and souls by telling them not to do this and not to do that?"

"I've the right to do those things."

"Don't give me that kind of talk. You are not talking to a peasant. And by the way, you have almost called the peasants dumb and stupid and dirty, forgetting the ugly fact that you yourself were a dirty peasant until, of course, I sent you to school."

Hassim turned to the priest. He had not known that before. Even Old Bio was surprised. His mouth hung wide open.

"Sure you have the right to exploit the peasants now by using the abracadabra of religion," Dante said. "You Filipinos, when you have a little education, are worse than anybody else I've ever seen. Especially when you wear the cloak of Christ."

"Even in the house of God you blaspheme."

"You are talking to a man who knows more than you will ever know in a thousand years. Don't use those phrases that you have borrowed from silly men. 'The house of God,' indeed." He beat his breast. "This is where the house of God lies, Father Bustamante! Not in your house of wickedness and treachery!"

"Yes, I see that you are truly an atheist. And I suppose, being with these people, you have also become a communist."

"Wait a minute there," Old Bio said, leaping away from the fire. He strode across the room and lifted a shaking finger at the priest. "Don't you call me a communist! I am a patriot!"

Father Bustamante looked at Old Bio with a steady gaze. Then he turned to Dante.

"Your companions must take me for an idiot, Dante," he said.

Dante studied his brother's face.

"Yes, I know your new name," Father Bustamante said. And slowly turning to Hassim, he said, "I congratulate you for your silence and self-control, Hassim. And you old man, Old Bio they call you, don't point your finger at me again. I'm a civilized man, if ever you saw one."

Old Bio looked at his obesity with disgust. He grabbed the

decanter and put it to his mouth. He drank. He choked. He smelled the stuff. He had never tasted it before. He looked at Dante.

"Are you bewildered, Old Bio?" Dante said. "That's brandy in your hand, imported from Spain, and probably fifty years old. The best that the church money could buy."

"I thought it was poison."

"No, go ahead. You'll not find one like it again. Don't be conscience-stricken. It's paid for by the people."

"Our people?"

"Who else?"

"Ay!"

They all watched the old man drink a mouthful of the brandy. He put the decanter back on the table and said, "What were you saying, Father Bustamante?"

The priest looked at the old man's glaring eyes, but he turned away and did not say anything. His hand was slowly moving to the table drawer, but almost imperceptively, as though his hand were moving that way by accident.

"Now that we are all acquainted with each other," Hassim interrupted at last, "I would like to have an explanation."

"Meaning how I came to know you?"

"Precisely."

"I thought you are really alert and intelligent," Father Bustamante said, slowly turning to the wall above Hassim's head. It was a document in a frame, with a huge black cross on the left-hand corner, above, and the Philippine flag on the right-hand corner, above, and in the center was the priest's name in bold letters, followed by the name of the governor of the province. "Read what it says if you can read," he added contemptuously.

The three of them looked at it, and Hassim and Dante read it:

CITIZENS' LEAGUE PARTY

FATHER BERNARDO BUSTAMANTE

DISTRICT DIRECTOR

And in that brief instant, when they were reading the document, Father Bustamante's hand leaped quickly into the drawer and brought out something dark and cold; he sat down on the chair noiselessly and put it between his thighs. Old Bio had almost seen him, for he had turned toward him suddenly; the document did not mean anything to him, for to him it was one of those mysterious parchments that he had signed without knowing what was in it.

"So even the church is in politics now?" Dante said.

"We have as much stake in the country as any of the other parties."

"Naturally."

"I suppose your organization has all our pictures and dossiers. It didn't take you long to recognize us, even this old man who probably has never seen a camera."

The priest opened the drawer again and picked a pamphlet from several others stacked inside and threw it on the table beside Dante. Hassim and Dante glanced swiftly at its title:

KNOW THE ENEMY:

THEIR BACKGROUND, PICTURES, CHARACTERISTICS .

Hassim and Dante looked at each other, but they did not touch the document. It was incredible, too incredible. The church had all that information about them? If they had, how did they get it? If they got it, who did the work?

Hassim was bewildered. It was his first time to come out of the jungles in so many years that he did not realize what was going on outside. No wonder this obese priest was so arrogant!

"You must have a neat organization," Hassim said.

"Better than any in the land."

"Explain."

"We have the people."

"You mean the church people."

"Yes. And others."

"You have me," Old Bio interrupted. 'I am not a church man, but I surely believe in the teachings of the Lord."

The priest looked up at Old Bio and wondered how much was the old man involved in the underground. Because the old man was at this point lifting the decanter to his mouth, Father Bustamante sneered. Then he dismissed him with a snarl and turned to Dante.

"You might as well know that we are preparing for the national election."

"You have a candidate for the presidency?"

"For the presidency, governors, congressmen, and mayors. Of course we are putting our very best forces behind the candidate for the presidency."

"Your candidates are all church people?"

"Of course not. Professional politicians, careerists, and the like. But they are all under our thumbs."

"You are violating the national constitution, especially that part where it definitely states the separation of the state and church."

"Don't be an idealist. Who made the constitution? Our men did. Who can undo it? Our men can. With our proper backing, of course."

"Nice setup," Hassim commented.

"Yes."

"My brother Bernardo," Dante said quietly, "what a pity that you've become a priest. You were once a man with a soul, so delicate and sensitive, so quick of pity and compassion and tenderness. I don't want to tell you what you are now, for you know it yourself. Do you still remember when we used to recite some verses of St. John of the Cross? You used to weep when we came to the 'Cantico Espiritual entre el Alma y Cristo su Esposo,' which runs like this:

> Adonde te escondiste,
> Amado, y me dejaste con gemido?
> Como el ciervo huiste,
> habiéndome herido;
> salí tras tí clamando, y ya eras ido.

> (Ah, where hast thyself hidden,
> Beloved, and left me all in lamentation?
> Like the stag hast thou fled,
> After thou didst wound me;
> I went forth crying after thee, and thou wert gone.)

Old Bio listened and felt guilty. He pushed the decanter of brandy away. He murmured the lines after Dante without wholly understanding what he was repeating. The priest sat uneasily. Hassim turned away from them and looked toward the window, where he could see the heavy rain beating against the tortoise shell of the panes. He had heard music too. The music of youth and young love. The music of family and living. Then there were other strains of music: of labor, of comradeship, of a dream. And there were still other strains: of fighting and death, of longing and loneliness, of pain and happiness. He had longed so much to hear the music of the land, of the mountains and rivers and plains and valleys, and of the people and animals and birds in them. How would he achieve that music? And where? And when? There was only the music of the cold rain left, and the thunder and lightning, and the long night, and the enemy hiding in the darkness.

"And do you still remember the part that you loved most," Dante was saying, "that we both recited one day on our knees? It runs like this:

> Buscando mis amores,
> iré por esos montes y riberas,
> ni cogeré las flores,
> ni temeré las fieras,
> y pasaré los fuertes y fronteras.
>
> (Seeking after my loved one,
> I shall go through woods and stream banks,
> Nor shall I gather flowers,
> Nor shall I fear the wild beasts,
> And I shall pass by ports and o'er frontiers.)

"That's enough!" Father Bustamante said.

"Yes, that's what I can show as passion for the Lord," Dante said. "That's passionate marriage of your soul to Christ. What has happened? Of course you are now a politician, and a landlord, and a priest. You have gone very far since the days when you ate snails and periwinkles from the river, Father Bustamante. Yes, indeed."

"What do you want? Is it money?"

"Not your kind of money."

"What is wrong with it?"

"It's blasphemous money. Forced out of the pockets of naked and starving peasants in the name of Christ. No, Father Bustamante. We don't take that kind of money. We use money that's freely given – and given in the sense that the giver knows why he is giving it and what it's for."

"You came back to provoke me."

"I came to tell you that in the name of Christ you are a bastard."

Father Bustamante's hand leaped from underneath the table. A sharp sound, like the screech of a cricket under a slab of stone, filled the room. A streak of fire struck Dante's shoulder, and the world seemed to tumble upon him, imprisoning him, squeezing him out of breath. Then the blood spurted out of his body, crimsoning his rain-soaked shirt.

And in that instant, Old Bio flung the decanter of brandy upon the priest, whose second shot was diverted to the floor. And almost at the same instant, Hassim brought down the butt of his gun on the priest's tonsure, digging a hole two inches deep; then brought it down again at the back of his right ear, and again on his temple, killing him. Then he motioned Old Bio to run to the door.

"The bastard got me, Hassim," Dante whispered weakly.

"You will be all right," Hassim said. If he had only not been meditating about music! Lucky the old man was around and at attention. He could have killed us all. Hell! He ripped Dante's shirt. "You are lucky. It's only the shoulder."

Old Bio ran back into the inner room. "I heard footsteps in the hallway," he said.

"Hold him."

Old Bio grabbed Dante. Hassim ran to one of the windows and smashed it with his gun. They were on the second floor, about twelve feet high. The rain beat upon him. Then he ran back to help Old Bio carry Dante to the window.

"Jump, old one," Hassim whispered. "I will go to the door, but wait for him."

Old Bio heard the heavy pounding on the door. He climbed up the window and jumped into the night, the gun held firmly in his right hand.

"Come on , Dante," Hassim urged.

"I can't."

"You can."

"What a way to die."

Hassim helped him climb up the window.

"Jump."

Dante sucked the air and jumped. Hassim ran back to the door of the inner room. The pounding on the outer door became louder. He waited breathlessly, guns in both hands. He began to perspire. His temple throbbed with pain.

Then the door broke open. And the hail of fire from his guns filled the room. He saw bodies falling at the door and in the hall. He heard someone running down the stairs. But he did not wait. He ran to the broken window and flung himself into the rain and the night.

## CHAPTER TWENTY-FIVE

. . . . . . . . . . . . . . . . . . . . . . . . . . . . . . . . . . . . .

**D**ante did not know how long he had been lying in the cold grass. It seemed as though he had been there for an eternity, his bleeding right shoulder crushed beneath him. Even his fall from the broken window of the rectory above him had seemed so slow, so quiet, as though he were falling from a great height on a magic carpet; but not exactly falling, for it had seemed that he was floating down on the carpet to the wet earth. Now as he lay immobile in the cold grass, he seemed to be crouching in the gray darkness of an old tomb in an abandoned cemetery. The silence seemed so profound to him that he could hear his heart beating against a blade of grass; indeed, so frightening that he could even hear his tears falling with the rain in the solitude of his helplessness.

Time was slipping away, second after long second. But he could not move; he could not even utter a cry for help. And in that agonizing passage of time he seemed, at long last, to have seized the citadel of his life of turmoil and pain. He saw it tumbling above him, all the scaffoldings cracking in several places, the pedestal giving in to the terrible weight and the sudden rumblings around him. It all seemed clear to him now: why he had been born poor; why he had left home when he was merely a boy; why he had gone to that other land called America, which he could not forget: his sufferings and longings in that strange land; why he had returned to his native soil; why his roots had been uprooted; why his friends had been gone. He moaned, and new tears blinded him; tears not of regret or surrender, but of a vivid understanding that it had seemed all so futile, so useless in the boundless panorama of human life. He knew he had joined the underground to give a meaning to his last days on earth, only to culminate in this rainful night, bleeding to death.

He felt the cold metal of his gun against his thigh, but only slightly and almost recognizably, for it seemed a part of his body, twisted finger underneath him. He opened his eyes, and all around him he saw the rain falling in the darkness through a mist of tears. Then he heard the muffled sound of running feet beating the earth, coming closer to him. With his free hand he tried to wipe his face, to have a better view of what was approaching him. But his sight was dim now, even as his life was dim; only his inner vision was sharp and clear, transcending time and space, focusing on the indiscriminate course of his life, all of his virtues and shames. He looked around him, with only his eyes rolling painfully in their sockets, his aching chest glued to the wet earth, his heart pounding, the rain-cleaned grass pouring upon him with all its fragrance.

"Come on, son!"

Who said that? Was it his father's voice when his, Dante's, stride could not keep up with the old man's long and hurried stride? When was that? Was it when he was ten and he and his father had gone to the village where his mother was dying? Yes, it could be. For the urgent voice came from afar, from a childhood day in the long ago, reaching him on the back of the wind of time, the wind of April and the strong rain, reaching him in the night. And he saw himself again, when he was ten, watching his dying mother under an oil lamp, turning to his sorrowing father when he said: "Is this all the meaning of life – to be born, to work hard, to die?" And he wanted to embrace his father then, to tell him that there was one comfort left; that he, Dante, would hug him through the darkness and coldness of life with his own warmth and light. Father, Father, where are you now? he murmured.

"Come on, son!"

That urgent voice again. If he could only move. If he could only get up. He would run furiously across the earth and shout to all the living: "I'll be damned, I'm alive!" If he could only shout. He would tell the whole world: "You devils, you didn't get me yet!" It was then that he felt a firm hand under his bleeding shoulder lift him up. He could not move; his legs were like soft clay. Even his head, dripping with rain, seemed out of place; and he wanted to touch it to be sure that it was still there, on top of him, a part of his body. If he could only move his hand. Now someone was helping him move his legs, step by step – slowly, painfully; it seemed as though his feet were weighted with stones, and somewhere someone in the night was pulling the stones away from the direction to which he was groping blindly, weakly. Then he felt another firm hand under his other shoulder, where there was a little feeling left. Then he was lifted up, and the earth flowed away from him. He was moving slowly through space without touching the ground, and only the rain falling upon his face told him that he was alive.

"Old Bio?" he asked weakly.

"Yes."

"Hassim?"

"Yes."

"Did the bastard get me?"

Silence.

"What happened to my legs?"

"They are all right."

"But I can't walk!"

"You lost plenty of blood."

"The bastard got me!"

"Take it easy."

Then he fainted. When he came to, he was leaning against a tree.

"Hassim?" he asked.

"Yes."

"Old Bio?"

"Yes."

"Where are we?"

"Not far from our hideout."

Dante opened his eyes. It was dark. It was still raining. He could hear the raindrops making a tremolo on the leaves. He sucked his lips. His right shoulder was numb, and he wondered why he could hardly feel anything. Then he saw Hassim standing in front of him, his back to him, and the old man sitting beside him, holding his head in his hands. From afar he could hear muffled voices. He could see torches moving in the darkness. What was going on out there? He wanted to ask the old man, but his mouth was dry and hot. He closed his eyes and swallowed his saliva; it went down his throat like boiling lead.

Hassim turned to him and asked, "Can you hear me, Dante?"

Dante nodded his head weakly.

"We have to take care of your wound. Is there any doctor in this town?"

"Yes."

"Show us the way. We'll take you to him."

"It's no use."

Old Bio helped him to his feet. "Come on, son," he said.

"No."

"It's the best thing to do, Dante," Hassim said.

"The mission – "

"It can wait."

"The mission first."

"Come on, son," Old Bio said again.

"Above all the mission, Hassim."

"You first, Dante."

Dante moaned. He knew that the risk would endanger their mission and the lives of his companions. He wanted to be alone now: to bleed slowly to death, to be wholly forgotten, so that they could proceed with the trip. With his left hand he felt for his gun. It was gone. Had he dropped it somewhere? Was it left in the grass where he had lain helpless? Now he could not even do one last heroic deed for the underground and his companions. He felt the edge of the buckle of his belt. No; it was too blunt. And he was too weak to use it. He licked his lips; his tongue was like sandpaper. He sobbed. Had it all come to this bitter end? All the protean struggle to gain a foothold on life? Damn it all, damn it all.

Hassim and Old Bio lifted him to his feet.

"The mission," he protested.

"The mission is useless without you," Hassim said.

"Yes," Old Bio agreed.

It's true, Dante reflected. The mission is truly useless without me. Who would identify Felix if I were dead? No one. The underground would be betrayed. I've got to live. I must live!

Dante walked with them, but he barely touched the ground. He turned his head now and then, directing them, avoiding the houses. And as he walked with them, barely touching the ground, he wanted to curse himself for being so useless, so helpless, so out of place. How many times had he dreamed of doing the very same thing to his companions, of carrying one or even two of them against great obstacles, facing danger and even close to death! But now, now that passionate dream had come true, only it had turned the other way round, only it had turned against him: against the man who had returned to his native land with a crystal-clear vision of awakening his people and showing them the true nature of the world in which they live: he, Dante, who had denied himself many things including women to prepare himself for the gigantic task ahead. And now it had all come to this bitter end.

Swept all over now that it had come to futility, Dante sighed deep within himself. There was a wintry sensation in the pit of his stomach. Must not die, he commanded himself. The world – is there a corner left in the world where I could have peace? Yes. Peace. What a beautiful word! How many glorious men and women have died for it? I've read many books about it. I've traveled through history, following its path. Peace, peace, peace to the troubled world! They told me to salute a flag and fight for it. But what flag? There were flags everywhere, and in many colors, and I saluted them all, sometimes with tears in my eyes. But which was the right flag? And in what color? Damn it to hell! They made me blind with my eyes open. God, how they reduced me to a slobbering beast, an imitation of a man! They told me man is free, is even divine. They told me man is pride and nobility. Where is that man now? Where is that noble man, that free man now? Peace. Where is the place for me to go? I've been everywhere in this world and in every corner was the huge sign: "We don't want your kind here. Now get out through the back door!" To the moon, maybe? Almighty God, let me live! Give me a gun! I could show them who is man enough to stand with both feet on the solid earth. But why is it that only in killing do they want me? Is there no place for me in the making of nice things? Once when I was a little boy I had a garden in the corner of our yard where I planted beautiful things, roses and things like that, because I liked growing things springing out of the richness of the earth, like vines creeping on the fence and reaching for sunlight and air. But they came, the proud men came, the cruel men came and crushed my beautiful plants with their boots, and they whipped me with their leather whips, and I didn't cry. They shouted, "You can't plant things here. We own this corner, this land, this country. We own the sunlight, the air, the whole world. We own your life. Now get out!" Yes, they own everything. Even in my dreams, my very private dreams, I see them with their crushing boots and leaping leather whips. I see their snarling forked tongues. I see their hate-corroded faces coming to seize my dreams away from me. No. No. I'll not go to them on my knees. . . .

"Are you all right, Dante?"

That must be Hassim's voice. He nodded his head. Strange. It seemed to have come from afar, brushing his ears like a melody.

"Take it easy. We'll soon be there."

He nodded his head again. That must be the old man's voice, concerned, gentle even. The voice of age and wisdom. The voice that had said many things in many places – in other times, other conflicts.

"Are you sure we are going in the right direction?"

"Yes." His own voice! He heard his own voice! He could talk. He was still alive. How precious it was to be able to talk! To express one's desire! Talk, Dante! Talk your head off! Say Yes!

"Here we are."

He opened his eyes.

"What's his name?"

"Jack O'Brian."

"American?"

"Yes."

The house was dark. Hassim motioned to the old man to knock on the door. Old Bio rapped twice. A window lit up. The sound of slippered feet approached the door. Silence. Old Bio knocked again. The door opened and a white face appeared. Old Bio kicked the door wide open and walked into the house before the man could protest. Hassim and Dante followed him. The man looked at them with indignation.

"What's the meaning of this intrusion?" he demanded.

"You are a doctor, aren't you?" Hassim said.

"Yes."

"Then go to it."

The doctor looked at Dante.

"He is hurt," Hassim explained.

"It is obvious. But what an ungodly hour!"

Old Bio understood the doctor's gesture of protest. He stirred and showed his gun.

"You'd better do it," he said in Tagalog. "And I mean it."

The doctor studied the old man's face, then Hassim's, and in an instant he knew that he was powerless.

"Is he threatening me?" he asked.

"The gun is threatening you," Hassim said sharply.

Dante regained consciousness. He was still leaning against Hassim; through the gathering mist of his memory he recognized the doctor. Then he saw Old Bio's menacing gun.

"Doctor O'Brian – " Dante said weakly.

"You know me?"

"I am – or was – a resident of this town."

"I see."

"You'd better do as the old man says, Doctor. He's not kidding with that gun. That gun of his has a long history. But there's no time for that now. You and I, we are both Americans, as the saying goes. But the old boy is a primitive and a peasant; he doesn't believe in the niceties of civilization the way we do."

It was Dante's last brave act; for even now, in his semidelirium, he had succeeded in building a bridge, at long last, scanning the chasm between the two lives he had lived, joining the land he could not forget with his native land, fusing the two personalities in him at last, and completely, the American and the Filipino; an act that took him thirty-five years to arrive at and execute, which was the ultimate fusion of his two selves; he, Dante, who was an American one moment and a Filipino the next, complete now at the very door of death.

"You've lived in the United States?"

"In more ways than you think, Doctor. My heart is divided, as it is. So from one American to another, in this wilderness of the world, do as the old man says. Otherwise – " Dante turned to Hassim, who seemed so far away and inscrutable now. The doctor followed his eyes, and he saw in Hassim's face something strange, remote, and even cruel. "Otherwise – " he repeated, and fainted.

"Take him to the back room," the doctor told Hassim. "There is a table there. Put him on it."

Hassim told Old Bio to stay at the door. He carried Dante to the back room. He found the table, and put Dante on it. Hassim studied his face for a moment, and it came to him suddenly and sadly that he was dying. When the doctor entered the room, Hassim looked at him with inquiring eyes. Doctor O'Brian avoided his eyes. He walked to the stove where a glass jar filled with surgical instruments was in readiness. He lit the wick under it, and motioned to Hassim to strip off Dante's blood-soaked, rain-soaked shirt. Then he put his rubber gloves on and started to operate.

In the middle of the operation, Dante regained consciousness again. And in that sudden awakening to reality, so brief yet so eternal, he tried to grope for a prayer. But he could not pray; he could not remember the words hovering in his fading memory. He felt the doctor's fingers on his body, but there was no pain; there was only a slight sensation, as though he were being brushed by a feather. Desperately he wrestled with his memory; somewhere in the forested darkness of his subconscious, he flung himself wildly, searching for the last comforting words to a troubled life. He moaned. Then he fainted again. When he came to, he remembered a friend of his in the long ago, a young poet who had lived with him in Seattle for a while. What did that sonofabitch tell me when we were rooming together in that cold room? he reflected. "Now, now, Conrad," he had said. "Violence doesn't settle anything. It only breeds violence." And he had asked in anger and desperation,

"What is the way then?" And that bastard of a poet, who was dying of tuberculosis, had answered, "Well, Conrad, understanding and tolerance are our best weapons in this our fight for a better world." And he had screamed, "Hell! Hell! Hell! I hate this world! I hate the whole human race!" And the dying poet had looked at him with sad eyes. And it was that look of sadness that had followed him everywhere, even to the jungles where he had been fighting for years, and even to this very room where one of them, one of those proud men who had inflicted a cyst of hate in his being was touching him and yet not touching him, measuring the shrinking length of his life. Now he could feel the weight of death on his body, and once more he heard the animal roar of the howling mob that had pursued him down the streets of San Diego, when vigilantes chased him out of town because of his organizational work. He could not hold himself any longer. He wanted to cry out to the world that had pressed him to a dark corner of life. "I hate the whole world," he murmured. Then he lost consciousness.

Was that all that he could remember? Think, Dante! In the depth of your soul were the embedded wondrous words, lost to the world for a while. Remember, remember! How did it go? Yes –

When Thou hast fled me, the world fleest from me;
Through thickets and woodlands, across seas and oceans,
I followed Thee, seeking Thy path: O Most Beloved,
Thou hast forsaken me, Thy wandering lost son. . . .

Doctor O'Brian looked at Hassim; beads of perspiration had bearded his face. The dull glow in the doctor's eyes told Hassim that it was too late. It was really too late, and Hassim sighed with sadness.

"There's nothing I can do now," the doctor said.

"Is he – ?"

He nodded his head. "I did the best I could," he explained.

"I understand," Hassim said, and left the room. He found Old Bio leaning against the front door, facing an American woman silently. "Mrs. O'Brian?" he asked.

She nodded her head.

Hassim turned to the old man. "He is dead," he said.

Old Bio looked at Hassim for a long time without speaking. Then he put the gun inside his shirt and bowed slightly to Mrs. O'Brian.

"He is apologizing to you, Mrs. O'Brian," Hassim said. "He does not understand English."

"Thank you. Is he dead?"

"Yes."

She got up and went to the operating room. Hassim and the old man followed her. They stood around the table where Dante lay lifeless. The doctor was sitting in a rattan chair, smoking a cigarette. Mrs. O'Brian studied Dante's face.

"He seems to be a sensitive person," she commented.

"He is," Hassim said.

"We call him Dante."

"Dante of the underground?"

"Yes."

"But of course. I should have recognized that face."

Doctor O'Brian stirred in his chair. "Who did it?" he asked.

"His brother."

Mrs. O'Brian looked askance.

"Father Bustamante," Hassim explained.

Mrs. O'Brian flicked an eye. Then she rushed out of the room and came back with a book.

"This is one of the best books," she said. "I would like to give it to him."

Hassim saw the title: *Tales of My Own People.* Old Bio took the book from Mrs. O'Brian and leafed through the pages with his wet fingers, as though he were reading it. But he was only fondling it. Then he returned to Mrs. O'Brian, who tucked it inside Dante's shirt.

"I've never seen him alive," Mrs. O'Brian said. "But I've always enjoyed his books. I don't know what he had been doing since he returned to the Philippines, but now he is dead. I would have liked to have known him."

"I have never really understood him," Hassim said. "But he must have gone through a great ordeal in the United States. I don't know what to say, because he had always praised and hated the American people at the same time."

The doctor rose from his chair and looked at Hassim fiercely. He said, "You come into my house and speak of hate, as if you were looking for it. Well, hate is in every heart. Whoever started it is none of my business. But remember this: I hate the Filipino people too!"

"No, Jack," Mrs. O'Brian intervened. "Not that, dear." It was a whispered scream, the call of one who had known pain: the call to stop the flow of blood from someone who had let blood flow into the world of hating men, who was always alert to violence like animals that feed on blood. Then she said to Hassim, "Have we not done enough for you? Have we not endangered our lives for your safety? Let us live in peace. Please go now."

Quietly Hassim walked to the window. The rain was still falling, and he could hear it beating against the pane. And as he stood there looking out into the night, the cigarette dangling in a corner of his mouth and illuminating his profile, he knew that he had to say something to this proud man to remember him by. He had to grapple with space and time, wrest away from the silence of years a land called America and fling it upon this room, beside this proud man, and point to towns and cities where fragments of Dante's life had been lost and where drops of his blood had been spilled to make the soil of that land rich for vegetation. He could provoke him into an argument and gunplay. He could slay him and his wife. And no one would ever know; no one would ever find out. He turned away from the night and walked back to the table.

"Yes, I understand now why Dante was bitter about you people," he said to the two Americans. "Even in our own land you try to run our lives. But you will not succeed this time. History has turned the other way round, and the reckoning is not far off."

"Please go," Mrs. O'Brian pleaded.

Hassim nodded to the old man, who bent over the table and gathered Dante in his arms. "Let us go, son," he said.

They walked to the front room and stood by the door.

"'We will leave you now," Hassim said to Mrs. O'Brian. Then looking at the doctor, he said, "But I will see you and your kind again, Doctor. I will meet you again across a barricade in this land, or even in your own land, or in some land somewhere in the world, for you will be defending all your beliefs and we will be defending ours. But until that day comes, I will save one bullet for you." Then he opened the door, and they vanished into the wet night.

So say good-bye to the world, Dante. The world that you had known was filled with troubles, unkind, ugly. But now it was all over. And you would never again see the world, never again sit on the green grass of the earth, never again hear the birds sing in the trees. And Mameng? Mameng was gone too, Dante. She who in all the world had given you a brief passage into joy, that Mameng was gone too, gone with all the others that you had tried to find in this unfriendly world. Mameng of the hillside and the cane field, she was gone. Only the eternal star of your sleep was left now; it was there fixed in the firmament of your sky to guide you always. So good night, good night.

And good-bye, comrade of the dark night. The world that you never made was left behind you now; it would be here now that you are gone; it would not trouble you anymore. And Hassim and Old Bio were left now to carry you down the hill and across the field, to locate a final resting place for you, since you belong to time and the wind now. There in some unmarked corner of your native land, there where birds would sing for you, there where the moon and the stars would shine over your mound of earth, there where the sun would creep into your sodden home, there in your resting place at last, at long last. You are home from the dark voyage, home from the perilous seas of life. Home, home.

So rest forever now, Dante.

## CHAPTER TWENTY-SIX

. . . . . . . . . . . . . . . . . . . . . . . . . . . . . . . .

**O**ld Bio carried the dead Dante in his arms through the town and across the flooded fields to their wet hideout in the canebrake. Hassim walked beside him in silence, casting a sweeping sidelong glance once in a while to see if they had been discovered. Or if the doctor had called the police. It seemed to them that there was no need for words; they still could not believe that Dante was truly dead. The transition from life to death was so swift that, even as they walked sadly in the darkness and rain to their companions, they were thinking simultaneously of the living Dante sitting at the edge of the immaculate table in his brother's rectory. For that was the real Dante, dripping with rain and talking in a somber, quiet voice, molding and remolding the unforgotten years with carefully modulated words, as though what he wanted to say was the last to come from him; so protean was his message that he thought he could encompass the glissando of time, capture the pulse of life in the glittering anarchy of that room in the rectory. The real Dante, who had known many solitudes and transitory loves; he had returned to his country to live, but death came instead to silence him forever.

Hassim glanced at the old man's burden and rubbed his itching nose. He could not shed a tear; it was unmanly for him to cry. How many times in the last few years had he carried comrades who had fallen in battle the way the old man was doing now? Even as he walked in the rain he remembered that frightful night when he had carried the bleeding Cy, the first Political Director of the underground and his mentor, through the thick jungles to their hidden camp. He remembered how he had felt that night: the numbing anguish welling up in his heart, for he knew that the loss of Cy would be a great blow to the organization. Creeping through the jungles he had murmured a prayer many times; in those early days of the struggle he still remembered that prayer from childhood. Now he wished he could remember it, for he had another burden not unlike that one a long time ago. Dante was a propagandist for the underground; who would take his place now? Who? He rubbed his itching nose again and sighed.

The gray darkness of the rain was impenetrable. And the sky was a huge blackness above them. But they walked on in silence, the rain pelting them with all its ferocity. It seemed to them that they had always lived in a world of rain; of silver rain, gray rain, black rain. In the fields it was gray rain, in the valley it was silver rain, in the jungle it was black rain. But it was always rain, sometimes cold and sometimes warm. And the ferocious rain in their hearts matched the ferocity of the rain in the world, cleaving their lives mercilessly into two irreparable parts. And these parts were impaled on the crossroad of their nights and days, on the wall of their dangerous task.

When they reached the hideout, the rain had lessened. The sky was clearing; there were even a few faint stars filling the bowl of night. And the dragons of darkness were speeding away, chased by cataracts of spearlike luminance leaping from every corner of the earth. It was bright enough for them; they who were comrades of the dark; they who lived in the shadows of night. It was bright enough for them to perform the rituals of their tragedy, not as phantoms but as clearly defined characters. Indeed, as men who could even hear the growth of a blade of grass in the darkness.

It was Dabu who first knew the tragedy, even before Old Bio laid down his burden on the grass before them. He knelt beside Dante and crossed his hands; then, looking up at Hassim with understanding, he rose to his feet and motioned to Legaspi. The two men started digging a shallow grave not far from the body with their knives. They worked with steady, expert hands, as though they were used to this kind of work, as though, in the shadows, they could see even the threadlike roots of the canes weaving a pattern of intricate motif below the surface of the wet earth.

Mameng leaned heavily against Linda Bie's breast and cried soundlessly. Her body shook in anguish and desperation, and in the pit of her stomach, because of her sudden loss, she felt a nausea rising up with a rending coldness, shattering her foothold on life. Now her heart seemed to be drying up, squeezing her lungs and throat with steely tightness. Then all at once she seemed to be bursting with an agony so great that she lost control of herself, at last, and cried out, "My God!"

Linda Bie gently stroked her shoulders, for there was nothing else for him to do. He could hear Mameng's heart hammering against his ribs, and it seemed, through contagion, that his heart was also beginning to murmur against his will. Then he squeezed Mameng against his breast, for indeed his heart was not murmuring but thundering against his chest. His whole being seemed beaten into a certain shape under that thundering noise, and for a moment he wanted to repeat Mameng's desperate cry of loneliness. But he controlled himself; he held Mameng tightly for fear of falling down with her. When Hassim and Old Bio carried the body to the shallow watery grave, he turned Mameng's face away so she would not see it.

Dabu and Legaspi quickly pushed the wet clay with their palms over the body. When they had completely covered it to ground level, Old Bio cut a few stalks of corn and spread them over the unmarked grave. Then the four of them stood silently for a minute, looking down at the wreath of green corn leaves. Then all at once they were strapping on their knapsacks and checking their guns.

Hassim led the way out of the cane field. The others followed him in single file, with the old man at the end. It had been Old Bio's secret motive to be the last, because now he stopped and turned around. He made the Sign of the Cross and murmured a prayer. Then he picked up a handful of clay and threw it into the darkness.

At the edge of the cane field they stopped to wait for the old man. When he appeared, they walked in twos: Dabu and Legaspi ahead, Mameng and Linda Bie next, Hassim and Old Bio last. They marched southward, away from the town. They marched on for three hours, when the sky darkened with rain clouds again. They stopped for a minute, and Hassim and Legaspi exchanged places.

Then the rain began to fall. Still they had not said a single word. They had many things to say, but the shock of the sudden loss of their comrade made them speechless. It seemed as though they would all suddenly burst into tears if they began talking about Dante. Only the rain was speaking for them now; only the sky was weeping for them tonight. And the dark night was in mourning for them now. And the night itself wore in the darkness of its visage the blackness of their sorrow.

Still they marched on. They were now four hours away from the cornfield. Hassim made a sign to Dabu to light a match, which he did without asking why, and Hassim looked at his watch. It was five in the morning. Then a volley of pistol shots burst out in the night, a second after Dabu blew out the match. They dropped to the ground in a formation that was almost beautiful, if not magnificent, for they were moving in uniform, their breasts glued to the muddy field: three facing the north, three facing the south, their feet almost touching each other. And the moment they dropped on the ground they started firing.

Hassim saw a figure fall before him. Quickly his eyes probed the darkness. He saw three others who were dropping to the ground to take position. And he wondered how many there were on Dabu's side as he took aim at another figure. There was firing all around him. He fired. Did he get his target? He could not know. The figure of a man was stretched on the ground. The shooting became sporadic. Only Old Bio, at the end of the line, seemed to be shooting. Then the man before him fired. The bullet sang an inch above his head. He was wrong. The enemy was very much alive and a good shot. He glued his chin to the mud, thinking. He would pretend dead. Perhaps his enemy would be foolish enough to raise his head. He waited. And sure enough, he raised his head. Hassim fired. The man's head plopped into a puddle.

Hassim looked around him in the darkness and the falling rain. They were surrounded. How many were they? Ten? Twenty? If they were policemen, they would be about ten in number. A town the size of the one they had just left would have ten men in its force. Ten, then, would be the right number of their enemies, unless some special guards had come with them. Hassim looked straight ahead of him, but it was too dark for him to see if their enemies were wearing uniforms. He was sweating profusely; even in the cold rain, he felt warm. Behind him, Dabu was firing. He thought of Legaspi with all his paraphernalia, crouching behind his sack of food and liquor. Then he laughed a little, because he suddenly remembered Old Bio, who was probably firing with one hand and drinking with the other. Did the doctor inform on them? Had they been recognized by the attendants and servants at the rectory? He began to plan a strategy. They could not crouch all night in the open field, what with the dawn about to break. Slowly he began to edge back to Dabu.

Dabu was also crawling back toward him in the mud. Their feet met, and they spoke with their shoes.

Taptap-tap: Dabu's shoes asked. "What to do?"

Taptap: Hassim's shoes answered. "Break away."

Tap-tap-tap: Dabu's shoes asked again. "Tell the others?"

Tap: Hassim's shoes answered. "Yes."

Dabu crawled away from Hassim, who could hear his body
sloshing in the mud. Quickly Hassim glanced at his companions who were all hugging the earth, as though they were all dead; but they were not because he saw them firing. His fingers were getting numb. He blew at his hands without interrupting his aim, and his hot breath made them feel better. It seemed that Dabu had been gone for a long time, crawling inch by inch and repeating the message to get away. A few times in the past they had been trapped like this in the open fields, and Dabu had to crawl back to the end of the line to repeat the message; and then he would stay at the end of the line so that in the getaway he cover his companions at the back, while Hassim covered them in front. If they would make the getaway now, how many would fall? He would not think of it, but the thought persisted in his mind. He breathed hard and aimed.

Then there was firing beyond the line of their enemies. Their enemies were encircled by another group. Hassim had no doubt about it. What was going on out there? The fighting was now between their enemies and the other group. He glanced at his companions, and as he turned he saw them rise from the mud as one man; then they were all running into the night, Dabu and Hassim covering them at the back and in front. Two shots fired at them as they ran. Hassim and Dabu fired back, gaining distance. Then they were out of range, and Hassim surveyed his companions.

Old Bio was carrying someone. Hassim rushed to him, and saw that it was Mameng. He could not tell if she was badly hurt. There was a sudden pain in his heart. What now? What now, you friends of the night? There was still some firing behind them. But they were safe now. As he ran in the darkness, Hassim tried to look for a temporary hideout. He saw a dark mass before him. Trees? Houses? He kept guessing. He ran, hearing his companions dragging their feet in the mud behind him. Then he knew it was a hut, all in darkness. It was fenceless and the yard was overgrown with grass and weeds. Abandoned? he reflected. He stopped and motioned to his companions to wait, while he and Dabu entered the yard.

Dabu was puffing heavily; he was wiping his face with one hand

and holding the gun, which had become unbearably hot from too much firing, with the other. Quietly they approached the ladder and went up noiselessly, slowly, rung after rung. At the landing they stopped and pulled out their flashlights simultaneously, their guns ready. Suddenly two sharp blades of light sprang from their hands, crossing and crisscrossing the hut, searching from corner to corner, leaping from roof to floor. The investigation took only a second. The hut was empty. Hassim nodded his command to Dabu to bring the others into the hut. Dabu left quickly, and Hassim investigated further.

When the others came into the hut, Hassim told Dabu and Legaspi to go outside and be on the lookout. Old Bio carefully put Mameng on the floor. Hassim knelt beside her and clicked his flashlight. He ran the light over her, but saw no sign of blood. Gently he put an ear against her breast and listened. She was breathing, but his anxiety made his hands tremble. To be sure that she was really breathing, he brushed his wet face with a sleeve and put an ear against her nose. She was breathing! He could feel it tickling his ear! What could be the matter? Carefully he turned her over. But there was no blood on her. Not anywhere. Anxiously he looked up at the old man, who was bending over Mameng with the same anxiety that Hassim had, but his face showed no indication that he knew her unconscious state. Trembling, Hassim unbuttoned her shirt and started rubbing her neck and chest; then she began to warm up, the solid bases of her breasts began to tighten and the nipples tinged redly. Then she opened her eyes and yawned. When she realized what Hassim was doing, she bolted upright and pushed his hands away. Ashamedly, she buttoned up her shirt.

"I must have gone to sleep," she explained.

Hassim felt embarrassed. Old Bio's face lit up, and he almost roared with laughter.

"You mean that you slept in the midst of the fighting?" he asked.

"I guess so. I remember dropping to the ground. And that is all."

"Sheer exhaustion," Hassim commented. His fright was gone. He felt relieved. He said to Linda Bie, "Do you know where we are?"

"Yes. We are nearing my hometown."

"Go out and tell them that there is nothing wrong."

Linda Bie left.

"You scared me to high heaven, Mameng," Old Bio confessed.

"I am sorry, old one."

"Lucky I stumbled into you. Don't do it again."

"I will try. Was anybody hurt?"

"Some," Hassim said. "But of the others. We were helped out by an unknown gang that came to our rescue. I would like to know who they were."

"Possibly bandits," Old Bio said.

Hassim walked to a window and looked out into the night. The rain had stopped and the night was fading. He lit a match and looked at his watch. Five o'clock. Then he heard the sound of feet pounding the earth, and he pulled out his gun. Then he saw dark figures becoming visible in the dawning. Swiftly he looked around the yard and saw that his men were prepared. Dabu was crouching behind an anthill. Legaspi had flattened himself on the ground, using his sack of provisions and liquor as a barricade. He could not see Linda Bie.

"Who is there?" It was Dabu's challenging, sharp voice.

"Friends!"

"What do you want?"

"We want to meet you."

"Why?"

"We helped you out there in the field against the local police."

I hope he is not kidding, Hassim reflected. He aimed his gun at the approaching men. Old Bio was at the window next to him. Mameng was kneeling on the floor, where there was a big crack in the grass wall, her gun ready.

" How many are you?" It was Dabu's ringing voice again.

"Seven."

"Put up your hands."

"Sure, friend."

That Dabu, Old Bio thought. For even he could see from a farther distance that there were seven men, who had already put up their hands and were approaching the house side by side. Sure they are friends, Old Bio continued thinking. Otherwise they won't range themselves in that perfect formation for target. But they must be pistolwise too, for their formation reveals without doubt that they are really friends. That Dabu . . .

Hassim rushed out of the hut, followed immediately by Old Bio and Mameng. He approached the strangers. The early morning light had already streaked the dark earth, revealing the stranger's faces. Hassim saw at a glance that two men were wearing canvas shoes, while the others were barefoot. Their guns were in their belts.

"No need to put up your hands," Hassim said.

"Thanks, friend," a man said.

Hassim turned to him. It was one of the men who had shoes. The older one, for Hassim could see now that the other with shoes was quite young. The older one was evidently the leader. There was a merry twinkle in his eyes, and his face, which was grave a moment before, was now lit up with friendliness. Hassim liked him at once. He gave his hand.

"Thanks for helping us out of that debacle," Hassim said.

"When we heard the firing back there, we knew some people were in need of help. So we came. Whoever are the enemies of the police are our friends. We don't need to know who you are or what you do. To us, it is enough that we are brothers of the night and enemies of the police."

"Policemen don't like us," Hassim said enigmatically.

"We are in the same boat. Are you passing through this territory?"

"Yes."

"From where?"

"North."

"Where to?"

"South."

"My name is Rene," the leader said, addressing Hassim and his companions. "And these are my men. And this is our territory."

"Mine is Bando," Hassim lied. "And these are my relatives. We are going south where a job is waiting for us."

"No jobs for us." He laughed and looked at his men. "Come on, *amigos*: get acquainted with our friends!"

Rene's men introduced themselves to Hassim's companions, who gave false names. Merriment ensued. One of Rene's men was boasting about shooting a landowner. Hassim felt better.

"Did you break any of the bottles?" Hassim asked Legaspi.

"I will break my neck first," he answered.

"Open two bottles and let us all drink."

Legaspi opened a bottle and gave it to Rene, who took a mouthful and said, "A good strong drink after a battle warms the heart."

"You said it," Old Bio said, who had just taken the other bottle from Legaspi.

Rene looked at the old man and slapped his thighs. "Old one, you are really a man," he said.

"Yes, a real man, son" Old Bio said. "Not a holy priest."

Rene laughed. He swallowed another mouthful and passed the bottle to his men. Old Bio also passed the bottle.

"Do you need any cigarettes?" Hassim asked Rene.

"Well – "

"Give them a pack each," he told Legaspi.

Rene smiled with contentment. He said, "It seems you have come from a prosperous place."

"We have friends."

"We have friends, too. And enemies."

"Did you get them all?"

"One got away. But we will get him. We know him."

"Save him for me," one of Rene's men said.

"He is yours, Porto."

Now the sun was coming out of the east, lighting up their faces.

"I did not know you have a woman," Rene said suddenly, looking in the direction of Mameng, who was sitting on a log apart from the men.

Rene's men looked at Mameng.

"My wife," Hassim lied.

"I am glad we helped you out of that rough terrain."

"Thanks again."

They had all become friendly. They stood in groups and exchanged experiences without revealing too much about their backgrounds. They even laughed when Old Bio told a joke.

"You are too old to be running in the night," Rene told the old man.

"I can outrun any policemen," he answered.

They laughed.

"I used to outrun the wild boars in the mountains," Old Bio said seriously.

"You are a born joker, old man."

"Like a politician."

They laughed again.

Hassim thought of Dante in the midst of their laughter. Strange that he had to die; he who had so much to say. Now his lips were sealed forever. A word, a gesture: and he was with them for a moment of time. A quick action, a sharp bullet: and he was gone for all time. Soon he would be eaten by worms; then nothing would remain of his body to testify that he had once lived in the world. Death was the common denominator, for the rich as well as the poor, for the proud and the meek – for all, all. Soon he, Hassim would be dead too; and nothing would remain to remind the world that he had existed except that he had fought and died for an idea. That was it: to die for an idea. Was it better to die for an idea than live without one? Dante had the idea to re-create the lost folklore of his country. Had he died for it? Hassim could not know; he would never know. Time was the element; and then? He sighed: so great was his burden that for a moment he was tempted to shout at the coming sun.

But he said to his companions, "Let us get going."

"Go ahead," Rene said. "In case you are in these parts and in need of help, ask for Rene."

"We will do that," Hassim said.

They shook hands.

"God be with you!"

"Same to you!"

Hassim and his companions departed, and walked into the new morning.

Also in the ASIAN AMERICAN HISTORY AND CULTURE series

Cane Fires:
The Anti-Japanese Movement
in Hawaii, 1865–1945 (1991)
  *Gary Y. Okihiro*

Entry Denied: Exclusion
and the Chinese Community
in America, 1882–1943 (1991)
  *Sucheng Chan, ed.*

Making Ethnic Choices:
California's Punjabi Mexican
Americans (1992)
  *Karen Isaksen Leonard*

Asian American Panethnicity:
Bridging Institutions and
Identities (1992)
  *Yen Le Espiritu*

Reading the Literatures
of Asian America (1992)
  *Shirley Geok-lin Lim
  and Amy Ling, eds.*

To Save China, To Save
Ourselves: The Chinese
Hand Laundry Alliance
of New York (1992)
  *Renqiu Yu*

The Politics of Life:
Four Plays by Asian
American Women (1993)
  *Velina Hasu Houston, ed.*

The Asian American
Movement (1993)
  *William Wei*

The First Suburban Chinatown:
The Remaking of Monterey
Park, California (1994)
  *Timothy P. Fong*

Hmong Means Free: Life in
Laos and America (1994)
  *Sucheng Chan, ed.*

Organizing Asian American
Labor: The Pacific Coast
Canned-Salmon Industry,
1870–1942 (1994)
  *Chris Friday*

The New Asian Immigration
in Los Angeles and Global
Restructuring (1994)
  *Paul Ong, Edna Bonacich,
  and Lucie Cheng, eds.*

Filipino American Lives
(forthcoming)
  *Yen Le Espiritu*

On Becoming Filipino:
Selected Writings of Carlos
Bulosan (forthcoming)
  *E. San Juan, Jr., ed.*

WITHDRAWN

5310